JERRY LEWIS
TOLD ME
I WAS
GOING
TO DIE

Essays

Matthew Del Papa

Library and Archives Canada Cataloguing in Publication

Title: Jerry Lewis told me I was going to die : essays / Matthew Del Papa.
Names: Del Papa, Matthew, author.
Identifiers: Canadiana (print) 20230151043 | Canadiana (ebook) 20230151086 |
ISBN 9781988989624
   (softcover) | ISBN 9781988989631 (EPUB)
Classification: LCC PS8607.E48253835 J47 2023 | DDC C814/.6—dc23

Printed and bound in Canada on 100% recycled paper.
Cover Design: Heather Campbell and Chippy Joseph
Author Photo: Bennett Malcolmson

Published by:
Latitude 46 Publishing
info@latitude46publishing.com
Latitude46publishing.com

We acknowledge the support of the Ontario Arts Council and Canada Council for the Arts.

JERRY LEWIS

TOLD ME

I WAS

GOING

TO DIE

Essays

Matthew Del Papa

For my family—especially my parents—who made all things possible.

Contents

A Not-So-Happy Anniversary 1

Wheelchairs: A Primer 6

Driving Lessons 11

Too Smart for My Own Good 19

Conversing with the Physically Disabled: A How-To Guide for the Clueless 26

Medical Malpractice 36

Treading Water 42

A Real Mickey Mouse Operation 49

On Matters Scatological 57

Top Ten Things I Wish Someone Had Told Me Prior to Childhood Surgery 64

Helmet Head 78

Public Transport—It's Not Just for Crazy People Anymore. 83

And the Band Played On 92

A Face Made for Radio 98

Not My Finest Moment, Part One 106

The Ramp to Hell 113

Parking Lot Blues 119

In Case of Emergency 126

Cafeteria Fun and Games 134

Jerry Lewis Told Me I Was Going to Die 140

The Tickle Machine Scam 149

Sneaking Snacks 156

Good Old Accessible U 164

Drunk Driving is No Joke 176

Spitting on Shakespeare 183

Big Brother, Don't Bother 191

The Best Medicine 199

The Storyteller 211

The Obligatory Sex Chapter 218

"Lame" Claims to Fame 228

Not My Finest Moment, Part Two 238

Aim High/Straight Shooter 244

Hard to Swallow 251

Where's My Hover-chair?! 258

Why Media Matters 266

Balancing on a Soapbox 275

Acknowledgements 282

A Not-So-Happy Anniversary

Every summer I celebrate a not-so-happy anniversary—though come to think of it "celebrate" might not be the right word. Commemorate is better. It is the day I stopped walking.

You'd think that life-changing moment would be seared into my memory, but the truth is I don't recall many of the specifics. It wasn't sudden or traumatic. My final steps happened sometime during the summer of 1982, probably in late July or early August, while I was away at summer camp. And there was simply too much else, good stuff all, happening for me to dwell on the latest in a long line of physical failings.

Being born with spinal muscular atrophy (innocuously abbreviated SMA)—a genetic disease that causes progressive muscle weakness and impacts many abilities, such as sitting up and walking—means I have had lifetime of muscle degradation and can look forward to continued weakening until the day I die. The ironic thing is there's nothing wrong with my muscles. It's the nervous system in my spine causing me trouble.

Here is how I understand the disease (and bear in mind I'm no doctor): There are a bundle of nerves running up every human being's spinal column and these carry messages from our brain to various muscles. A healthy person thinks, unconsciously, lift with full strength and the muscles do just that. SMA causes that message to change. Somehow the message becomes lift with 80% strength.

That failure in communication means my muscles never get used to their full potential. And, since the human body knows better than to keep wasting valuable resources on unused tissue, that unused 20% is allowed to slowly atrophy. This causes a cycle of weakening.

The degradation starts with the "trunk muscles," meaning those closest to the body core. Hence the accurate but somewhat cruel nickname "floppy baby syndrome" given to the worst affected, those with Type I*—whose necks are never able to support their heads.

There are four generally recognized types of SMA with the most severe damaging the muscles used for breathing. Luckily for me I don't have that type.**

Having Type II means my muscles needed time to atrophy

---

* According to the SMA Trust, "although classified as rare, SMA [Type I] is the leading genetic killer of infants and toddlers, with approximately 95% of the most severely disabled cases resulting in death by the age of 18 months."

** Medical terminology is always changing and that's especially true for SMA. All my life I was told I had Type II but there are now as many as five types, depending who you ask: Type 0 and I are always fatal, with few children surviving past age two; Type II and III are more difficult to distinguish (according to this scale I am probably a II, a moderately-severe case); Type IV is adult-onset.

enough to become noticeable. Currently my biceps and thighs are incredibly weak, almost, but not quite, to the point of uselessness. Contrast those with my fingers and toes, which still retain most of their function merely at reduced strength.

Luckily this disease doesn't affect the autonomic organs, so important organs like the heart remain wholly unaffected. Unfortunately, the lungs are not immune. Breathing would seem a rather important part of life and my lungs are . . . compromised. Nothing major at this point—diminished breath capacity isn't fatal but, eventually, the slow-but-sure failure of my lungs is what will probably "get" me. The only real question is: When?

With SMA the muscle weakening isn't constant. No, the atrophying process is as unpredictable as is inevitable. The disease progresses differently with every patient. I've experienced lengthy "plateaus" where only minimal degradation occurs and then, without any warning, an ability I've always taken for granted is just . . . gone.

What could be a devastating loss of function for many has become "Tuesday" for me. Though frustrating, I've learned to take these setbacks in stride. At some point I overheard and adopted the one-time United States Marine Corps slogan—Improvise, Adapt, and Overcome—as my own personal mantra. This has allowed me to establish workarounds for many of the obvious physical shortcomings*** but these easy fixes are becoming more and more difficult as the disease progresses.

• • •

*** Can't lift a cup to your lips, use a straw. Unable to roll on a normal mattress, replace it with a waterbed.

Walking wasn't the first ability I lost—merely the most obvious one—and it won't be the last. Still, that one change marked a major milestone in my life. Being wheelchair-bound hastened the loss of other muscles which in turn affected still others. Is it any wonder that I long ago became convinced that all changes are bad?

Not that I walked all that well before the end. The entire year prior, I developed a distinct tilt. I'd lean on walls, letting the surface take some of my weight, and sort of slide along until I came to a door. Then I'd throw myself across the gap and, hopefully, reach the far jamb. This method didn't always work. Once in a while I'd come up short and, if the door was open, topple into the room like a felled oak . . . only with more complaints.

A few people, small-minded pranksters mostly, liked to leave doors ajar. Not enough to notice though, just ready to give way when a weight was pressed against them—say a physically challenged eight-year-old merely trying to remain upright.

There is no telling how much longer the entire leaning thing would have continued. Everyone knew the writing was on the wall—except where my shoulder rubbed it off. But then I went to a unique summer camp, one designed for special needs campers. It was there I started using a wheelchair. Purely as a convenience thing . . . just not my convenience.

The thing you need to know about Camp Northwood is this: a great deal of its activities took place out of doors, and if there's one thing nature is unable to reliably provide, it's walls. With nothing to lean against there were huge sections of the grounds I could not access without help. Even the places where I could manage, it was just quicker for the counsellors to push me around in a wheelchair.* By the time I got home, the damage had been done—my leg muscles had atrophied past the point of use. I was wheelchair-bound.

There is no one to blame. My time walking was coming to an end regardless, and to be fair to the camp counsellors, a lot of responsibilities were heaped on their scrawny teenage shoulders.

Each was tasked with managing an entire cabin-full of disabled children, sixteen in total, all with unique physical challenges. The poor counsellors—volunteers one and all—tried their best but almost immediately found themselves overwhelmed by conflicting responsibilities. Struggle brought out the best in some and the worst in others. Saving a few minutes by putting me in a wheelchair meant they could use that time for other purposes, like helping accommodate the needier kids or sneaking off to make out with their fellow counsellors.**

Luckily my grandmother had an old wheelchair gathering dust in her basement and lent it to me when I arrived home no longer able to stand.

---

* The place must have bought them in bulk—they had wheelchairs stored everywhere. Big, little. New, old. Manual, electric. Working and in need of repair. All the parked spares were a tripping hazard. I tried to count them all but gave up the job when I passed two hundred.

** That tired camp movie cliché turned out to be one of the few that lived up to the Hollywood hype.

Wheelchairs: A Primer

Squeak, squeak, squeak. That was the sound made by my first wheelchair—an ancient iron and canvas monstrosity—whenever it rolled. That manual device more resembled a WWI tank than the sleek wheelchairs now on display in the nation's healthcare showrooms. No amount of lubricant—not oil, grease, or liberal applications of that canned miracle-worker WD-40—could eliminate the annoyingly repetitive squeal. And we doused the noisy wheels almost to death.

Everywhere I went the embarrassingly annoying sound announced me.

Beggars, as they say, can't be choosers. With my leg muscles weakening seemingly overnight,* I needed a wheelchair in a hurry and my grandparents had one. What did it matter if it dated back well beyond the Stone Age?** The canvas seat, designed before the concept of "comfort" even existed, might have left a lot to the imagination—and you needed to be an internationally ranked weightlifter to move the massively over-engineered behemoth more than an inch—but, with the addition of a truly horrifying three-inch wide burlap-covered Velcro seatbelt, it did the job.

I learned early on that, much like the titular puppet characters in the seminal '80s horror-comedy classic Gremlins, bad things happened when that wheelchair (manufactured by Everest and Jennings—at one time the "world's largest supplier of wheelchairs") got wet. The canvas acted like a sponge, soaking up moisture and holding it clammily against my young posterior for days on end. It's a miracle I didn't develop hemorrhoids or rickets or some other old-timey disease riding around on that damp, cold, and probably mould-spawning seat.

Sure, at the ripe old age of nine, I looked ridiculous in a chair meant for an adult—and a good-sized adult at that—but this was just a temporary solution. A month or two, no more.

Unfortunately for my then-tender behind and even more fragile ego, I was—and still am—cheap in the extreme. Good enough is all I ever ask of my accommodating technologies. And that old chair met my young needs such that "temporary" morphed into approximately a decade of use . . . as back-up.

---

* "Seemingly" is the key word. The tissue had been degenerating for years—I had merely reached the point where it could no longer be ignored. My *tripping point*, if you will.

** Technically, as a "folding wheelchair," it couldn't have been built prior to 1937—that was when Harry C. Jennings and his partner Herbert A. Everest patented their breakthrough folding model.

There was no way that an almost-immovable wheelchair could remain my primary mode of transport—my atrophying musculature necessitated a more modern alternative. Only an electrically powered wheelchair would allow me to get about with any autonomy. Yet despite its many glaring inadequacies, that heavy, old, third-hand beast remained my trusty manual alternative for years. The long-faded green canvas and constantly flaking chrome carried me all the places my even heavier electric simply couldn't go—on field trips, up or down flights of stairs, and, most importantly, aboard the train, across the lake, and around my family's camp.

I need to give the old dinosaur its due—that primitive wheelchair endured.

No matter the abuse we put it through, the chair wouldn't die. Compensating for a stunning lack in aesthetics and a criminally difficult-to-use functionality with stubborn sturdiness, it could take a beating better than any assistive device I've ever seen since. Thrown about, dropped, bouncing about the bed of a half-ton truck trekking along on the pole-line, even strapped to the pontoon of a bush-plane—the wheelchair just kept rolling, sounding its mournful, squeak, squeak, squeak.

Finally, though, enough became enough. I ventured into Doncaster Medical, the city's local wheelchair-supply store, and chose a replacement. Sticker shock almost had me, crippled though I was, leaping up and running away. Being young, healthy, and having my parents paying meant I recovered quickly but it's a safe bet that many older and sicker customers suffered life-threatening coronaries seeing the prices on offer.

Even the bare-bones "stock" models came with price-tags bordering on astronomical. Every added feature, no matter how minor, sent the cost soaring ever higher.

Needless to say, I went with the plainest manual wheelchair available. Since black seemed standard, and changing colour also added to the cost, I stuck with the basic factory paint. It suited my then-teenage psyche to a tee. Other choices proved equally simple, leatherette seating with actual padding was an obvious decision. The only option I paid extra for was the spokeless wheels—the black rims set the entire thing off with a semblance of class.

Weighing less than half of its predecessor, this Canadian-made chair served me for another couple decades, until wear and tear—leatherette might be more visually appealing than canvas but it doesn't last nearly as long—sent me in search of a replacement. Once again frugality got the better of me. Rather than buying new, I decided to try my luck with a second-hand purchase. Unlike my first wheelchair, this one only dated to the late 1970s.

Cobbled together from the cannibalized remains of a half-dozen broken wheelchairs, this Frankenstein-type monster looked even less appealing than the ancient E&J model. Luckily, the price more than made up for its aesthetic shortcomings. Featuring a black synthetic seat-bottom and a maroon leatherette back, two different sized armrests, and handlebar grips clearly recycled from some kid's much-abused moped, the thing rolled smoothly enough. A neat trick considering none of the four wheels matched.

I used that particular abomination until it began to rust out from underneath me. Then came my current emergency back-up: the Costco Special.

Soured by second-hand buyer's remorse, I decided to purchase new once more. This time, however, on a budget. No specialty store could compete with Canada's favourite big box warehouse club and so I ordered a wheelchair sight-unseen over the Internet. It shipped via Fed-Ex, packaged snugly in half a forest's worth of cardboard, and arrived exactly as advertised. Nothing special, the cost-effective purchase still works . . . more or less.

Like every chair before it, the Costco Special has its own issues. One of the much more modern castors sticks, this means turning it is just as difficult as its antique predecessor. No doubt my using it in the shower immediately voided the manufacturer's warranty. But considering the astronomical price of purpose-built bathing chairs—ranging from hundreds to thousands of dollars—I'm happy to continue abusing the club-brand.

Four manual wheelchairs in nearly forty years of need isn't half bad. Of course, that modest rate of attrition was only made possible by the daily abuse inflicted on my electric wheelchairs. And, boy, did I do a number on them!

Driving Lessons

The last thing the salesman said to me, as I was oh-so-carefully driving my shiny new electric wheelchair through the store's ridiculously narrow front door, was "You won't ever need to go over three."

I had it at six—the highest speed possible—five minutes after I got home . . . and wished there was a seven.

You'd think they'd give comprehensive operating instructions before letting a child loose on the world in a high-priced, electrically powered assistive device. Mine consisted of "Here's the on/off switch. The turtle means slow and the rabbit fast. If the red light blinks, you need a charge."

That was it. Well, that and the thinly veiled precaution against speeding as I left, which I immediately ignored. Only the blinking thing proved useful. I came to dread that little red light.

My first electric wheelchair didn't have a warning light. It didn't have a lot of things: functioning brakes, adequate motors, or a user-friendly design. That particular chair—built, once again, by Everest and Jennings—was a slow, noisy deathtrap. I used it for a couple of years despite its repeatedly trying to murder me, somehow arranging for each attempt to look like an accident. Most notoriously when the motors' belt-drives slipped as I was descending Capreol's steepest hill, sending me plummeting out of control towards the river. Only a miraculously placed sapling saved me from a watery grave.

"Motivated" didn't do me justice when the time finally arrived to go shopping for its replacement, but even then, as a naïve preteen, I knew enough not to rush into a purchase. Fortunately, the options were severely limited.

Going in, I knew one thing for certain: I didn't want the same manufacturer a third time. That didn't leave a lot to choose from.

The wheelchair I bought proved an immediate improvement in almost every way. Following on its predecessor's psychotic heels this wheelchair, built by Fortress Scientific—a Canadian company—quickly rolled its way into my heart and became the one I still remember the most fondly.

I didn't use that wheelchair so much as abuse it. There were few places I wouldn't follow my friends on their Schwinns—through puddles, along forest "trails," and even over jumps. The little electric motors screamed as I tried to make them do things their designers never intended.

Terrain didn't matter to that wheelchair. I threw all sorts at it—dirt, mud, snow, ice—and, so long as the batteries were fully charged, my second power-wheelchair plowed through. I drove it up and down slopes that rivalled Everest. Certain death awaited a single misplaced tire. That assistive device tackled difficult surfaces so skillfully that I took to trying to stymie the thing. I didn't enjoy succeeding in that endeavour—being stuck in snow so deep it took three friends almost a half-hour to dig me free proved a chilling experience—but learning the machine's limits only endeared it to me further.

I liked the model so much that I stuck with the manufacturer through several subsequent purchases.

All told I think I owned five Fortress Scientific-made models. And never once during those twenty-plus years did the company ever quite figure out how to make a reliable controller. Excepting the fuses and tires, both of which "blew" regularly, no part failed more regularly than that vital interactive component.

For all their sophistication, early electric wheelchairs didn't devote much time to instrumentation. Fortress Scientific's joystick—a term that always elicited snickers—could be best described as "bare-boned." It featured one rubber-wrapped switch, one hard plastic numbered dial, and a single red indicator light. That was it. (Later models would expand to include a variety of gauges, dials, and, of course, buttons galore.)

As a warning system, the red light left a lot to be desired. It blinked when the batteries were low and it blinked the exact same when the batteries completely drained. There was no differentiating between extremes. Ignoring the light wasn't an option. Unlike a car where, even when the needle is on empty, there's usually enough gas left in the tank to get you to the next station. All too often, when the red light started to wink on and off, the chair immediately died.

It died crossing busy roads, it died outside at thirty below, and it died when I was home alone with no one around to help. But at least it didn't lie. Not like the speed dial. I hated that dial and its mocking little rabbit. My chair didn't run "quick like a bunny." It crawled. Even at full speed.

What I wouldn't have given back then for something with a bit more oomph.

• • •

Like most Canadians, my driving has changed as I've aged . . . and not for the better. "Cautious" is the most accurate descriptor of me now. As a young man, though, all I wanted was speed.

I dreamed of one thing: Going fast. Neck-snapping acceleration, eye-watering velocity, and a wheelchair capable of outrunning a coach bus at highway speeds. And movies were to blame.

A bit of context here. I got my first electric wheelchair in the fall of 1982. Meatballs Part II, the much-maligned follow-up to Bill Murray's 1979 breakout film debut, arrived in theatres in 1984. A totally forgettable film, it squandered a talented cast (including Richard Mulligan and early performances from Paul Reubens and John Larroquette) and garnered nothing but negative reviews, except in the eyes of me and my friends.

We were far too young to understand the two main plots. One involved an unscrupulous land deal which promised foreclosure on the underdog Camp Sasquatch and the other focused on a pair of hormone-fuelled teens seeking an intimate moment of "privacy" in order to express their affection "physically." None of that mattered to us. No, in our juvenile eyes the movie was saved by the ridiculously silly subplot about an alien. Pre-dating CGI, the low-budget E.T. clone looked like a Soviet-era Muppet knockoff—more creepy than silly, and not at all endearing.

Bad creature effects didn't draw us in. That task fell to the group of young campers helping the alien, named "Meathead," get back to his home planet. One of whom was in a wheelchair.

You need to remember this was during the Reagan era. Terms like inclusion and positive body identity hadn't been invented yet. If a film or television character had a handicap, he (or, more rarely, she) would be the villain.* Physical deformities dominated—scars, limps, withered limbs, and hunchbacks. So, to see a good guy in a wheelchair—and for that to be a kid who looked more or less like me—blew my then-young mind.

Unfortunately, Tommy "Wheelchair" McVee (imagine trying to get away with a nickname like that now?!) set unrealistic expectations for viewers, namely, that wheelchairs could travel in excess of sixty miles per hour and pass vehicles moving along the freeway with ease.

Not even a year later, the 1985 adaption of Stephen King's novella Silver Bullet hit theatres and reinforced the illusion that "suped-up" wheelchairs not only existed but could be jury-rigged by drunken uncles in rural garages. The fact that King added his signature horror element (in this case that meant werewolves) made it a must-see for anyone in our age bracket.

Influenced by such unrealistic standards it's no surprise that picking out my second electric wheelchair proved a disappointing process. Going into the store I had a badly skewed image of what to expect and found myself let down every step of the way.

• • •

Fortress Scientific wheelchairs had small, wide wheels. Early models featured deeply-treaded black rubber. Their seriously intimidating

---

* There were, of course, exceptions but these were rare and seldom aimed at a pre-pubescent audience. Raymond Burr's *Ironside* is, for example, a program I never watched growing up. Not even in reruns.

appearance contrasted with the skinny grey tires of my wimpy E&J wheelchair; those scrawny wheels made getting stuck a daily fact of life. I took to avoiding mud, muck, soft dirt, and anything else likely to catch those tires—shag carpeting, discarded laundry, or any lawn not trimmed to fairway length. The new chair's "guts" came covered in a sleek white plastic fuselage, giving the whole thing a futuristic feel. Best of all, the Fortress Scientific was fast, or so the salesman assured me, boasting, "It tops out at over six miles an hour!"

That doesn't sound like much but it seemed mighty impressive when first experienced in Doncaster Medical's small and crowded retail space. It became much less satisfying on the open roads of my hometown. Capreol's wide rural streets called for more and I yearned to lay down some rubber like those characters on the big screen.

So, imagine the dismay I felt on realizing that—far from breaking speed limits—my fancy new wheelchair couldn't match a limping octogenarian. The letdown was both immediate and soul-crushing. The fact that I needed a while to "get the hang of driving it" didn't help.

No one in the movies ever struggles to master a skill. Except during the obligatory training montage. Me? I required weeks just to stop driving into things. All ten of my toes got bruised—a hundred times or more that first week alone—none were broken, though. More a testament to my strong bones than my then-anaemic driving skills.

Every door in my house developed scrape marks while I learned my new wheelchair's fundamentals. It responded quickly and had stunning torque, especially when compared to the first underpowered belt-driven chair. Naturally, that meant the walls suffered too, as did each and every piece of furniture. Scratches, chips, and worse marked my failures. The suffering wasn't only limited to inanimate objects, my pets and parents all learned to step quickly when I was moving. Toes and tails got run over daily.

Gradually my driving got better. It took me a while, but I learned from my mistakes (pain and constant teasing are strong motivators). Eventually I got to be pretty good. After a year I could zip through the narrowest doors at full speed, leaving barely quarter inch clearance on either side, without a second thought.

Not that I didn't suffer my share of embarrassing "relapses."

St. Mary's School bore witness to many of the consequences, repainting my classroom door three times that first year. Evidence still lingers in the form of deep gouges.

And then there was the time the joystick got pinned in the "forward" position without my noticing and, after flipping the power switch on, the chair surged ahead like some unstoppable killing machine. My custom-made, battleship-sized desk was pushed from the back of the classroom through three rows of panicked peers. Kids were sent flying like bowling pins, scrambling for their lives while I shouted, "Look out!" and flailed at the controller.

That nightmare-inducing incident might have been the low-point of my wheelchair-driving career . . . if I hadn't taken our four rows of classmates a couple years later.

• • •

The one thing that movies never mention is consequences.

Black leather might look cool on the big screen but it has drawbacks in real life, especially as wheelchair upholstery. Not that any of mine ever featured real leather. Just some cheap synthetic substitute. I found out the hard way that wearing shorts while sitting on pleather was a painfully bad idea, especially for eight consecutive, sweat-soaked hours on an unseasonably hot June day.

That incident involved me losing some skin—actually, a lot of skin. Several chunks, many of them centimetres across, were left sticking to the not-leather after I'd been forcibly peeled from my chair. You know the sound Velcro makes when pulled apart? That was the noise my flesh made when some of it decided to remain attached to the seat. The backs of my thighs were a torn and bleeding mess—it looked like someone had taken a rusty cheese-grater to my legs—and that proved a scaringly traumatic lesson.

I didn't abandon black or faux leather. In fact, every wheelchair ordered since has featured the exact same set-up. The experience did convince me to stick to long pants. Better to sweat through the sweltering summer sun than risk a repetition. It's been more than thirty years and I still have not worn shorts since.

Too Smart for My Own Good

I don't know who was more embarrassed, me or the woman anxiously leaning over me.

Concern radiated from her every pore as she bent in far too close, putting her face right into mine, and, hand tentatively touching my shoulder—almost as if I were made of spun-glass and the merest contact might cause me to shatter—asked, enunciating each word with special care, "Are. You. Okay?"

It was late August and the mall was packed with back-to-school shoppers when this random stranger accosted me. No one took the slightest notice of my predicament. Too wrapped up in their own transactional affairs to care for the plight of a fellow human being, I guess. A valuable, if humiliating, lesson in overestimating the inherent goodness of the species . . . provided I were capable of learning such (I wasn't then and still am not).

I'd been sitting outside a women's clothing store, resting with my eyes closed, quietly minding my own business while waiting on my mom. She enjoyed shopping. I did not. The crowds, the costs, and the insanely ridiculous variety of choices combined to exhaust and frustrate me. I had rushed through gathering my school essentials—four different coloured binders, a couple packages of lined paper, and a bag of cheap Bic pens—only to be dragged around after finishing for what felt like days as my mom went in search of "One more thing."

Needless to say, I wasn't in the best of moods.

My eyes snapped open at the gentle contact and an involuntary jerk shook my body. Finding someone in my personal space—something that I've always hated—sent adrenaline surging. Startled by the unexpected, if obviously well-meaning, assault I managed a semi-coherent, "Hghmph!"

"Are. You. Lost?" this woman continued, speaking even slower than before since I hadn't managed anything intelligible. Then, patting me in what she probably thought of as a reassuring gesture, she added, "Do. You. Need. Help?"

To me that condescending contact felt like the sort of treatment one would offer a stray dog—the kind of mangy mutt that needed a good meal, a flea-dip, and a week in a canine spa. The temptation to bite her almost overwhelmed me but I got that instinctual fight-or-flight reaction under control quickly. Still, it took a heroic act of will not to snap at her.

"Um, no," came my delayed reply.

What I wanted to do was slap her intruding hand away and demand to know what gave her the right to touch me. Instead, I forced a reassuring smile and, voice somehow cordial, added, "I'm fine, thank you for asking. Everything is fine."

The polite response was automatic. Courtesy is my default mode. And it drove my able-bodied friends mad.

They hated my unending civility toward intrusive strangers; especially those who assumed physical disability equated with cognitive shortcomings. Me, I tried to stay positive. "They're just trying to help," I'd explain, not sure who I was hoping to convince—those same disgusted friends or me. Instead of arguing with them further on the topic, a losing proposition, I preferred to change the topic.

The one simple question I never voiced: "What good would being rude do?"

That day in the New Sudbury Shopping Centre I didn't need to get into the presumed helplessness debate. The woman's stunned reaction—no doubt surprised that I, an obviously "special needs" young man, could string two sentences together without assistance—proved that ableist assumptions never die. (Ableism, for those unfamiliar with the term, is a surprisingly common form of social prejudice wherein it is believed that those with disabilities are somehow lesser than people of more typical ability. This type of discrimination is based on the belief that all disabled people require help or fixing.) My coherent response clearly didn't fit into her world view; where all the handicapped* were "poor unfortunates" incapable of living life to the fullest and so constantly in need of rescue.

I could have been an arse and asked why, of all the people crowding the mall that day, she decided I alone needed help. There was potential for a scene. It wouldn't take much to find offence in

---

* Smarter people than I have tried and failed to explain the difference between *handicapped* and *disabled*. For the purpose of this book, however, think of the terms as roughly synonymous.

either her words or tone and make a fuss. None of which would have made the situation any less embarrassing for either of us.

• • •

Being part of a visible minority—even one as diverse and difficult to categorize as the disabled—means I've faced judging stares most of my life. Finding myself pigeonholed is bad but to be mis-categorized based on nothing but prejudice* is frustrating beyond belief.

Most of the handicapped people I know, those physically able to communicate verbally, are well spoken. And a surprising number of non-verbal people manage to make themselves understood provided they have access to the proper accommodations.

That is, of course, old news to anyone who has ever met or spoken to a disabled person. I remember reading a study that claimed most people with physical handicaps tend to have IQs scoring well above average. Which makes sense. If you think about what life is like for children in a wheelchair, you'd realize why so many disabled youngsters are so eloquent and/or intellectually advanced—we spend an inordinate amount of time with adults. Not by choice, mind. But when left behind by the able-bodied kids as they run off to play, we usually end up sitting with the grownups, talking, listening, and learning.

Such a situation certainly sums up much of my childhood. At first, I mostly managed to maintain my place amongst the other kids—stumbling behind while the rest ran and tiring quickly at most physical endeavours—but gradually, as my disability worsened, even this limited participation became more and more difficult.

---

* Ableists assume that the handicapped are defined by their disability, often treating them as objects of pity rather than autonomous people in their own rights.

By the time I ended up needing a wheelchair, that assistive device seemed a blessing and not the curse you'd expect. It allowed me to once again be part of the activities, if in a modified fashion. That wheelchair dominated most conversations thereafter, sometimes directly—commenting upon it made a great conversation starter for people unsure of what to say to a handicapped kid—but most often its spectre lurked beneath the surface. Sitting there, obviously physically disabled, influenced how others treated me. And not for the better as my earlier, all too common, anecdote clearly shows.

Such assumptions seldom even penetrate my awareness anymore. Those ignorant interactions are far too common to get worked up about. For me, the daily frustrations of disability now come in two foul-tasting flavours: The things I want to do but can't; and the things people insist on doing to me that I wish they wouldn't. The first is obvious—I would have loved to go golfing with my grandfather, play catch with my dad, or skate on a hockey team with my brother—but the second category takes some explaining.

As illustrated in this chapter's opening, strangers touch me. Nothing perverted. These people are trying to be kind, placing a reassuring hand on my shoulder, arm, or knee. Pats on the back or head are also disturbingly common. Others think they're helping by wiping my face or straightening out my hair, at least back in my glory days when I still had a full head of thick, black hair.

A bit of free advice for dealing with the disabled: Do not touch us unasked!

In today's world you'd think the idea of consent would be front and centre but when it comes to handicapped people, those social niceties go out the window.

Which is why most of the disabled people I know are just . . . resigned. Sure, some people get angry about every slight. But most of us know that it takes energy to be mad all the time. And the longer you deal with disability's chronic frustrations the more you learn the importance of spending your limited energy on life's more productive aspects.

The thing about being handicapped that few able-bodied understand is its sheer exhaustion. Even something as relatively minor as not being able to stand upright wears you down. The entire world is made for standing—shelves, cupboards, workstations, cash registers—try living life sitting down and you'll soon see how tiring it can be.

I bring that up as an introduction to Spoon Theory. Developed by Christine Miserandino, and explained on her website But You Don't Look Sick, this concept uses spoons to represent the amount of energy she as a woman with lupus* has available on any given day. Doing tasks and chores obviously requires a certain number of spoons (energy), but the same is true for those commonplace everyday occurrences healthy people never think about, like getting out of bed, putting on clothes, or eating. Depending on your particular ailment and its severity you might only have a handful of spoons . . . so you need to spend them wisely. The disabled quickly become experts at measuring the amount of effort an activity requires and weighing the required spoon expenditure against what they need to keep in reserve to conclude their day.

And it doesn't take you long to learn the importance of always holding a couple spoons back, just in case.

Spoon Theory has been adopted by a broad cross-section of people facing serious health issues to explain what life with

---

* A chronic autoimmune disease.

a chronic illness** is like. Many have even taken to identifying themselves as "Spoonies." I'm lucky in that, as a relatively healthy cripple,*** I have a fairly large number of spoons. Unfortunately, to paraphrase a famous Canadian chanteuse, even ten thousand spoons are useless when what you need is a knife.

What good is unlimited energy when you can't get through the door to use it? That question still frustrates people with disabilities. We're just too exhausted to waste spoons complaining about it.

** Note that while all people suffering from chronic illnesses are disabled, not all people with disabilities have chronic illnesses.

*** Thirty-six years in a wheelchair means I can use this term—I'm "reclaiming" it and, in doing so, removing the word's power from those who would use it to insult. If you are uncertain whether you can drop "crippled" into a casual conversation then you're probably better off using a less divisive synonym.

Conversing with the Physically Disabled: A How-To Guide for the Clueless

I've soured on small-talk and it's all my family's fault. They're too damn friendly.

There's no point naming names but certain of my relatives have a God-given knack for making friends. It's like their superpower or something. Two minutes of conversation and they've turned complete strangers into bosom buddies. The location or circumstances don't matter. I've emerged from a store in the mall to find my mom exchanging life stories with someone she just met; I've attended hockey games and listened as my dad found a new friend in the front row and dissected fifty years of local sports history; and I've spent hours in the hospital waiting room only to find that the long-suffering nurse on duty still remembers my grandparents . . . from a chance encounter thirty years back.

Not only do I lack their garrulous gift but I have grown to resent it. For me, approaching a stranger involves nothing but awkwardness. Looking up while making introductions puts wheelchair-users at immediate disadvantage. And, frankly, that's a hole some of us never dig ourselves out of.

For me, conversations require the sort of step-by-step planning usually reserved for carefully coordinated multinational military manoeuvres. Gone are the days of "Hot enough for you?" That once solid opening gambit has fallen out of favour. (Climate change's ridiculous partisanship has rendered any reference to the weather politically problematic.)

As society slowly splinters into increasingly insular camps, it's becoming clear that taking time to talk to strangers is not something many of us are comfortable with. More and more we're falling out of practice in polite chit-chat. And that's just common everyday encounters. Add in the complications of a visible disability—should you ignore it or address it, if the latter then the issue becomes how—and difficulties multiply, both immediately and exponentially. Nervousness ensues and small talk, that once commonplace grease keeping personal interactions civil, becomes much more difficult.

Not that the handicapped are all fragile flowers or sensitive souls. Far from it. Most of us have been part of plenty of awkward conversations . . . if usually on the receiving end.

Occasionally, however, we prove just as inept in dealing with the disabled as the rest of you.

• • •

Someone had to say something, the situation was becoming ridiculous.

Every day for two weeks I'd met this same guy. He'd be getting off the elevator at the exact moment I was hurrying to climb aboard. We did this same little dance—me backing my big electric wheelchair up so that he could slowly manoeuvre his much smaller manual wheelchair out of the way and let me slip past.

Nods of acknowledgement were the most we'd ever exchanged. Our respective schedules didn't allow for more. Both of us were always rushing.

Attending university in a wheelchair meant mapping out the quickest routes became a matter of survival. I'd established a path that let me race from the seventh floor of the Parker Building to the second floor of the Library Building in under six minutes. It wasn't the most direct route between classes, requiring some zigging around hallway bottlenecks, doubling back to take advantage of automatic doors, and waiting for elevators to arrive empty enough to squeeze me in. It was merely the best any handicapped person could manage.

Any delay ate into my allotted travel time. And I hated running late. But it seemed my destiny given this daily encounter.

I'd been trying to work up the nerve to offer a casual greeting. Perhaps, an off-hand, "Afternoon," an oh-so-casual, "s'Up?" or the always appropriate all-Canadian apology, "Sorry."

Today, however, he came bursting from the elevator in a shiny new electric wheelchair and, in surprise, I blurted, "Nice chair." Only to instantly regret it. I recognized the look he directed at me—surprise and pity combined with genial good humour worn down almost to breaking—because I'd worn that exact same expression myself whenever someone—usually someone able-bodied—said something equally stupid to me. Doubling down, I asked, "Is it new?"

Clearly not enjoying the encounter he answered, "No." Then,

sensing the awkwardness, threw out a desperate, "Yours?"

Using the open doors of the waiting elevator as a convenient excuse to make my escape, I rolled aboard while saying, "Not even close." Turning about I offered, "Have a nice day," and vowed never to talk to that guy again.

Our indifferent nods returned the next day but they lacked their previous companionable undertone.

• • •

I try to believe the best of people, I really do. But there are days when it's hard. Oh boy, are there days. Sensitivity training is needed by a surprising number of people. The number of asinine comments directed at the disabled, most made in ignorant innocence, are truly astounding.*

People think they're doing the handicapped a favour by introducing themselves or starting with the small talk. No doubt there are some few special needs individuals who appreciate having others take the initiative. I am not one of them. Despite being a "people person" and enjoying a friendly chat more than most, I prefer to make the first move. Doing so spares us all the embarrassment of thoughtless conversation starters like:

I.   "It must be nice being chauffeured around all the time, eh? I bet the bus comes right to your door!"

---

* I give children a pass on this bit of invasive social discourse. Minors cannot be blamed, either for their curiosity or lack of couth. In fact, I try to be as honest as possible answering kids, and occasionally take things too far, like the time I introduced the topic of recessive DNA to the six-year-old sitting beside me at a wedding dinner.

That is one of the most annoying assumptions that the able-bodied have made to my face. Trust me, there isn't much "nice" about wheelchairs. I use mine out of necessity, not choice. I've accepted the need for assistive devices but that is not the same as enjoying them. Most handicapped people reconcile themselves to their situation. Again, not because they like the so-called "special treatment"—it quickly becomes galling—but rather to maintain their sanity.

And though the bus does come to my door, "nice" isn't exactly the term for relying on others to drive you around, needing to book every trip in advance, or being forced to share the ride with an ever-changing cast of characters—many of whom don't get out often and so struggle with basic social niceties.

II. "Why do people in wheelchairs always get moved to the front of the line? You lot are the only ones sitting down! It's the rest of us who should go first, standing around waiting like suckers."

Unless you're a professional comedian, don't try making light of someone else's handicap. Your "attempt at humour" probably isn't funny and I can guarantee you're not the first to think of that line. All you accomplish is to force the butt of your joke to make an impossible choice: laugh awkwardly at your lame witticism or call you out on your "poor taste" like some sort of thin-skinned politically correct vigilante. Generally speaking, I go with the former. A pain-filled chuckle or sympathetic smile, often accompanied by a derisive eye roll, conveys my disdain more eloquently than any drawn-out dialogue.

The only exception to "joking" is if you are a person with a visible disability. And, even then, you're far better off laughing at your own situation. Belittling someone else is tricky business and it is very easy to slip from good-natured teasing to flat-out insults. Should you cross that almost imperceptible line, chances are high that it won't be a handicapped individual calling you out. The able-bodied tend to police that line much more vocally, shouting down such irresponsible language louder than any disabled person could or would.

III. "It's SO good to see you out!" or, worse, leaning in close and offering a teary-eyed, overly sincere comment along the lines of, "People like you are just so inspiring."

I get it. You want to believe the best of people. And thinking that the handicapped overcome unimaginable obstacles on a daily basis provides many able-bodied with hope. "If they have the strength to deal with their challenges," the thinking goes, "then surely I must be able to fight through my problems."

Admittedly, there are some disabled people who face immense obstacles. But for most of us it is not some great miracle every time we leave our homes. Doing so might require more effort and planning but not divine intervention. I manage to haul my fat arse outside quite a bit during pleasant weather.* Don't feel obliged to compliment me on that feat.

IV. "But you're so smart/talented/funny/attractive?!"

Offering a compliment as a defence for a handicapped person's failure is not helpful. It is not our qualities that hold us back.

---

* An occurrence that happens with far less frequency and much more difficulty during the eight months those of us living in Northern Ontario call winter—an unfortunate side-effect faced by many of Canada's rural communities.

Ignorance, prejudice, and lack of opportunities do that just fine, thank you kindly. Trust me, we know our capabilities and shortcomings far better than you. Pointing them out usually only serves to remind us how unfair life can be.

V. "What's, ah, wrong with you?"

I'm not going to sit here and claim that there is nothing "wrong" with me—though I know cripples who would. Getting out of this wheelchair has always been front of my mind. But that doesn't mean I like people assuming I'm broken. Perhaps I should answer with a challenge, something along the lines of, "Nothing. What's wrong with you?" That might prove an effective reply, if I utter it with sufficient scorn.

Responding with aggression just isn't in me (unless we're talking politics, then watch out). Politeness and reason are a better bet. I find it best to simply shoot the elephant in the room, especially when someone's pointing the giant pachyderm out so helpfully.

If curiosity gets the better of you and there's simply no resisting the intrusive inquiry, then phrase it in a neutral manner. "Why are you disabled?" works fine.

VI. "Have you tried prayer? I know a great priest, I bet he could help fix you."

It's that "fix" bit that gets to me, though the religious overtones tend to rub the wrong way too. I've heard the secular version often enough, too; merely substitute "stem cells" or "gene therapy" for prayer and replace "priest" with doctor.

The thing I try to remember when someone trots out these or similar suggestions is that they're trying to help. There's no point acting snarky or growing angry. A simple "Thanks" can usually end the conversation.

VII. "Here, let me ..." invariably accompanied by an unasked intrusion into my personal space as some well-meaning busybody jumps to my aid uninvited, usually ruining what little effort I'd already accomplished.

There's big difference between helping someone and just shouldering them out of the way to do it yourself. Yes, the second is quicker—especially when dealing with the disabled—but just because you can do something better/easier/faster doesn't mean you should. Think of the sense of accomplishment completing a task brings you and now multiply the difficulty setting by several orders of magnitude.

Tying that shoelace is a nothing moment for you, done and immediately forgotten, but for many handicapped it is a challenge of Herculean proportions. Completing that seemingly simple task might require every ounce of their dexterity, cost them an enormous expenditure of energy, and could very well be the high-water mark of their day. And you did it in seconds, like it was nothing, which it now is.

• • •

Ignorance makes fools of us all. You worry about saying the "wrong" thing and so end up saying something even worse. That said, in the interest of fostering a better understanding between the able-bodied and those of us living with some sort of obvious physical disability, I'm offering some simple all-purpose suggestions.

DO:

- Feel free to approach us.
- Acknowledge our disability.
- Remember that we are human.
- Allow us our individualism.

DO NOT:

- Assume we are deaf, stupid, in need of rescue.
- Joke about a disability you do not share.*
- Get offended if not every disabled person is a cheerful inspiration all the time.**

Even with those helpful conversational tips steering you away from the worst missteps, interactions between a visible minority and someone more "mainstream" will remain something of a minefield.

Sitting where I do, it's often a challenge biting back laughter on seeing people's horrified reactions to the use of certain "trigger" words in my presence. "Walk," for instance. You would not believe the number of times I hear something like, "And so I took my dog for a walk . . . oh, I'm so sorry!" The regret is palpable.

Those hasty apologies and comments like, "No offence," only call attention to the issue. It's not as if I'm likely to forget that I cannot walk. Using that word—or others like run, stand, step, etc.—is not some jarring reminder. The mere mention of some activity beyond me is not enough to prompt an emotional collapse.

---

* While most handicapped people are capable of laughing at their predicament, most is not all. Some need longer to reconcile themselves to their particular situation. Others are just humourless a-holes.

** Even the best of us has the occasional bad day, short temper, or other serenity-busting aggravations.

You are not breaking the sad news that life is inherently unfair. Hurrying to reassure me of your sympathy just makes it weird.

So, to summarize, stop worrying. If you say something hurtful or offensive, we'll tell you. Chances are we've heard it, or worse, before. Probably not uttered in ignorance either.

Medical Malpractice

Me and medical professionals don't agree on much—and, since I live with a chronic disability, that poses something of a problem.

I've witnessed first-hand the best (life-saving surgery at a world class facility) and the worst (being misdiagnosed with a fatal form of SMA) of what socialized medicine can do. Seeing our hospital system up close and personal gave me a certain sympathy for the impossible jobs Canada's health providers undertake daily. That familiarity, however, has yet to engender any affection. If anything, this proximity reinforced my suspicions of socialized medicine.

It's easy to be cynical about health care. Few of us are at our best when accessing medical services. Being forced to sit for extended periods in cramped and crowded waiting rooms hardly endears the bloated bureaucracy to the user*. Stressed doctors and nurses—each lacking the time and the energy needed to communicate individually with patients and form a one-on-one relationship built on trust and understanding—too often fall back on impersonal tests, stock treatments, and expensive drug therapies pushed by faceless pharmacological giants.

And who can forget the endless joy of hours spent navigating the automated "Help Lines." These byzantine phone systems make trying to reach an actual human being a torturous ordeal. The time spent on hold listening to annoyingly repetitive music loop away our lives can never be regained.

Much as I admire the dedication of our nation's health care professionals, accessing their care is too often a labyrinthine process full of government regulation and impenetrable red tape. Our medical system is like an iceberg, only a small portion is visible. Doctors, nurses, and other "front of house" staff interact with the public but much of the real work takes place behind closed doors or off-site.

It's become clear to me that healthcare professionals, though appearing as God-like figures to us during times of pain and suffering, can all-too-easily act no better than squabbling children. Petty jealousies and staggering levels of incompetence run through the medical industrial complex just like every workplace.

I've always tried to remain an impartial observer, especially in hospital. That careful emotional separation acts like a defence mechanism, distancing me from the frequently devastating experiences taking place around (or occasionally to) me. Given that purposeful separation, it sounds strange to hear that I hold some fond memories of my experiences with health care. I blame Sally.

---

* "Triage" is, after all, just medical slang for "prioritizing."

Sally Spence was one of the best people I ever knew. Her big smile and bigger laugh brightened every building she occupied. No mere room could contain the infectiousness of her personality. We met when I was a child of three and she was a young physiotherapist, awash in energy, caring, and bright pink lipstick.

Back in the late 1970s, she was just starting out at Sudbury's Children's Treatment Centre—a place she would work for the next thirty years, ending as Clinical Manager before retiring from the CTC in 2011—but had already discovered how to bring endless joy to all around her. I experienced her professional passion firsthand. She celebrated the children around her, cheering their successes with the sort of enveloping positivity that pulled everyone along in her wake. It was clear to me, even at that ridiculous age, that this woman loved life.

Though every one of the children under her care bore the label "special," it was obvious to anyone meeting Sally that the term fit her even better.

Things were different in the late 1970s. Expectations for the disabled were low—the era of institutionalization was just ending—but somehow Sally rose above that.

The CTC was down the hall from Laurentian Hospital's pool and comprised just a couple well-intentioned but vastly overwhelmed employees. The space was small and their budget much smaller. I remember a lot of gym mats—none of which were new or seemed to have much padding—and a big, mirrored wall (though that last might be imagined).

Various foam pads and crudely build pieces of specialized equipment took up one entire side of the facility, none of which ever got brought out for my use.

Sally put me through my paces every week, focusing almost exclusively on stretches and the most basic of exercises, such as push-ups, sit-ups, limb raising, etc. Her contagious enthusiasm found itself put to the test by my unending petulance—she was the irresistible force and I the immovable object—arguments abounded. Mostly good natured and always respectful.

Working out struck me as pointless, even when first starting out at the ripe old age of three. I never got any stronger and complained throughout every session. It was only years later, long after I quit physio in disgust, that the importance of that frustrating weekly ritual became known—my various joints began "tightening."

Though most of my trips to the CTC came via bus, the earliest visits and the drives I remember most fondly all took place via carpool. Me and my mom would join my oldest friend Stacey and her mom for the drive in from Capreol. The two women sat up front and us two kids crowded in the back. I remember congratulatory cartons of milk, sharing boxes of Timbits, and chatting pretty much nonstop the entire way there and back. Somehow those friendly conversations always ended up adversarial, and there's no denying who was to blame.

I remain contrary and opinionated to this day, but at least back then I had a certain "cuteness" factor working in my favour.* In fact, Sally's first impression of me—recounted with her signature good humour at my grandfather's funeral—was watching that kind-hearted gentleman walk me down the long hospital hall and into the centre, him holding my then three-year-old hand and me arguing every step.

Maturity softened this annoying trait but failed to fully dispel it. Too often I find my opinion conflicting with those around me. I

---

* At the time I was a chubby-cheeked towheaded little urchin, who could pull off soulful-eyed innocence like the most cherubic of fallen angels. A bit of mugging always got me my way.

have, by default, become an expert at impromptu debates and will happily argue with anyone, anytime, on (almost) any topic. This is a defence mechanism, one I deploy whenever uncomfortable. Like while, say, undergoing so-called medical "tests."

This dependency on testing is another problem area betwixt me and the medical profession. Not the screening sort or even the diagnostic type. Those have value. No, my grievance is with measuring tests, and it started young.

One machine, used to test lung capacity, has been the bane of my existence for decades. Let me tell you, there's a special place in Hell for the designer of that device. Failing a breathing test is not like flunking Algebra—breathing is actually important—and the colour-coordinated lights left no doubt as to how you scored. I never got into the green, topping out in the yellow no matter the effort I put forth, and walked away feeling badly about myself.

The pressure proved devastating. Especially on those occasions when I travelled all the way to Toronto for a check-up.* There, the same insanely intense female technician would signal me to begin in the subtlest and most reassuring manner: screaming directly into my face. "Blow!" she would shout. Followed with an even louder, "Blow! Blowblowblowblowblow. BLOW!!!"

Were these encouragements or threats? I never did find out, but my numbers always scored higher with her, regardless. Fear is a wonderful motivator.

Learning how poor my results compared to a "healthy" kid put me off that test for more than two decades. Not even Sally's

---

* Once a year, Sick Kids held its neuromuscular clinic and I endured the same annual routine, being weighed and measured, getting a series of X-rays, performing a series of lung capacity tests, then meeting with a doctor for upwards of ten minutes. Their advice never varied: "Eat right, lose weight, and exercise more."

perpetual positivity could sway that stubborn stance. I shelved the exercises—even the embarrassingly feeble efforts I reluctantly went through at home—and tossed the one device that might have actually helped improve my breathing into the closet to gather dust. It didn't look impressive being nothing but a ping-pong ball in a clear plastic tube. Blowing in the mouthpiece would lift the ball; flipping the tube over reversed the effort; inhaling would cause the ball to rise. The challenge was to hold it aloft for as long as possible. It didn't take much to move the ping-pong to the top but keeping it there required real effort, meaning the lungs got a workout. I hated working out. Especially once I learned it was "good for me." I associated that phrase with foul-tasting medicines and fouler tasting vegetables, both forced on me by people who should have known better.

Sally knew me. She knew how contrary I could be. If health care in Canada had a persona half as welcoming and one-tenth as humanizing as the late Sally Spence, people might actually enjoy "going to the doctor." Not me, mind, but less-argumentative people.

Treading Water

Fat floats. You need to know that first or nothing which follows will make sense. It also helps to keep in mind that I was once a skinny kid. It's hard to believe now, given that I'm currently just over 200 pounds (or 91 kilograms to be exact), but "scrawny" best described me back in the day, at least until I ended up in a wheelchair. From that moment on the weight just sort of . . . stuck.

During childhood, me and my friends ran, played, and fought pretty much non-stop from late June to early September. Only the hottest weather slowed us. Copious amounts of well-sugared Kool-Aid and jumping through hose-mounted sprinklers mostly prevented heatstroke, and when the temperature rose beyond their combined cooling capabilities, there was always "the river."

Growing up I loved the water. Like generations of Capreol

youth, I swam in the local river—known to residents as the Vermillion. The town's small but neat beach drew a crowd every summer. It was a mark of honour amongst Capreol's youth to swim, unaided, from the dock to the island and back—a total distance of roughly ninety yards—with bonus marks to anyone who could manage to remain underwater the entire way. I never managed that heroic feat but did get to the island on my own before age eight, coming up for air numerous times, and even took several levels of formal swimming lessons in those familiar waters, complete with official government-regulated certification badges. These weren't modified for "special needs" either. No, they were the real deal and I earned them the hard way . . . by shivering in my too-small swim trunks.

From the river I took to spending an hour at Laurentian Hospital's therapeutically heated pool every week. Swimming formed the only fun part of physiotherapy. Starting at the age of three, long before I even know how to pronounce the word, I ventured to Sudbury for my weekly torture session.

If you think your job is stressful, try motivating a disabled kid! Let's just describe my sit-ups as half-hearted and my push-ups as laughably futile. Not one of those exercises ever mattered to me. I was just passing the minutes until I could escape to my happy place: the welcoming warmth of Laurentian Hospital's well-chlorinated pool.

I did the commute to and from the Children's Treatment Centre for years. Enduring the old school treatment* so that I could

---

* "Physio" might be big business these days—with therapists routinely performing wonders, both for people recovering from injury and those working to alleviate more permanent conditions—but back in my youth there were few "modern" technologies. Innovations like lasers, ultrasounds, and electroshocks were not even dreamt of then.

go splashing about the specially heated waters without a care in the world. Being underwater made me happy. I found a stillness hiding beneath the surface. Calming loneliness embraced me. Call it serenity if you want, but in that bath-like water's ridiculous warmth—they kept the temperature at almost ninety degrees, all it needed was soap-bubbles and a rubber ducky—it was just me, my heartbeat, and my burning lungs.

I still remember my time in that eye-burning exercise pool fondly. It was the highlight of my week and the only reason I ever attended physiotherapy. Swimming, unlike sit-ups or push-ups, was something I excelled at. In the water it didn't matter that my muscles were weak, I swam like a porpoise, diving down to pop back up and spitting out mouthfuls of water, splashing about until wrinkled like an ancient prune.

Since I liked to open my eyes underwater but didn't like the sting of chlorine on my naked corneas, I brought goggles into the pool with me. Sure, the oversized black and yellow headgear made me look like some sort of weird insectoid-alien but that never bothered me. The hour I spent in that pool belonged to me and I made full use of every second . . . to traumatize everyone around.

During my time in Laurentian's water, I loved nothing more than to float face-down, arms and legs outstretched, fingers and toes splayed. Having trained myself to hold my breath for nearly two whole minutes at an early age meant my drifting across the water's surface like an unmoving corpse freaked the heck out of people. The fact that all the pool's regulars knew and ignored my antics didn't help. Their casual indifference to "the poor drowned crippled boy" only made the sight more shocking to newcomers.

More than once someone panicked, jumped in the water, and pulled me up thinking I needed CPR. But no, I was fine. Better than fine. The pool was my sanctuary.

Until, one day, my happy delusion was despoiled.

It shouldn't have come as a shock. The copious chemicals keeping the water clean weren't added solely to annoy me. I never gave their presence much thought. Nor the fact that it took many of the disabled swimmers' long minutes to get helped in and out of the water. Long, bladder-bursting minutes some of them didn't have to spare while racing to use "the facilities."

"Just pee in the pool." Those were the five words that ruined everything.

Hearing the allowance uttered aloud caused me to suddenly realize why the hospital added so much chlorine ... and it wasn't for the taste. Swimming in that pool lost its shine after that. The water felt polluted. And I hung up my trunks. If only someone had offered me that vital piece of advice, "Don't drink the water."

The point is: I've always been very comfortable in the water.

So, naturally, when my elementary school went for lessons at the nearby Howard Armstrong Complex in the mid-1980s, everyone assumed I would drown.

No one said anything aloud, but the lifeguard kept one eye on me, the lone "special needs" kid, and one on the rest of the class as we made our way into the pool. Getting me in the water proved something of a chore. Not only did I require help changing into my swimsuit, but I needed assistance entering the pool. Luckily the complex had a ramp and a wheelchair specially designed to be submerged.

I didn't flounder in the complex's big pool. Instead, I laughed off the proffered buoyancy vest and dove into the deep end.

Okay, "diving" is a bit of an exaggeration. Unable to stand, jump, or even fall in a controlled manner, I sort of rolled in ... but with attitude. In my element at last, I cut through the water like some sort of prepubescent merman and easily outperformed the entire class. Swimming, it turned out, was the one and only time that I, an obviously physically disabled Canadian, beat my contemporaries un-aided by assistive devices or accommodating rule changes.

Naturally, I cheated.

Remember how this all started? Fat floats.

Well, after years of being in a wheelchair, I'd packed on a few pounds. Almost every ounce of which was fat. Don't get me wrong, I wasn't obese or anything (that would come later) but there were signs, especially around my expanding middle and bubbling butt. In the water, all that recently gained weight buoyed this boy up better than any personal floatation device.

No one noticed or much cared why I swam so well, at least not until the instructor challenged the advanced part of the class—meaning those not in imminent danger of drowning—to a competition to see who could tread water the longest.

Unlike the other two swimmers in the advanced group, I didn't have to work to stay afloat. No kicking necessary. I didn't have to paddle either. The fat accumulating in layers under my skin functioned as my very own life-vest. All I needed to do was take a big breath of air and keep some in. Easy.

I could be there still, floating without effort.

Beside me, my friends Aaron and Alyssa scissored and splashed. Soon they each were struggling, clawing at the water in desperate attempts to remain above the surface. I forget which of the two reached for the pool's rim first but the other wasn't long behind. For my part I kept moving my arms, pretending to work, kicking occasionally for artistic effect. Eventually the instructor gave up, announced me the winner, and moved on to another exercise.

I aced that too. Along with every other water-born challenge that day. Sadly, the school never went swimming again. But my one shining moment of pool supremacy sustains me still.*

• • •

It would take a few years but all that budding body fat, so beneficial in treading water, almost killed me.

My second cousin Rose has a pool. Her husband ran the local oil business and so didn't blink at the fuel necessary to keep the temperature at a balmy eighty-two degrees. They were kind enough to let their various relatives (even those not especially close-knit) use these luxurious facilities, a privilege we were careful not to abuse.

One afternoon, three decades back, my friend Stacey** and I called ahead to use the pool. Getting permission proved easy enough and my dad drove us over already in our swimsuits. We climbed in and began splashing about, having fun. Then I tried to swim, just as I'd been doing most of my life, laying prone across the surface with my face in the water. Only this time when I went to change position, I couldn't get my legs to go down. The copious amounts of fat collecting around my thighs and calves, unused leg muscles atrophying from years of neglect, floated. I tried and tried to force my legs underneath me, to get myself upright and take in a breath, but those functionally useless pins refused. Finally, lungs on fire from lack of air, I used every ounce of limited strength in my crippled core to twist and shout, "Help!"

---

* It proves a much happier memory than other field trips—like the bowling debacle (where I rolled my ball with such delicacy that it stopped after striking the first pin, without knocking anything over) or the curling catastrophe (I got frostbite on my butt from sitting on the ice for over three hours).

** Not my oldest friend Stacey, a different Stacey. Let's call her "prim Stacey." She was one of those children who brush their teeth after every meal even at school or when eating at a friend's, you know the kind adults adore and all the other kids quietly resent.

Half a mouthful of water came in with the yell but my dad, reading a newspaper by the pool, heard and jumped in to save me.

It took me years to venture near the water after that terrifying incident. The element I considered my second home tried to kill me that day and the betrayal stung. Only twice since almost drowning have I dared try swimming again, and both times the problem persisted. There will never be a third attempt.

St. Mary's one-time champion swimmer can no longer tread water.

A Real Mickey Mouse Operation*

Sing it with me: ♫ M-I-C-K-E-Y M-O-U-S-E! ♫

That was the criminally cheerful refrain to The Mickey Mouse Club's saccharine theme-song. To this day I cannot help but shout along whenever I hear "The Mickey Mouse March" and I entirely missed out on that generation-defining television program . . . three separate times.

Everyone knows the Walt Disney Company, a highly litigious corporate behemoth of unimagined reach. Though currently an

---

* Talk about your misleading phrases. Disney is one of the world's biggest and most successful corporations and yet its iconic "spokes-mouse," Mickey—who ranks among history's most recognizable global mascots—is routinely used as a byword for childish incompetence.

omnipresent, and occasionally evil*, media empire it once confined itself to "family" programming. But even at its most innocent the studio never met an idea they wouldn't happily exploit. Clean-cut kids performing on a weekly variety show fit right into their carefully cultivated cultural wheelhouse.

Launched in 1955, the original program proved so successful at targeting the youth demographic—helped by the Mouseketeer's breakout star, a then-young Annette Funicello—that they happily recycled the singing and dancing concept twice,** first in 1977 as The New Mickey Mouse Club and then again in 1994 as The All-New Mickey Mouse Club (often shortened to MMC). And that doesn't even count the 2017 internet-only Club Mickey Mouse (or the Korean and Malaysian revivals).

I was born to a disheartening dearth of cartoon-mouse-themed televised fan clubs, being too young for the original mouse-ear-wearing program and its first follow-up and too old for the reboot. Despite this sad lack, I grew up fascinated by Walt Disney and everything branded with his iconic signature. Even the primitive thirteen-channel TV dial of my youth featured plenty of Disney productions, ranging from The Wonderful World of Disney airing a different family-friendly movie every week—featuring made for TV slop and the occasional "classic" from the studio vaults—to Saturday morning cartoon fodder like The Adventures of the Gummi Bears.

---

* Google the plight of Alan Dean Foster if you're curious about the ridiculous lows a multi-billion-dollar company will go to just make a buck, including depriving a contracted author of overdue royalties.

** You might recognize some of those involved in the reboots: Britney Spears, Christina Aguellera, Justin Timberlake, and Canadian Ryan Gosling achieved global superstardom after being featured on the 1990s show.

My best effort at public speaking involved painfully memorizing and then haltingly reciting a fawning speech about the company's then-new president, Michael Eisner. Why was it my best? Because I actually cared about the subject. The inner workings of the "House of Mouse" fascinated me, and not just because I dreamt of someday working there as an animator.

This is all a longwinded set-up for the life-changing trip my family took in 1981 to spend a week in Florida.

The thought of actually visiting Disney World, a place that held an otherworldly dream status to me at the time, like Shangri-la or Never-Never Land, had me physically vibrating with pure excitement. I was too young to know that the actual corporate headquarters were located elsewhere. Ditto for the legendary film studios. Worse, we arrived just as EPCOT was being constructed.

At the time we toured its massive grounds, Disney World was, essentially, an overgrown theme-park, and an expensive one at that. With ridiculously overpriced food, obscene markups on merchandise, and lines long enough, even at those costs, to suck much of the joy from the experience. Not even the most hyper-enthusiastic Mickey Mouse fanatic like me could be blind to the venue's faults.***

We only managed one day at the self-proclaimed "Happiest Place on Earth," dividing the rest of our time between the Sunshine State's other famous attractions (SeaWorld and Ringling Bros. and Barnham & Bailey's Circus World are two that most stand out).

***   Like the fact that they sold replicas of their mascot's severed scalp for park-goers to wear as trophies! Children sported plastic mouse ears in perverted pastiche of their rodent hero—a twisted tribute to their tailed idol. Seriously, how demented is that?

But nothing could compare to Disney . . . even then.*

Though far different from today's super-sleek operation, Disney World in the early 1980s was still a must-see tourist destination. It marked the highlight of any visit to Florida. Unless, of course, you were in a wheelchair. In which case it was probably best to just stay home. This was especially true when we went, in the summer of 1981. Disney World hadn't yet developed their insanely liberal handicapped policy, otherwise I'd have been whisked to the front of every line.

Not that I was in a wheelchair at the time. No, that summer I still managed to walk, neither far nor well and never very fast. Tiring quickly and being just that little bit too big to be carried everywhere for an entire day, my parents picked up an oversized stroller to push me around while on vacation. I can still picture its blue and white striped synthetic cloth seat. Synthetics don't breathe well. A fact I discovered to my sweat-soaked surprise under Florida's unforgiving summer sun.

Since my time visiting the park, Disney has revised its policies towards accessibility, first by creating a policy and then, upon seeing their corporate largess abused, scaling things back considerably after fraudsters ruined the VIP treatment for all of us.

No resort, regardless of expense, can meet every conceivable need. The spectrum of disabilities is simply too vast. But, to their credit, Disney makes an effort to cover most mobility issues and the majority of visual and hearing difficulties. Included among the wide variety of accommodations currently offered are: Rental wheelchairs, Rental electric conveyance vehicles, Accommodations for service animals, Assistive Listening systems, Reflective Captioning, Sign

---

* Without three decades worth of later additions, constant renovations, and continuing technological improvements.

Language interpretation, Text Typewriter telephones, Handheld Captioning, Video Captioning, Audio Description devices, Braille guidebooks, and Digital audio tours.

Walt Disney World categorizes its attractions for Guests with mobility disabilities thus:

- May Remain in Wheelchair/ECV
- Must Be Ambulatory
- Must Transfer from Wheelchair/ECV to Ride Vehicle
- Must Transfer from ECV to Wheelchair
- Must Transfer from ECV to Wheelchair, and from Wheelchair to Ride Vehicle.

All of which are helpful, but it was skipping lines which almost brought the park down.

Being stared at is nothing new for the handicapped, but seeing suspicion on those staring faces proved a new low. Basing VIP-status on something so difficult to categorize as "disability" was a disastrous decision. People, naturally, exploited the system. It didn't take long for the unscrupulous to begin faking disabilities just to take advantage of that particular piece of preferential treatment.

Disney managed to find a compromise with its current Disability Access Services. The DAS allows guests to schedule their experience without having to wait in line—a difficult feat for many people with handicaps—but doesn't push them through to the front. Since I sat during the majority of my visit to Disney World, those delays didn't affect me overmuch.

Unfortunately, most of the rides were beyond me. Not only were me and my brother both young, seven and five respectively, but many involved spinning or other physical motions. I could barely manage one "gee." Being tossed about at multiple gravities was out of the question.

The gentler attractions—Jungle Cruise, Walt Disney's Enchanted Tiki Room, Country Bear Jamboree—all moved at something closer to my speed. Not exactly "fun," they nonetheless each proved "entertaining." I'm still disappointed forty years later that The Hall of Presidents was closed for reconditioning during our visit.

I did manage a few rides—the Mad Hatter's Tea Party and "It's a Small World"—without difficulty. My dad carried me into one of the submarines, a difficult feat, and lifted me onto the small steam engine for a sedate trip alongside a group of amazed toddlers. Much of Pirates of the Caribbean sailed over my head—the designers used "historical accuracy" as an excuse for some inappropriately "saucy" humour. Space Mountain called but even at seven I knew a roller coaster that intense wouldn't work out for me.

My brother fell hard for Haunted Mansion, going through it three times with my dad, but nothing impressed me more than the remote-controlled boats. Large steering wheels, the sort found on old-timey steam ships, guided them and I spent a full hour gripping the handles and shouting vaguely nautical movie dialogue like "All ahead full!" and "Hard to port!"

Being able to fully enjoy that attraction proved a novel experience. The early 1980s didn't stand out for its accommodating attitude. Not even a major tourist locale like Florida bothered with accessibility. My visit predated the ADA—which didn't come into effect until 1990—and it was that piece of federal legislation, more than anything, which brought monumental change . . . to the United States.

Back home, in the "Great White North," things took longer to evolve. Our attitudes towards inclusivity might have been more forward-thinking than our American cousins but their laws had teeth. In Canada, enforcement has always been much less rigorous. Even today a shocking number of buildings fail to offer even the most basic accessibility.

Travelling this country reveals a disheartening variety of disappointing set-ups. Especially in rural areas like Northern Ontario. These were real Mickey Mouse operations—even those branded as national chains.

In the bad old days, when I still ventured out of town, staying at a hotel or motel proved a constant crapshoot. I never knew what lay beyond the threshold. There were no industry wide standards then and certainly no government mandates as to what sort of accommodations these rooms needed to make toward the disabled. Many didn't even feature extra-wide doorways. You'd think facilities would ensure that their paying customers could at least enter the premises, but a surprising number failed on that, the most obvious of business basics. Calling ahead to confirm that their rooms were wheelchair-accessible as advertised, became second nature. It didn't take me very long to learn not to trust any assurance until seeing the quarters in person. More than one hotelier explained, straight-faced and without the slightest apology upon handing over the key, that their property was all one level "once you make it up the steps."

The only thing special about those rooms designated as "wheelchair friendly" seemed the price. Paying extra for "handicapped accessible" all too often meant nothing more than a grab-bar shakily installed beside the toilet.

Roadside motels featured all the comforts of home, provided home leaned toward industrial carpets, particle board furniture, flame-resistant curtains, and bedding of dubious origin and uncertain cleanliness. Those accommodations truly were the nadir of comfort, but, being dry, at least they beat sleeping outdoors—except for the leaky faucets, the showers that drip-drip-dripped all night long, and the toilets flushing for no reason. And who can forget the nearby ice machines? Their off-kilter motors screeched and the clank-bang of dispensing could wake the dead. Even the high-end hotels left a lot of room for improvement—at least in my experience.

There were notable exceptions. One hotel, in Sault Ste. Marie of all places, went the extra mile and had a track installed into the ceiling above the bed. There was no lift provided—guests were expected to bring their own I guess—but, still, that marked the highwater point of corporate renovation. Most places, even multinational chains, got by with the minimum effort to accommodate disabled guests.

I won't even try to count the number of times I was offered a room several floors off the ground. Patient explanations could usually get us moved to a more reasonable level—second or third—where I might have a chance at egress in case of fire (or other emergencies).

Travel is not something I bother with anymore, especially not overnight. Have things improved since my early days abroad? I'm sure they must have. But there is zero chance of me even finding out first-hand, unless I can luck into a cheap flight to Florida. Disney World still holds special meaning for me.

Good old Uncle Walt—and the company he founded—dominates twenty-first century mass entertainment on screens both big and small. The House of Mouse controls iconic franchises like Marvel, Lucasfilm, and Pixar, runs a world-wide network of resorts, a fleet of cruise ships, and, in Florida at least, enforces its own laws.

Now bow to your cartoon rodent overlord, sing his song, and be happy . . . or else.

On Matters Scatological

Here it comes, the toilet humour. Brace yourself, things are going to get lowbrow. I don't want to go there, truly I don't, but I have to. Everybody poops, or so a popular children's book tells us. And, given that the second most common question I (and, from what I've heard, every other wheelchair user) get asked is, "How do you . . . you know? Go?" It's probably best to address the issue in an honest and forthright manner.

In most societies men are supposed to urinate standing up. The fact that I cannot stand confuses the issue, especially for kids. Patience is necessary to describe the mechanics. It never ends with a simple, "I sit." That, despite the benefit of being true, isn't enough to satisfy inquisitive young minds. The truth seldom suffices these days.

Most kids, on hearing the answer, look at me and demand, "What, like a girl?!"

Curiosity is a great trait in children . . . until it's directed at you. Then their never-ending questions and brutal honesty become a torturous trial. Anyone who's ever tried to reason with a pre-teen—or worse, a toddler—knows the special hell involved. Each answer, no matter how exhaustive, is invariably met with the repeated refrain of "Why?" As each increasingly frustrated explanation hits that same one-word roadblock, epiphany dawns: the Spanish Inquisition wished it were as effective at getting under people's skin as your average five-year-old.

Most kids don't even have to try to fluster the adults around them; they naturally hit upon the most embarrassing subjects and question them with such open innocence that no right-minded person can ignore them. I have to respond to children—maybe it's because I'm sitting and so closer to their level*—their sense of wonder is infectious and, even though I'm ninety-nine percent sure neither of us will find the result satisfying, it forces me to try and answer.

So, here goes: Not to get into too much sordid detail but using the "facilities" is something of a procedure for people like myself. It usually involves carefully choreographed assistance—both human and mechanical.

Of course, I'm not the only one with embarrassing bathroom-related issues. A certain unnamed (and unlamented) former US president and his notorious "Pee Tape"—the existence of which would explain a great deal about his pro-Putin agenda—springs to mind. My difficulties, at least, don't involve Russian prostitutes. No, for me the problems tie back to an overlarge bladder.

---

* Seriously, try looking a kid in the eye and then denying them!

I used to joke that I had "iron innards." Not to brag but I used to "hold it" indefinitely. Fourteen, sixteen, eighteen hours, no problem. No amount of liquid phased me. Beverages both hot and cold passed my lips without issue, from oversized travel mugs to the legendary Big Gulp knockoffs sold at every corner store. My capacity knew no limit. One memorable evening put me to the test. I sat beside a decorative fountain all night long. The water feature's merry tinkling reached every corner of the large hall but was most noticeable for those nearest, meaning my table. It was a family event—my cousin's wedding—so, naturally, everyone pounded back the toasts. Despite matching everyone in the hall, drink for enthusiastic drink, I was the only one not subconsciously prompted to make repeat use of the venue's facilities. The sound of constantly running water, nature's diuretic, pushed whole tables to run for the bathroom in stampeding unison, usually at the end of an especially long speech, but not me. I was immune.

This wasn't "shy bladder," or anything related to my disability. No, the whole wilful retention of liquid started long before I lost the ability to walk.

Even as a kid I despised being out of the loop. FOMO—Fear of Missing Out—dominated my consciousness and, somehow, I got it into my young mind that all the really interesting events in the world happened when I was absent, either in bed sleeping or in the bathroom tending my "business." Not willing to allow events to pass me by, I began putting off life's necessities. First for minutes, then hours.

Years of strict self-control meant that I conditioned myself to urinate twice a day and to defecate once every week or so.

Needless to say, no toilet was safe when I finally voided my bowels. Clogs were common. And my visits to the facilities tended to be lengthy, noisy, and pungent. I probably owe the custodian of St. Mary's Elementary a long overdue apology.

That, of course, was an unhealthy and unsustainable bathroom regimen. It came back to bite me on the butt at the advanced age of seven when I became so constipated that I needed medical grade laxatives and thirty-eight painfully embarrassing hours of bedrest—on rubber sheets—to get things moving. Did I learn my lesson? No. No, I did not.

Things changed when I stopped walking. From that point on I required assistance transferring to the toilet. For decades that responsibility fell to my dad. He would lift me from bed and carry me across the hall to the bathroom. This system worked well at home but both of us had reasons to be away from home—he worked and I had school.

Fortunately, the groundwork for intestinal success had already been laid. My weird obsession with witnessing life first-hand paid off. Years of training meant that only the direst bathroom emergencies caused me difficulty and, if ever I couldn't wait, well, St. Mary's Elementary sat not far from my house. I could be home in under ten minutes.

Oh, don't get me wrong, I've had my share of "accidents." Bladder infections are the usual culprit. Sitting all day, every day creates ideal conditions for some embarrassing ailments, and that particular annoyance is my bane.

It doesn't sound all that bad, having to urinate frequently. I know a lot of people, seniors mostly, who'd happily trade that side-effect for their much more discomforting issues. Those people do not require assistance to us the restroom, however. I do. And, since bothering someone to help with toileting is both intrusive and humiliating, I've long scheduled my bathroom visits to be more convenient.

That remained true even in later years when school took me

away from Capreol for eight to 14 hours a day. Bladder control proved easy. Bowel issues proved a much tougher nut to crack. It took some embarrassing trial and error but eventually I developed a successful strategy to deal with the sudden and unexpected onset of stomach trouble.

When nausea, heartburn, upset stomach, indigestion, and diarrhea couldn't be ignored or willed away, what better solution than Pepto-Bismol? It had a century of proven effectiveness as a résumé. For more than a decade I popped those capsules like some sort of stomach-soothing candy whenever I needed to poop. This was prior to "Chewables" revolutionizing the business and long before Cherry Flavour arrived on the scene to make the medicine palatable. Sufferers today don't know how good they have it. Modern LiquiCaps, Ultra Caplets, Kids Chewable Tablet/Bubblegum or the so-called Herbal Blends—Peppermint & Caraway or Ginger & Chamomile—all render patented "Five-symptom Relief."

If Procter & Gamble even decides on a spokesperson, they need to look to me. No one on Earth field-tested their product more rigorously nor valued it more highly. Being unable to use the toilet unaided meant bathroom considerations featured prominently in my daily planning. And there was no more effective treatment than what I, to this day, refer to as, "My little pink miracle pill."

At first, a zip-lock baggie held everything, and not a big sandwich bag either. But that soon changed as I discovered unexpected contingencies. A variety of other over-the-counter cure-alls joined PB. Headaches prompted me to begin stocking Tylenol. Sinus medicines, Vicks cough drops, and throat lozenges like Fisherman's Friend kept seasonal colds at bay. Allergy pills, caffeine pills, and various vitamin supplements grew my onboard pharmacy until I carried a "man-purse" full of pills.

Soon I had a none-too-small duffle bag loaded with "medicines."

More than once the question circulated through parties, "Who's carrying?" It didn't take me more than once to learn that my "stash" didn't count. Disappointment, pitying looks, and humiliating laughter resulted when I made the mistake of pulling out the Pepto-Bismol.

No matter where I went or what I did that iconic pink bottle went with me. It held pride of place in my travelling pharmacopoeia and was never allowed to dip below half-full. At the first tinge of tummy turmoil, I popped a Pepto. One always did the trick. Whatever intestinal issues caused me distress immediately tightened up.

And if the chalky mixture occasionally worked too well, better being constipated at home than experiencing an excruciatingly embarrassing excretion in public.

• • •

When it came to scatological matters my life settled into a comfortable routine. At least until I discovered my porcelain nemesis.

Having a flush toilet at camp was an unheard luxury when I was young. None of this outhouse BS, with spiders, snakes, and other vermin lurking in wait. No, our place—thanks to the handiness of my grandfather and great-uncle—had a fully functioning commode. Located in a large, clean, tiled bathroom, including sink with running water. A large window made it both bright and airy. Sure, in spring and fall the room was insanely cold but it beat running outside to the "crapper" through rain or snow.

Everyone in the family happily used that modern-ish marvel for years. Then, one day, I fell off.

Toilets and me have had a long-running feud. Needing help

to get on means I also need help to debark. While informing someone of the former is easy enough, sitting on the throne in a bathroom during a noisy party makes the latter more difficult. I've been forgotten in the loo more than once. On one memorable occasion for three hours. Good thing that house had a selection of reading material to pass the time.

I became somewhat notorious too for the trail of clogs left in my wake. Even "industrial-strength" facilities weren't immune. People made sure the plunger was handy before inviting me over, just in case I "had to go."

None of which mattered at camp. There my weakened muscles proved unable to hold me in place and I landed on my crossed legs, managing to sprain both ankles.

Having full feeling in my limbs combined with little useful muscle to make a miserable combination. Three extra-strength Advil took the edge off. But what followed was a long and pain-filled night of not-sleeping. The next morning, we left camp for the hospital but not before I wrote of my humiliation in the camp book. I promised to return, vowing that the toilet would not defeat me.

But it did. I have never returned since.

That tragic toileting experience proved enough to put me forever on the edge of the seat. Paranoia has removed the age-old dog-themed choice of "Setter" or "Pointer." Fear of falling has me gripping with all the tenacity of a "Terrier" whenever precariously perched upon the porcelain throne.

Top Ten Things I Wish Someone Had Told Me Prior to Childhood Surgery

I take a lot of pride in being a smart man.* Probably because, growing up, I was such a know-nothing kid. I didn't read anything not forced down my throat at school and wasn't especially curious about the world around me. My academic accomplishments never amounted to much—I won no meritorious awards and earned no accolades—but all that changed when I learned the thrill of knowing things others don't.

Call it "The Cliff Clavin Principle."

For those unfamiliar with 1980s sitcoms, that character appeared as part of the regular cast on NBC's long-running series

---

* Smart enough, for instance, to regret boasting of it here.

Cheers. Played to perfection by John Ratzenberger, this mailman know-it-all gained a devoted following for his eager-to-please enthusiasm, nagging self-doubt, and non-stop efforts to regale the iconic bar's exasperated patrons with interesting trivia . . . or at least trivia interesting to him.

Cliff often found himself the butt of jokes. Such a fate seemed inevitable given his annoying habit of claiming expertise at absolutely everything, regardless of skill or experience. No matter what he said, be it earnest or well-meaning, his superior tone quickly annoyed all around him. Perturbed by Clavin's antics, his fellow barflies resorted to teasing and thinly veiled insults as inevitable retribution.

I share one trait with TV's most boring fact-machine: We both love knowing things others don't. These don't need to be important or, in Cliff's case, even factual. Odd bits of obscure history or bizarre facts are enough to establish our bona fides.

Unfortunately, back in 1985 I hadn't learned the joys of thinking myself smarter than everyone else in any given room (an assumption that only ever proved true when alone). Ignorance and naïveté dominated my personality then. Questioning life, let alone the adults in my life, never occurred to the younger me. I took things as they came, both good and bad, and simply made the best of them.

Then I found myself facing major surgery. A situation no one thought to prepare me for.

I went under the knife late in the summer of 1985. Spinal scoliosis is a side-effect of SMA and my back was bending in a worrying way—onto my lungs. There didn't seem to be any effect on my breathing . . . yet. But all the doctors agreed it was only a matter of time. So, at the ripe old age of eleven (and three-quarters), I ventured to what I imagined to be the unhappiest place in the world: a children's hospital.

Going in blind left me drifting from unpleasant surprise to even more unpleasant surprise.

"Forewarned," the saying goes, "is forearmed." I arrived uninformed and unprepared. Thinking back here are the top ten things I wish someone had told me prior to childhood surgery:

I. That hospitals are not supposed to be fun—not even children's hospitals.

Immortality is the default for most kids. Few children suffer serious illness or face the prospect of an early death. I found myself among that happily ignorant crew on arriving at SickKids. The entire hospital works hard to hide the more depressing facets of modern health care from their young patients. Brightly coloured murals, friendly faces, and an underlying ethos of genuine kindness succeeded at this monumental challenge.

Those undergoing treatment at the world-class facilities are not only allowed to be kids but actively encouraged to have fun. I fell in amongst that crowd during my brief stay. Gangs of us raced down the wide but busy halls, wheelchairs rolling and crutches swinging with wild abandon. At the time, SickKids maintained an on-site arcade, complete with all the latest gaming cabinets, a pool table, and more. Being all of 12, too young to participate in the "Teens Only" activities despite various entreaties, I moped for a bit before pulling out my deck of playing cards and teaching my ward roommates how to play cribbage. We shared comic books and copies of MAD magazine, took turns turning the radio dial trying to find a station we could all listen to at an inappropriately loud volume, and otherwise made our own amusement.

Getting in "trouble" from the nurses became so commonplace

for the hospital's patients as to have long since become a tradition.

Those over-worked angels in white put up with our antics, smiling good-naturedly as their charges worked off nervous energy in inappropriate ways, until we pushed too far, and they launched into a series of cautionary "horror" stories. Most revolved around the sorry fate of previous "rambunctious" patients.

II. What an "enema" was and that these are administered before all major surgeries.

I was eleven, okay. And, despite the SMA, ridiculously healthy. Other than the usual childhood illnesses (colds, flus, chicken pox) and my weekly visits to the Children's Treatment Centre for physiotherapy, I had no real first-hand experience with the medical system.

The morning of my operation a nurse arrived in my room while I was still getting out of bed. She had in her hands a harmless-looking tray and announced, in a weirdly cheerful voice, "Time for Matthew's enema."

Not knowing the term, but assuming it meant a needle, I nodded and said, "Sure thing. Let me just go to the bathroom first."

Moments later I got why everyone laughed. It didn't seem particularly funny to me, though. I was too busy clinging to the toilet so as not to blow myself off while enduring the most extreme BM of my young life.

Cleaned out, I was thrown aboard a gurney and wheeled off to the operating room.

III. That daytime TV in the 80s sucked. Even in Toronto.

Kids today don't know how good they have it. On-demand programming, entire series at their fingertips, and the collective knowledge of humanity—including music, books, and movies—are just clicks away. When I was young, we had radio stations whose reception varied according to the weather, libraries organized around card catalogues that some joker always messed up, and cable television with actual cables featuring all of a dozen channels— several of which were French—ending their programming schedule at midnight.

But that was in Sudbury. Rural entertainment left a lot to be desired. Surely Toronto, the centre of culture in English-speaking Canada, could do better?

Turns out they couldn't. In fact, Hogtown's pedestrian television left a bigger scar on me than the surgery.

I went under the knife Thursday morning at 7:23 am. Despite my pleading, the OR nurses steadfastly refused to wait until the TV show I was watching in "pre-op" ended. Instead, they callously clicked the program off before wheeling me into the operating theatre. To this day, I still don't know how Hercules rescued the cute blond in a too-short toga.*

More than 12 hours later, I awoke, clawing my way to consciousness through layers of lingering anaesthesia. Still groggy, I immediately ripped the annoying oxygen canula out of my nose and tried to work some moisture into my mouth. That action brought a concerned-looking nurse rushing to my side. She brought a cup of ice-water with her and allowed me periodic sips while gauging my consciousness.

---

* I'm willing to bet it involved the titular hero putting on his signature ring, in that often-recycled cut-scene, and holding it to the heavens while dramatic music played in the background.

Smiling encouragement, she asked all the usual post-surgery enquiries: Can you tell me where you are? Do you know who's president? Do you know what day of the week it is?

The second almost tripped me up. I was still trying to argue, "This is Canada. We don't have a president," when the last question penetrated. "It's Thursday!" I almost shouted. Even through the post-operative fog that answer held significance to me. Hurriedly turning the tables on her, I asked, "What time is it?"

Turned out it was just prior to eight. Hearing that I demanded, "Get me a TV." NBC's weekly programming powerhouse, marketed as "Must See TV," aired every Thursday at eight p.m. And I was not missing my programs.

IV. That the food would be more of a challenge than the surgery.

Mention hospital food and you're sure to elicit groans. The "meals" served might be healthy but that's about all you can say about them. Low in sodium, low in fat, with mild flavour profiles and few difficult to chew pieces—those are choking hazards—leaves little I'd call appetizing.

It doesn't help that most patients are sick. Nothing tastes right when you're ill. Even mom's universal cure-all, chicken soup, isn't always up to the challenge. Food prepared off-site, as most hospitals now outsource that service, arrive cold, congealed, and stomach-turning.

I arrived in hospital with a well-earned reputation for "pickiness." My first meal, rubbery chicken served alongside mushed potatoes leftover from the War of 1812, set the tone. Things went downhill from there. I lived on Jell-O and packages of soda crackers during my entire stay . . . all while lamenting the dinners missed back home.

Obviously, something in my plaintive complaints struck a chord with a young nurse because she surprised me with a plate of smuggled spaghetti. Not being of Italian heritage, her idea of quality pasta came out of can. I, of course, knew better. My entire life I'd been given homemade sauce and noodles, each lovingly made by experienced hands of various relatives.

Gratitude should have been my reaction to her well-intentioned gesture. Instead, I turned my nose up at her meal and stuck with packaged soda crackers.

V. That there were books written especially for boys. You just couldn't find them in the hospital gift shop.

Damn that Judy Blume! Her books, delightfully quirky accounts of youth—almost always from a girl's perspective—were all that my mother could find to read during my recovery. They were better than nothing, I'll give them that much. Blubber is the one I remember most, about the bullying of a fat girl and how her tormentors come to terms with her weight issues, probably because at that point in my life I was beginning to noticeably pack on the pounds.

My parents were great throughout my surgery, both before and after. Taking turns sleeping in our van so as to always be near to hand. But neither was up-to-date with the new releases or particularly well-versed in the sort of literature aimed at boys. Thinking back, I'd have killed for some YA or even a bit of science fiction—Heinlein's so-called "juveniles" would have helped pass the hours while I lay bed-ridden. Instead, there was Mrs. Blume. I suspect my mom enjoyed them far more than me.

VI. That you can refuse treatment for any reason.

At the time of my operation, spine-straightening surgery was still new. The first successful treatment had occurred far too recently for anyone with sense to even consider undertaking the still technically experimental procedure. I didn't have an option. My life didn't quite hang in the balance. I could have put it off for months or possibly even years. The worsening spinal scoliosis would need medical attention sooner or later and, being young and naïve, I chose sooner.

It was a point of pride for me that my surgeon had pioneered the operation and, as far as I knew, I was the fifth or sixth person in the world to have it done.

"Twelve hours under anesthesia followed by weeks of bedridden recovery." Or so everyone involved warned me. The surgeon, the anesthesiologist, the nurses, my parents. But they didn't stop there. No, everyone added two ominous words, "Painful weeks." That last was stressed, repeatedly, and until I grew sick of hearing it.

Which left me confused. Following the operation, I didn't suffer from any noticeable pain. Not on first waking and not in the days that followed. Sure, there was some soreness—you can't be split open from top to bottom, get steel rods attached to your backbone, then have your spinal column stretched several inches before being stitched back up again and not expect a bit of discomfort—but nothing near the level of agony I'd been promised. In fact, I found the injecting of my "medicine" much more bothersome.

Why they insisted on jamming that obscenely large needle into my leg, I'll never know. It hurt every time. Until, finally, I begged them to stop. No one believed me when I said my back felt "fine." Across the hall the young woman who had the same surgery the day before me complained nonstop. She lived in agony, desperate for the brief release brought on by the carefully timed pain medications. Meanwhile, I wanted the injections to stop.

There's a frustration known almost exclusively to two groups: children and the chronically ill. It involves having others think they know what's best for you better than you do. Everyone claimed to be working in my best interest while I was recovering from major surgery, but it was one old nurse who did me the most meaningful service: she told me I could say no.

I promptly did just that. It became my new favourite word, like I was some sort of contrary toddler with a limited vocabulary. I declined every painkiller on offer. And, though that didn't go over well with the medical establishment, my discomfort never increased. What's more, my appetite started to return. I couldn't get home fast enough after that.

VII. That our nation's pride and joy, socialized medicine, can be manipulated by the vain, entitled, and unscrupulous to their own advantage.

My release from hospital was hastened by a temper tantrum. Not mine. No, even as a child of eleven I knew better than to behave in such a disrespectful manner. Some random parent threw this fit. Raising her voice in outraged indignity, this woman verbally berated the over-worked health care professionals as if they only existed to serve her needs and couldn't even do that right.

Lying in my bed and listening to her self-absorbed rant—it was impossible to ignore her strident complaints even at the other end of the floor—I recognized the practiced rhythm to her grievances. No doubt she spoke with the same level of disrespect to every lackey that dared cross her, be it some teenage server spilling her ridiculously overpriced expresso or an underpaid valet delivering her beloved Benz with a smudge on the paint.

I didn't think she could sink any lower but then out came that phrase known far and wide as the universal arsehole calling card, "Do you know who I am?!"

What prompted this pique? SickKids, the foremost children's hospital in Canada, dared to try and discharge this woman's daughter. Too self-important to permit such a slight, she would have none of it. Instead, she belittled, browbeat, and all but held her breath in order to get a room for the girl. Name-dropping did nothing to endear her or her daughter to the staff. Unconcerned at the scene she was making, the woman repeated four words like some arrogant mantra, "I demand immediate satisfaction!" When that didn't bring instant action, she stepped up her pettiness and began threatening expensive lawsuits, embarrassing exposes into her "shocking treatment," and promised swift retribution if her daughter wasn't provided "proper space to recover" while waiting to see the specialist—a "friend of the family"—the next day.

Like most of our nation's medical facilities, The Hospital for Sick Children, worked with resources stretched to the limit. Finding a spare room took time and effort. Several nurses and even a couple of the less busy doctors tried to explain the harsh reality of medical triage, but the woman remained adamant. Finally, through sheer petulance she got her daughter assigned accommodation.

Her outraged screeches on hearing it was to be a "ward" room almost took the roof off the building. "You expect my daughter to share?" she asked, voice a disbelieving whisper. The explosion of anger that followed the unnatural calm rivalled a supernova. While not uttering a single swearword, the woman insulted everyone with such upper-crust courtesy that it could have been amusing. . . if it weren't so shockingly inappropriate.

This was a children's hospital, after all. Kids suffered unimaginable pain, parents dealt with devastating diagnosis, and doctors made unconscionably difficult choices on a daily basis.

Unfamiliar with the sheer selfishness of the rich, I listened in horror to the staggering cluelessness and marvelled that anyone could speak so selfishly to another human being—until the head nurse came into my room (my private recovery room) to ask if I'd be willing to move. The troublemaking woman's arrogant entitlement had become too annoying to tolerate and, to shut her up, I was being put in the ward.

I could have refused. My major surgery pre-empted most other treatments. But having heard the hateful words spouted at the staff, I decided to cooperate. Moving didn't much matter to me. I was scheduled to fly home the next day. Back to my own bed and the familiar comforts of Capreol.

The satisfaction on that woman's face as I was wheeled out of the way—like so much garbage—turned me forever against the wealthy. To her, I didn't matter. I might not even have been human. She was too busy instructing the nurses in how to "best prepare" for her daughter's arrival to spare me more than a dismissive smirk. The last I heard from her wasn't "Thanks" but a shrill demand to "scrub every inch, please." But, of course, she left out the pleasantry.

Her daughter, a real chip off the old block judging by the superior smile she shot down her surgically perfected nose at me, clearly needed the private room. The plaster cast enveloping her tanned forearm must have been exhausting.

VIII. That "bedrest" is not all that different from "torture."

Not being in pain after major surgery made me miserable. I didn't want to suffer. Far from it. I considered my recovery a blessing and even heard the nurses gossiping about my "miraculous" recuperation a time or two. The problem with feeling good is you want to do stuff and I couldn't . . . by doctor's order.

One of the innovations my surgeon brought to spine-straightening was to keep the patient on their back, unmoving, during recovery. Prior to that, patients were suspended face-down to keep the pressure off their spines. His literal "flipping" of the treatment sped the healing process significantly and eased the discomfort level astronomically. Which meant I was anxious to get up, out of bed, and do something—anything!

Watching bad daytime TV quickly paled and being read Judy Blume only distracted me for so long. I stared at the hospital ceiling counting tiles for hours. Then, as the days passed, I grew frustrated. Anger followed. My increasingly short temper had me snapping at everyone, visitors and staff, for no reason. The smallest trigger would set me off.

I didn't raise a ruckus but my increasingly foul mood was clear to all. The longer I stayed in that bed the worse I acted.

Finally, the doctor gave me what I needed. It wasn't a prescription but a date—as in announcing the day of my release. Sure, it was seventy-two hours away and he included several worrying wriggle-words like "If all proceeds smoothly" and "Should there be no complications" but I didn't care. The important thing was I was getting out of that damned bed!

IX. How much a "Get Well Soon" card could mean.

Arriving home, I settled into my own bed. Another five days of enforced bedrest lay ahead of me but that didn't look so onerous. Not when surrounded by the familiar quiet routine of family and small-town living so hard to find in a big city.

Even on those rare occasions when the hospital wasn't awash with activity, at all hours and loud enough to cut through even the industrial-strength sedatives, the streets produced more noise than a Northern Ontario boy ever expected. Horns honked, tires squealed, and people insisted on screaming every word so as to be heard over it all.

That all changed in Capreol—until a group of familiar students arrived at my door. Friends one and all. The half-dozen visitors represented my classmates, all thirty-one of them, and they came bearing gifts. Unbeknownst to me, the first day's entire art class—all forty-five minutes—was dedicated to making me "Get Well Soon" cards. Sure, none could match the store-bought for professionalism or pithiness—cut cardboard and pencil crayons limited even the most creative imagination—but those thirty-one individual pieces of folded paper did more to restore my spirits than any Hallmark-produced wholesomeness.

I have them all still, tucked away somewhere safe. It's been almost forty years now since they were delivered but I remember the welcoming feeling those thirty-one hand-made cards brought. Sometimes the simplest things make all the difference.

X. Above all, I wish someone had taken me aside and explained that my upcoming surgery wasn't going to "cure" me.

Naïve didn't do eleven-year-old me justice. Somehow hearing that the doctors were going to fix my back got conflated in my young mind with being "cured" of SMA. No one said that or even hinted at it, but hope had me hearing what I most wanted to hear.

Prior to leaving for TO, I convinced myself that, following surgery, there'd be no more wheelchair, no more muscle weakness, and no more reason for me to be different. I honestly believed the delusion. Worse, I made the mistake of mentioning it to some friends. One of them told her parents, who, in turn, told mine . . . and they set me down to have a little "talk."

And I lied throughout the entire thing.

I may be naïve but I'm not stupid. Body language alone told me something wasn't right. Their tone of voice provided warning even before their words sank in. "You don't think this operation is going to fix you, right?"

Until that conversation, I had. But answered, "Of course not." Dying a little inside as I spoke.

Hope is a truly great thing. It keeps me going to this day. But back then, having that hope shot down set me into a tailspin. I didn't voice my feelings—that wasn't me, then or now—but I wondered why I was even bothering with surgery if I'd come home the same.

I decided then and there that living in ignorance was no life at all. A more determined person would have embraced knowledge, studied up on their disease, and become an expert on it. Me? I went the opposite way entirely. Ignoring the proffered information with malicious glee.

It would take me several more years to learn the power of random facts and the pleasure to be found in knowing things other don't. Becoming a fan of Cheers and its resident smarty-pants showed me the way. So, let's all raise a glass to network TV and the influence it holds on our society's young.

Helmet Head

Head trauma is no joke. I know people whose lives have been forever changed as a result of concussion.

Traumatic brain injuries (often abbreviated as TBI) impact millions every year, resulting in nearly 30,000 deaths in the U.S. annually. Though those most affected tend to be older or younger (accidental falls are the number one cause of brain injury in North America), damage to the brain affects all ages and can be both serious and debilitating.

Fortunately for me, given the ridiculous amount of abuse my cranium has suffered, I've a thick skull—a fact exasperated teachers loved to mention on report cards.* Blows that would lay others unconscious I have somehow shaken off without seeming repercussion. Laughing at knocks to the noggin may seem juvenile but the humour hides some serious worry.

• • •

When I was a kid, I fell a lot—always backwards,** strangely—weak muscles, lousy reflexes, and a somewhat "wonky" sense of balance meant my poor head hit the ground (or the floor, pavement, coffee table, what-have-you) with what we'd now call "concussion inducing" regularity*** and the doctors repeatedly told me to start wearing a helmet. I, of course, refused. How many concussions did my stubbornness cause me . . . dozens? Hundreds? Probably more.

Why did I ignore the doctors' well-meaning advice? Hard-headedness only explains so much. The reality is, even at a young age, I knew one thing about helmets that science is only just acknowledging: They're goofy looking.

That's right, I avoided helmets for fashion reasons.

Not the most serious complaint, true, but, to a then-young and insecure me (I was self-conscious as an eight-year-old) searching for any excuse, it was reason enough. The appearance aspect was a big problem for me. My walking was already "iffy" enough that

---

* Seriously, my mom still has the first note sent home, it called me "uncontrollable, un-teachable" and worse . . . I was all of three-years-old at the time! I am still inordinately proud of my badass younger self.

** It is some pernicious law of nature, much like how a dropped piece of toast always lands butter-side down, that my head would strike something when I toppled. With no way of protecting myself, those collisions often left a mark.

*** Traumatic brain injury might explain my decision to become a writer.

people stared. I didn't want a giant piece of plastic-armoured padding strapped around my head. You might as well have looped a sign around my neck reading, "Freak."

No one at the time, outside of athletes mandated to do so by their sport, wore helmets. This was decades prior to the dawning of the nanny state and the arrival of helicopter parents. No one coddled citizens' craniums then. Kids were practically thrown out the door and told to endanger themselves on a daily basis. "Growing pains" was meant literally.

Thinking through my childhood, I can easily list a hundred different ways me and my contemporaries risked our very lives. Predating seat belt laws (Ontario passed legislation in 1976), car seats (originating in 1933, these weren't regulated until the 1960s and didn't become commonplace until the 1990s), and airbags (early versions proved dangerous and it took until the 1980s for a reliable model to enter production), meant every commute posed a threat. And don't get me started on our daredevil antics while on bike, toboggan, or skateboard—all undertaken without even the most minimal amount of safety gear.

Things have changed quite a bit since those concussion-filled days. And so have helmets. People of all ages wear them now. It is rare to see a cyclist or roller-blader without some sort of head protection. Even some curlers put safety before fashion out on the pebbled ice.

Protective headgear has become commonplace. Helped, no doubt, by the rather dramatic design changes helmets have undergone over the past four decades. Slimmer than ever—with increased comfort and a wide variety of colours—they now come in "stylish" options and are, in many cases, a fashion statement in their own right.

That's a far cry from back in the day when former Capreolite

Doug Mohns became one of the first NHL-ers to "don a lid."

Helmets are so prevalent in modern society that some people even argue they're becoming a problem. Most of us harbouring "special needs" like the increase in usage. After all, when everyone else has helmet head there is no reason to point and stare.

Thinking back on my many traumatic brain injuries—the ones I remember anyway—I noticed a strange trend: my head injuries always declined in winter. You'd think they'd increase during the slippery season. Icy sidewalks should have combined with heavy boots to pull me down more often. And, in fact, they did. So, what saved my tender young noggin? Toques. My grandmother knitted me these god-awful woollen monstrosities—three sizes too big and fully an inch thick—and they protected me better than any CSA-approved padding. Especially since there was no way I'd ever be caught dead in such obvious protective gear.

So, here's my million-dollar, life-changing idea—disguise the helmet. Start with the assumption that some protection is better than none and build it into commonplace headwear like toques and ballcaps. An inconspicuous bit of padding, a few strips of plastic, all sewn inside (with some colourful pattern to disguise the stitching) and . . . voila! We've transformed the helmet into something no one can recognize as a safety feature. Not a perfect solution I know, but it's got to help some. And, according to research out of Virginia Tech, even two hundred dollar professional grade hockey helmets can't promise more than that.

• • •

Hard-headedness runs in my family—it inspired our unregistered heraldic motto Semper Caput Edurus (meaning "Always Hard-Headed") —but, of all the Del Papas, I take that phrase the most literally.

Even spending most of the last forty years in a wheelchair, I've suffered my share of blows to the head. Baseballs, two-by-fours, steel rods and more have "rung my bell." I once bounced my skull off a bed's headboard so hard it left a dent in the wood and had me seeing both stars and little twittering birdies dancing about.

Did I suffer concussions? Probably. No one much worried about head injuries decades back. "It don't look that bad," seemed the de-facto diagnosis. Usually followed by, "Walk it off." Not the most apropos of advice to give a cripple. Still, being treated with such casual disregard—just like anyone else in a similar situation—proved preferable to me.

After all, as the song goes, "Never trust a fellow with a helmet on his head." *

---

* "Helmethead" by Great Big Sea, from their 2004 album *Something Beautiful*.

Public Transport—It's Not Just for Crazy People Anymore

Being chauffeured to and from school gave me a big head. Not that I ever needed much help in that department. My cranium is, and always has been, on the gargantuan side—both physically and metaphorically. But the special treatment didn't help.

Many North Americans are suspicious of public transportation, and rightly so. Mass transit in this part of the world leaves a lot to be desired. Trains are expensive to ride. Subways, according to popular lore, are dirty and crowded. Airplanes require invasive security screenings and usually involve obscenely frustrating delays. Then there are buses . . . and buses seem worse yet—especially if you believe the media.

Listening to the "if it bleeds it leads" news is enough to convince a person that riding a bus is akin to taking your life into your hands. The seats are crowded with would-be murderers, ravaging potential rapists, and serial killers on the hunt for their next victim. And, while there is more truth to those exaggerated claims than bus company publicists would like, the press still paints a bleak picture. Almost as if every bus—be it city, school, or charter—is something out of a dystopian nightmare . . . where it's a good ride if commuters don't get stabbed.

Despite all the horror stories, plenty of people ride the bus. Some even more than once. I just wasn't one of them. Not at first, anyway.

Starting in September 1978, I joined every other physically disabled elementary student in Capreol—all four of us—in being treated to an all-expenses-paid school commute. Via taxi.

Why no bus for young Matthew? All the town's other Kindergarteners got put aboard the big yellow school-bus for their daily commute. The answer appears obvious: My wheelchair. Only that wasn't the reason. No, my earliest schooling took place before I stopped walking.

Prior to needing the use of a wheelchair, most of my problems involved steps—taking them and climbing them. Stamina marked my biggest difficulty. I tired easily. That made the quarter-block journey from my home to the nearest bus stop an exhausting ordeal for me. And that didn't count standing around waiting or the challenge presented by the bus's stairs.

I might have managed walking until age eight but never with anything like grace. Even at my best I seldom did more than shuffle my feet along the ground. Anytime I needed to lift them more than a handspan left me stymied. Going up stairs proved an insurmountable challenge* and the bus featured a riser bigger than most.

Getting aboard would have required assistance and, since neither children nor drivers have much patience, I found myself routed to a different form of transport. I was the youngest (by several years) of a young lot and so don't remember much of the ordeal. In fact, for me, the modified daily commute seemed . . . normal. Having the canary-coloured cab pull up to my door and being helped in and out by the driver became routine. I didn't know any different. And besides, there were three other kids sharing the ride with me: Stacey, Richie, and Bradley. The last two were both older and close friends; they chatted in the backseat while Stacey and I sat up front beside the chain-smoking cabbie. I spent most of the drive fiddling with the electronic meter—it seemed so advanced to my young eyes—pushing the beeping buttons until someone told me to stop.

That all changed when I got my first wheelchair. Too big to fit in the taxi's trunk, it put an end to the familiar commute and necessitated a shift to wheelchair-accessible bus for the rest of my extended education.** Seventeen long years.

And so I can say with absolute confidence that you meet the strangest people on the bus. Good strange, annoying strange, and "Let me off this bus right now!" strange. None though, in my experience, were stranger than the drivers themselves.

---

* The only steps I ever managed to climb unaided were at my family camp. There my dad got set the task of building the stairs to our dock's flat-roofed sitting area. As a youth he didn't measure, just eyeballed the job, and produced a riser never reaching three inches, let alone than the standard height of seven to seven and a half.

** Honesty demands I admit that during the 1993-94 school year I rode in a privately-owned van, one that had an extended roof and an electric lift.

It takes a special sort of person to drive a bus. Beyond the ability to handle several tonnes of speeding iron, drivers must deal with maurading cyclists who think they own the road and jaywalking pedestrians harbouring some sort of death wish—not to mention every other vehicle on the road and the aggressive lunatics behind their wheels. Then there's the little fact that you have all the passengers' lives in your care. The stress is immense.

Now add in tight schedules, increasing traffic, deteriorating roads, constantly changing weather conditions, and the ever-shrinking well of human decency . . . and you can see it requires nerves of steel and the patience of a saint to take on the job.

And that's on a normal bus. My bus riding experiences were somewhat different than most. I rode the Handi-Transit—aka "the short bus."

Most of my views on life have changed as I've aged but nothing compares to my shifting stance on public transport. As a child I thought it a treat to have a special vehicle carry me around. Then, right about the time I got my first wheelchair, all I wanted was to be with my friends. For a time, most notably during high school initiation, riding alone seemed a relief. Hearing of the hurtful hijinks taking place aboard the regular bus made me grateful for the security of solitary transport.

Then I reached sixteen and I watched my contemporaries begin to drive. I envied that newfound independence. Muscle weakness combined with glacial reflexes make me a poor candidate for a licence. Even if I wanted to try the test, which necessitated travelling to Toronto, it meant ignoring the fact that my super-charged, easily distracted imagination would put others in danger every time I sat behind the wheel.

All through high school the vehicles contracted to carry me were privately owned and payment for their services came from the schoolboard. Upon graduation that changed. Getting to and from university became my problem and my expense. That awoke me to the cost of transportation like a bucket of ice-water dumped on my head.

It's amazing how paying for a service makes you aware of every detail. Suddenly I wanted to get full value for my money. It wasn't a complete transformation. I didn't go from blissfully ignorant child to demandingly cynical adult. Waiting upon the bus to arrive never triggered an entitled sense of intense outrage, like it did with so many of the older riders. Nor did the constantly malfunctioning heaters freeze my humanity—though I came to dread the vehicle's door opening. Twenty long shivering minutes were required for the bus's struggling temperature control system to combat the invasive chill, usually right around the time of our next stop.

Most of the Handi-Transit vehicles were old, sorry-looking dinosaurs only barely kept on the road. Besides always needing a good scrubbing, both inside and out, many of the more essential creature comforts required maintenance. Prioritizing safety might have made sense, from a liability point-of-view, but whoever oversaw the service could never fully commit.

I'd have believed their claims to safety except for the worn condition of the straps used to tie my wheelchair down. And don't get me started on the "hasty" training given to the drivers on attaching these restraints—it was more good luck than good planning that no one got seriously hurt. Luckily for me, my wheelchair had its own seatbelt.* That luxury was not shared by

---

* I will never forget the one time it failed. The schoolbus made a sudden stop at a light and my seatbelt, each half bolted to the back of the wheelchair, let go. How I didn't end up on the bus's none-too-clean floor remains a mystery. But every belt since has been one continuous piece, just to prevent a repeat incident.

my equally vulnerable but more ambulatory fellows. They made do with just the thinnest padding on the leatherette-covered bench seats while the driver was secured in place by the sort of three-point harness usually reserved for Formula 1 drivers.

"Handi-Transit" isn't, despite the name, the handiest form of transport. I should know, I've been in a wheelchair for almost forty years now and spent thousands of hours aboard those instantly recognizable vehicles . . . or, more accurately, waiting for them. Punctuality is another thing lacking aboard the Handi-Transit. In fact, there are a lot of terms no sane person would ever apply to those buses: luxurious, comfortable, and cost-effective spring to mind.

Like most of my fellow passengers I found myself labelled as "special." That one-word catch-all covered a myriad of users. No one I ever talked to seemed entirely sure what criteria went into earning the coveted label. Most boarders' needs were obvious: the disabled and the old needn't explain themselves . . . at least not to me. Judging others suitability for the plum service never appealed, bracing myself to remain upright while whipping around corners kept me busy enough, but a lot of riders speculated—some none-too-quietly—about who "deserved" the select Handi-Transit treatment. The door-to-door delivery, complete with assistance boarding the vehicle, put the city's regular bus service to shame. And having the price "set" no matter where or how far we travelled didn't hurt either.

I rode that bus for six years, almost the entirety of my university studies. It proved a highly educational experience. You can learn a lot about the human condition aboard a bus. That most egalitarian mode of public transport exposed me to a wide cross-section of society, including parts otherwise outside my circle of experience. Seniors, I was surprised to discover, made for the most amusing bus-mates—one meandering anecdote could encompass the entire forty-five-minute journey—but could also be the most difficult riders. No one knows the bus's schedule like the old and woe unto any driver who arrived a minute late or left one second early. That precise, often passive-aggressive, punctuality tended to be the pensioners' worst quality. Other riders dreaded their long, often repetitive stories. Several of my fellows avoided sharing a seat with certain seniors, unable to take another conversation starting with "In my day" or "I remember when" and proceeding downhill from there. Reminisces dominated almost every conversation I shared with senior passengers. I enjoyed each and every one, but then I seldom had to listen for more than half an hour at a time—the poor driver got it non-stop.

Given the dizzying array of disabilities the driver needed to deal with—each with its own unique set of specific instructions—it's amazing that they could keep their daily duties straight.

Not to toot my own horn but I was an easy passenger. My needs were simple: someone to work the lift,* secure my wheelchair, and drive. Most of the other physically disabled were the same. Most, but not all. Some few proved far trickier. I remember one girl who lived in discomfort and gasped in pain if her legs were so much as slightly jostled. For those who don't know, securing a wheelchair for travel necessitated much rougher treatment than mere jostling and that didn't count the difficult of climbing around—and sometimes over—the various assistive devices. I always felt sorry for the driver and the girl, neither of whom enjoyed their encounters. Just not

---

* Preferably someone fully caffeinated and paying attention. One disinterested bus driver lowered the lift and encouraged me to drive onto the platform even though it was already on the ground, three feet below. Needless to say, I always double-checked before following any of her instructions after that.

nearly as sorry as I did for any seated near to the one mentally challenged young man. Tactile sensations fascinated him. He spent the entire drive rubbing his fingers back and forth across the seat, the window, and the walls. If things stopped there, we'd have had no problems, but this guy couldn't resist touching anyone next to him—fingering their hair and clothes with wondrous admiration. It got to be so bad he had to be seated separately . . . an imperfect solution at best.

Most memorable, and dangerous, was the wrestling-obsessed teen. Every day he would regale me with the latest WWE excitement, even enthusiastically performing the moves as best he could in his wheelchair—causing those seated nearby to dodge his flailing limbs. His biggest dream in life was to have his hero, Stone Cold Steve Austin, ride to the ring on the back of his wheelchair.

The Handi-Transit riders came in all sorts of out-there flavours and the person behind the wheel had to deal with our "quirks." This could be pleasant—as with Howie and his unflappable, ever-optimistic love of the Toronto Maple Leafs or difficult like the man who refused to bathe and stunk so badly we opened every window while he was onboard, even in winter.

Some passengers were heartbreaking. Getting to know those visiting the Alzheimer's Society proved the hardest. Watching these people steadily decline, from friendly and talkative bus-mates to quiet and detached shells, wore on us more than them. The same could be said of the childlike innocence constantly displayed by one teenage girl. Her mental development never progressed beyond that of a five-year-old, leaving her perpetually cheerful and eager to make friends. Every day she generously gifted a painting to the driver—who promptly taped each above his head. By year's end the entire bus was papered with the teen's art and it seemed a much cheerier place.

You want to know the dirty little secret of Handi-Transit services? The passengers weren't the only ones aboard who were special. The drivers proved equally . . . unique.

Finding steady drivers for the "special needs" bus was a perennial challenge. Over the years I was witness to a wide assortment—all of whom were, invariably, kind. But that kindness couldn't hide their weirdness. Here's my list of most memorable drivers: a reformed ex-biker—complete with neck tattoos and requisite facial scar—who alternated between regaling me with stories of his violent gangland past and preaching his newly-accepted Christianity; a practising witch who thought, wrongly, she could sing; a young woman utterly convinced that my dog smiled at her every morning; and a noted local psychic—I scoffed at her supposed "powers" until she successfully assisted the police on a case and then went on to win the lottery.

Each day aboard bus was an adventure. Sure, the rides were long and roundabout, the company unpredictable, and the heating systems never quite up to the job come winter but I wouldn't change the years I spent aboard.

Still, nothing could compare with the taxi. It spoiled me on public transport forever after.

And the Band Played On

There have been studies that show introducing children to music helps create fuller, more rounded personalities. I'm sure a lot of highly qualified psychiatrists and expertly trained psychologists were paid good money for that research. Whether there is any measurable evidence to support their conclusions is for others to decide. All I know for sure is that schools across Canada bought into the notion. My alma mater proved no exception.

Too bad I began music class in a hole and never really dug myself out.

Capreol's own St. Mary's Elementary School reserved "band class" for the two most senior grades, seven and eight. When I was in Grade Seven the music room was in the basement and, since the building lacked anything as sophisticated as an elevator,

92

I was "excused" from attending. When my contemporaries trudged downstairs for music lessons, I remained in our main-floor classroom and did homework. That didn't seem like such a bad deal. The long-time teacher, Mr. C,* made a point to keep me occupied; giving me little jobs whenever I appeared bored or talking sports to help pass the time. In truth, rather than feeling left out of music class, I enjoyed the hour spent with him. The one-on-one time seemed a rare privilege.

But by the next year things changed. Someone must have complained because, when I started Grade Eight, accommodations were made. Too bad no one seemed particularly happy with the compromise . . . especially me.

Everyone else had a full year to learn the basics of their instruments. Me? I got thrown into the proverbial deep end—only weighted down with cement shoes—and commanded "Swim!"

The first order of business involved testing. That's right, my musical journey began with me trying every instrument in the school orchestra, all under the judgemental eye of some "important" imported expert. He criticized the way I sat, bemoaned that I failed "to hold it right," and pulled several from my grip when my diminished lung capacity left me unable to blow strongly enough to make the brass or woodwind instrument work. That man's attitude annoyed me no end but didn't come as a shock.

My experience with music had started years earlier and involved a most traumatic introduction to the art—with my grandparents buying me a piano. I know . . . first world problems, right?

I didn't know the word "shrew" when I began piano lessons but that term, I later realized, would have fit my first instructor to a tee.

---

* He retired at the end of that school year, leaving a large hole in the school's faculty, and depriving following cohorts from his gentle wisdom and stern-but-fair code of conduct.

That sounds harsh but, trust me, anyone unfortunate enough to take a lesson from that woman would agree. She worked out of the school gymnasium. Students went into her little "office"—barely big enough for an upright piano and her chair—with reluctant, fearful faces and fled at the end of the hour inevitably awash with tears.

Talent level didn't matter—and I'll admit here I had none—she tore into each one of us placed under her oh-so-tender care mercilessly. Neither age nor enthusiasm lessened her whip-like tongue, the woman zeroed in on each of our young faults with the unerring instincts of an embittered Marine Corps drill instructor. She dehumanized the teacher-student relationship to the point many gave up on music rather than put up with her abuse for another second.

It seemed to me at the time that I could do no right in her eyes. The fact that I never practiced might have had something to do with my constant failure to measure up. But I know several of her other students rehearsed diligently, performed flawlessly, and still emerged from her cramped cubicle crying.

Every "lesson" progressed the same, with me kicking my feet—lacking all sense of rhythm—as I sat on the bench, tongue sticking out in concentration, while the instructor reduced me to a quivering wreck. Two minutes in I'd be looking up at the ceiling in vain attempt to hold back the tears. That habit invariably led to her wholly inappropriate criticism, given the school's oft-stated Catholicism, "Quit looking to Heaven. God can't help you here!"

To say piano wasn't my priority would be a colossal understatement. Sports distracted me. So too cartoons. I undertook music lessons for one reason and one reason only: To please my grandmother. That dear woman applauded no matter how mediocre my efforts. Pride shone on her face as I ham-handedly butchered the classics.

The most vicious serial killers in the world would wince at witnessing the massacres I made of beloved tunes. "Twinkle, Twinkle" flummoxed my fledgling fingers and the intricacies of "She'll Be Coming Round the Mountain" placed so much strain on me that I nearly suffered a breakdown while I pecked at the ivories.

It fell to a later teacher to make those eighty-eight keys approachable. Not easy mind, just less like torture. This man came to my house and, in just a few good-natured lessons, I learned more from his brief words of encouragement than enduring what's-her-name's hellish histrionics.

To be fair, that only amounted to the most elementary of basics—like reading staff notation—but being able to plunk out the simplest of tunes in an almost recognizable fashion proved a balm to my embittered soul.

My grandmother's approving delight didn't hurt either.

• • •

There was only one instrument on offer at St. Mary's Elementary not requiring strong lungs: the drums. These weren't the cool-type drums found in rock bands, both professional and aspiring. No, rather than a tight little set, the school had three individual "stations" in the percussion section—the snare drum, the bass drum, and the cymbal—and each was played separately. It proved an ineffective strategy.

I guess I should have been grateful there was no triangle or else I'd have been assigned that nerdiest of orchestra staples.

As it was, me and my two fellow percussionists—Alyssa and Theresa—rotated daily. That bit of fair-mindedness meant each of us got a turn on the snare—the most desirable of the three instruments. It also meant none of us ever truly mastered any one of our noisome trio.

Having several years of piano under my belt meant I felt confident. That didn't last long. It took me half a year to learn that the baton being waved at the front of the class was meant to keep time. Prior to that I thought the teacher merely needed to feel important.

Two shining moments and one poorly thought-out comment dominated my one year in band. I cannot quite remember when the first highlight occurred but, thanks to class-clown Scott and his perfect comedic timing, we embarrassed the music teacher and set the entire band to laughing. It was Scott who approached me and asked if I'd participate by punctuating his "joke" with a rim-shot. That instantly recognizable bit of old-time vaudevillian showmanship—snare-snare-snare-cymbal, Bah-da-bah. Ching!—stretched my skillset to the limit but when he raised his hand mid-rehearsal and said, "Miss. I think we need to put Jason back on the saxophone. Even bad sax is better than no sax at all," my drumsticks flew.

The second incident occurred at our Christmas recital. I'd been moved to the cymbal for this particular carol and the notation gave me an opening four-note solo. The classic song started with me laying down steady metronomic beat on the cymbal for the rest of the band to come in on. Up came the music instructor's baton and, on the downswing, I began . . . only to be furiously waved off.

My one chance to shine had been squandered.

The teacher frowned at me and I glared back, confident since the sheet music sat in front of me. It took her a moment to confirm that I was, in fact, correct. She offered a hasty apology, saying, "Sorry, Mat. You're right. Let's try that again."

And we did. Unfortunately, the moment had been despoiled.

My first cymbal strike sounded tentative even to me. But by number three I'd gotten into the swing of it and managed to keep up that steady rate throughout the entirety of the song. "Jingle Bells" if I recall correctly.

My unintentionally insulting comment came during the last day of school. Our music teacher, a kind woman who not only enjoyed her job but actually liked spending time around children, took the last few minutes of class to express her appreciation to us. Like many teenage boys, displays of honest emotion discomforted me and so I began tapping out an unconscious rhythm on my drumsticks. The sound proved louder than I intended and she heard. Stopping mid-speech, the music teacher appeared more curious than angry as she asked, "What is that you're playing?"

Not even aware that my hands were moving the sticks I paused. "Nothing," came the self-conscious answer. Then I added, "It's just something I made up."

"Why didn't you show such creativity during the rest of the year?"

Rather than admit the truth, that it never even occurred to me that deviating from the assigned music was even possible, I said, "I only do it when I'm bored."

That answer wasn't meant as a criticism of her raw, heartfelt goodbye. But it seemed clear from her face that she took it that way.

Good thing that music class was ending for us graduating students, because it seemed highly unlikely the teacher would be letting me join in any more lessons after that. In fact, the class moved back into St. Mary's basement the next school year. The era of accessibility had ended. And because of me it did so on a sour note.

A Face Made for Radio

Try as I might, I cannot sing.* Not even a little. There is, in fact, zero musical talent in me. I have no rhythm, am completely tone-deaf, and I possess a truly terrible memory for lyrics. (As a child, the local Catholic church used my disability as a convenient excuse to keep me out of the loft-rehearsing choir—thinking, no doubt, that a less cruel choice then telling me I seemed incapable of hitting a note on cue.) What I can do, however, is talk. You'd be hard pressed to find anyone more naturally gifted at talking than me. I've been known to monologue for extended periods, barely even coming up for air, pontificating on subjects I know very little about. Worse,

---

* And I tried for years ... even though people asked me to stop. And not everyone did so politely.

thanks to my voracious reading, I'm able to sound convincingly authoritative while spouting barely understood facts—to any but an actual expert, at least. And, above all, I love nothing more than telling long, rambling, and ultimately pointless stories . . . often for hours on end.

Naturally, well-meaning people told me to get into radio.

This advice peaked after my local elementary school graduation ceremony, where my big mouth combined with my runaway enthusiasm—seldom a good combination—to get me into yet another wacky sitcom-style predicament.

I never intended to speak at the commencement, and I certainly didn't volunteer to do so but, after the latest in a long line of failed attempts to outsmart a teacher backfired, nobody gave me much choice.

Being volun-told to stand before friends, parents, and faculty to recite a prayer still seems like a violation of religious liberty—a bold move for a Catholic institution—and an outright crime against most, if not all, of my inalienable charter rights. If I hadn't brought the humiliation on myself there might have been more complaining on my part. As it was, I pouted throughout the hours-long ceremony until suddenly my turn in the spotlight arrived.

The sterile gymnasium of a small-town elementary school is hardly the best place to make a public speaking debut. The hardwood floor and cinderblock walls don't provide complimentary acoustics, the high ceiling creates a sound-deadening effect, and that doesn't even count the crowd. Restive from being kept sitting too long in unseasonable June heat—without air conditioning, fans, or even a hint of ventilation—the proud onlookers squirmed on squeaky seats, grumbled low-voiced complaints, and gossiped with their fellow sufferers to pass the time.

So, you can see the situation wasn't ideal.

Most of those who preceded me mumbled their passages into their chests, struggling to enunciate the words, and leaving anyone not in the front row guessing as to what was being said. Nervous giggles or panicked frenzies marked their attempts at reading solemn Bible passages or inspirational poems.

Nobody expected my contribution to be any different. In fact, most of my peers thought I'd do worse.

My inability to stand meant no one in the crowd would be able to see me over those seated ahead of them. Flop sweat soaked my newly purchased white dress shirt, and my bright red bow-tie—yes, I made that unfortunate senior-centric fashion choice at age 14—seemed to be strangling me as I gasped for breath on the drive from the anonymous safety seated alongside my fellow graduates to the awkward, lonely prominence reserved for each designated contributor. And, unlike everyone who chose to be part of the ceremony, I'd never once shown the slightest flare for the dramatic in my ten years attending St. Mary's.

Unbeknownst to all, this wasn't my first performance, nor the most hostile audience I'd ever faced.

Way back in my summer camp days, half a decade prior, I'd spent most of a week doing "theatre." Dying on that wheelchair-accessible stage seemed relatively painless to me since it followed my repeated unhorsing at the stables.

Still sore from my epically agonizing falls—don't ever buy into the, "Got to get back up in the saddle" logic, it's just an excuse for further humiliation—my badly bruised ego had me fleeing after the fourth failed riding attempt and adamant in refusing to go anywhere near a horse thereafter.

If I'd known how critical a camp full of disabled kids could be of their fellows' amateur theatrical efforts, I might have tried climbing aboard saddle a fifth time.

Once in the limelight I failed miserably. Turns out me and Uta Hagen didn't share much in common. Even the rudiments of acting proved beyond me. Not only did I find memorizing lines a challenge, hitting my mark proved a constant distraction, and I never knew what to do with my hands—moving them awkwardly from front to back with zero resemblance to any actual human being.

Unnatural as my early attempts were—and not even a team of MIT's best engineers could build a robot less natural at emoting than me—things got worse as Camp Northwood's resident acting coach worked with me. That harried nineteen-year-old tried her best. The rest of the erstwhile cast made noticeable progress under her tutelage, even coming to shine under the footlight's proverbial glare. Me? I only became more self-conscious. Second-guessing every instinct meant I trod the boards with all the charisma of a week-old corpse and carried less charm than a flatulent skunk crashing an all-bean church picnic.

Wooden may best describe my summer stage presence. But I did learn one valuable skill: How to "project" my voice. Mastering that bit of verbal volume to the extent that, years later—when it came time to read my brief prayer—I found myself easily filling the school gymnasium.

Heads turned as I uttered my first syllable. Speaking from the diaphragm gave power to the words and they echoed throughout the gym, clear to the farthest corners. People began standing trying to see over the heads of those in front before I read through the first sentence. Unaware of the stir, I continued the prayer—one of five I composed for the occasion, no doubt divinely inspired.

Since I have an unfortunate tendency to rush when reading aloud, as if the punctuation were a mere suggestion and racing to the end marked some sort of victory, my mantra that day was simple: Slow and steady. It must have worked because people lined up to congratulate me after the event ended. Hands were shaken, compliments shared—including several directing me into radio broadcasting—and I went home feeling pretty good about myself. Sweat-stained shirt notwithstanding.

Word of my voice spread and I found myself helping at our town's Youth Games. These Olympic-style sporting competitions centred on the 400-metre track not far from my home. It was my job to announce the winners, using my booming voice to be heard over the children's chattering excitement. Nothing difficult . . . except pronouncing the names. Capreol is hardly the most ethnically diverse town in Canada but over the years people from dozens of countries have come to reside withing its limits—Germans, Poles, Ukrainians, Finns, Italians, Russians, and more. And, somehow, I butchered every name. The harder I tried the worse things became. By the end of the day even the simplest pronunciations gave me fits. Bets were being taken on just how badly I would mangle each successive winner's surname.

I had found my kryptonite. Any hope of a career in radio came crashing back to earth. My future cratered, I went home an emotional wreck.

Then, as if by some miracle, I appeared on CBC radio. Twice.

The first time happened at the Scotties (aka The Tournament of Hearts—Canada's preeminent women's curling championships) and, even though my comments aired without any form of credit, they went nation-wide. Praising the event with succinct sincerity earned me repeat play across the entire network. On the hour. Through the entire week.

Unfortunately, my second stint with CBC went horribly wrong. I'd forgotten the first rule of publicity: Always be positive.

There'd been a last-minute cancellation and I got called out of the blue as an emergency fill-in—if I "could get there in under an hour." Interviewing for my second self-published collection of railroad-themed short stories should have been an easy publicity win. Turns out live radio is not my forte. Most of the blame is mine but shame on the mother-corporation for not warning me on how to behave. No, I didn't scream obscenities into the microphone (though the urge definitely struck). Instead, I focused on the most inappropriate tale in the entire short story collection and elaborated with incriminating detail. The more I spoke the wider the host's eyes grew. I ended with an offhand, "Good thing the statute of limitations has expired, eh?" Which earned a nervous chuckle then a professional throw to commercial. Needless to say, they never invited me back.

More recently I guested on CKLU's Poetry broadcast, answering questions, insulting poets, and reading an embarrassing short story to the amusement of Sudbury's then-Poet Laureate.

The city's current Poet Laureate hosts The PL Pod and has tentatively proposed I guest on the podcast. Given my previous failures this doesn't strike me as the most promising of ideas. Though I do have an unexpected take on poetry, namely that I hate it. If announcing that bit of bias doesn't get me kicked off the program then I plan to go on and explain the admiration with which I hold all poets, the envy I feel toward their elegant efficiency with language, and the raw emotional power they pack into each beguilingly beautiful verse. Jealousy is an ugly look on me but it's far from the only obstacle between me and a successful radio appearance.

Fate has conspired against me too.

I would have tried my hand (voice?) at the university radio station while attending Laurentian—I even had a program planned out Crash's Can-Con, playing nothing but Canadian content—

except CKLU wasn't wheelchair accessible at the time. The student-run station sat in a tiny portable at the edge of one of the campus's smaller parking lots. Sure, I could have made a stink and the school probably would have moved it—the campus had plenty of space—but that sort of complaining just isn't in me.*

There's no doubt in my mind that I'd have been a terrible DJ. My musical tastes tend to be seriously uncool** and I always find myself lagging behind my peers in discovering, let alone appreciating, the defining artists of any given year. (Have you heard this band, Nirvana? I think they might be big.) Worse, I have this innate need to educate, amuse, and impress. Nothing can restrain my impulse to expound and elucidate. Then there's the fact that most of the things I think sound smart and funny—humorous allusions to obscure bits of pop culture—seldom resonate with others. My best material usually earns me confused stares and uneasy, get-this-crazy-man-away-from-me, smiles.

Reading the news might have been more my speed—current events have always interested me—if it weren't for my aforementioned habit of horrendously mispronouncing names. Place names get mangled just as badly . . . heaven help me if there's an accent mark!

Interviewing others is where I would most shine. I like people, individually anyway, and love listening to them talk. An attentive audience is key to any interview. Listening to others is one of my

---

* It wasn't all that long since I received threatening phone calls "encouraging" me not to attend Capreol High School. Many residents figured the local school board was itching to close the community institution and assumed, rightly, that the expensive renovations needed to make it wheelchair accessible would be the deciding factor. That episode left a sour taste in my mouth for years and gave me a less than favourable view of CHS and its supporters. (The school was shuttered less than a decade later and not because of me.)

** I'm listening to Weird Al Yankovic as I type this and think the man is a genius.

few redeeming qualities. Nothing draws people out like someone hanging onto every word of their story. It is a useful broadcasting instinct, being able to prompt and cajole others with nothing but a smile, encouraging nod, or well placed, "Really?" Larry King credited his phenomenal success to that oft-overlooked trait.

Did I miss my calling? Maybe. But I'm still a talker. Always have been and always will be. And given the explosion of podcasts there are more venues out there than ever before. Who knows, my voice might still be heard.

Not My Finest Moment, Part One

Regrets. I have a few. Too many really. But one sticks out. It involved needless cruelty—on my part—and changed the entire direction of my life as only a youthful indiscretion can. Try as I might, there is no excusing my actions that night. I can only relate the facts and hope that the following anecdote conveys the depth of regret I still feel regarding my unthinking behaviour.

Courtesy has since become my default persona. I choose politeness—even when it isn't always warranted—thanks in no small part due to this incident and the shame subsequently seared upon my soul.

The day in question marked the first time in my then-young life that I understood words and actions have consequences beyond my control. It was when I realized that other people have problems.

That believing the best of those around me and living in such a way that they think the same of me, mattered. All of which prompted me to become the kind of a man who prides himself on his positivity and actively works to put more "good feelings" out into the world . . . no matter my personal circumstances. That sounds naïve. Nonetheless, I'd rather look on life with hope and be disappointed than live as a cynic and gloat about being right.

Admitting to past mistakes is the first step towards a brighter tomorrow. All the self-help books agree. Not that owning up to our missteps is an easy task. Most of us prefer to gloss over our errors. I will be the first to confess a worrying tendency to forget or misremember many of life's failures. There's a comfort in rewriting our personal histories . . . at least in our own minds. Each of us is, after all, the hero of our own story. Or in this case, for me, the villain.

Unfortunately for my fragile psyche, it is more important that this book contains the truth—even when such honesty is unflattering. Creative non-fiction can't all be amusing anecdotes and slapstick humour. And, though most of my stories skew toward funny, I've had my share of darker moments. Making a 14-year-old girl cry proved one of them.

In my defence, I was also 14 at the time and the incident followed a stress-filled day.

• • •

Even back when I graduated St. Mary's Elementary, long ago in the mists of time though it was, the final day of primary school marked a pivotal turning point in life. Today, students recognize the moment's significance with elaborate ceremonies, a plethora of awards, commemorative photos, and even formal-dress parties but in the late 1980s we took things more casually . . . and that proved the first of our mistakes. Scheduling the two events we did bother to hold all on the same day was our second.

Being a Catholic institution, prayers got recited at length—both before and after the diplomas were handed out. I don't remember a lot of details beyond a lot of waiting around and constantly tugging at the constricting unfamiliarity of my too-tight bowtie the entire time. Receiving my "sheepskin"—in reality a photocopied document with the individualized particulars penned in after the fact—came as a welcome relief. The day, one of the longest and most awkward of our then-young lives, ultimately culminated with a dance, the first most of us ever attended.

If you were to ask me to list my own personal versions of Hell, dances would rank near the top. Loud and crowded, the dance floor is not a place I've ever felt comfortable. Not only do I have zero rhythm, but physical contact of any sort is repellant. The idea of grinding against some stranger holds no real appeal for me. Add in the discomfort of "dressing up" and it's easy to see why I was on edge.

I can't speak on behalf of all disabled persons but, for me, watching the able-bodied gyrating to the music—regardless of their skill or grace—is bittersweet. I enjoy seeing the joy and affection shared between dancers but it also serves to reinforce the difference between us. Oh, sure, plenty of handicapped people can cut the proverbial rug. There's no physical reason keeping me on the sidelines. My electric wheelchair could have me out there easily enough. But doing so would draw attention and pity—two things I work hard to avoid.

As it is, someone always feels sorry for the "poor soul in the wheelchair" and asks me to dance. My reactions to those offers haven't always been kind. In fact, during my youth, I tended to reply rather . . . badly.

Hard though it may be to believe—and the stories in this book probably aren't helping—disability doesn't dominate my mind on a daily basis. In fact, I often go whole minutes without thinking about the fact that I'm in a wheelchair. Lifestyle changes, various accommodations, and four decades of "getting used to" my condition means I sometimes forget that I'm even handicapped.

Dances, however, serve as a constant reminder of my physical shortcomings. And that is the only explanation for how I treated Jane Doe,* the 14-year-old I drove to tears.

Everyone knew Jane. She had a generous smile and, even as a teen, showered kindness on everyone around her. We had been classmates for a decade—having met in kindergarten—and I counted her a friend long before graduation day arrived. There was a small-town wholesomeness to her. Blessed with a warm heart and a warmer personality, Jane projected a "motherly concern" rare among our age group.

And, for some unknown reason, she liked me. Anyone who's ever been a teen knows the importance of that word.

Early in the evening, Jane came over to where I sat in an out-of-the-way corner and asked me to dance.

Naturally, I turned her down.

And if I had stopped there—with a simple, polite, "No thanks"—things probably would have ended. A two-minute explanation on my part could have prevented a night full of awkwardness and misery. Being 14, however, such maturity proved beyond me. Instead of answering her kindness with corresponding

---

* I'm protecting her identity out of shame. No doubt Jane Doe has long forgotten the entire incident. But I have yet to reconcile the childish behaviour and needless cruelty with the man I like to think I am. One night's callousness has shaped the rest of my life and out of such moments is character made . . . or not made.

kindness I gave into anger and cut her down. Adding something needlessly caustic to the initial reply.

Jane must have forgiven the snotty tone—there was a good-nature to her soul—because she came back throughout the night, asking me again and again to dance. And, each time, my reply grew crueller.

The first few weren't actually intended that way. My initial words might have lacked kindness, but it was only when I realized my friends—teenage boys one and all—were laughing that I really stepped up the insults. It never once occurred to me she'd take them to heart. I was only joking, after all. My friends and I insulted each other all the time and never took a word of it seriously.

At first, I thought Jane enjoyed the game. She stormed off after each increasingly callous rejection to go huddle with the other girls. Turns out she wasn't muttering angrily but crying.

I only learned the truth late in the dance. One of Jane's friends, outraged on her behalf, marched over and told me point blank that she was really hurt by my thoughtless comments.

Immediate regret washed over me. Sure, to my mind Jane Doe was a bit of a nuisance. Everyone knew of her unconditional kindness, she shared that daily, but I bore the brunt of her mothering nature. She directed constant concern in my direction—always asking about my well-being in a manner that somehow felt intrusive, cloying, and demeaning. I resented that she went out of her way to help me, the class's lone disabled member. All I wanted was to just be one of the guys and she kept treating me different . . . better.

Discovering Jane was in tears hit me like an ice-cold shower.

Not having ever caused a teenage girl to cry before,* I found myself at a loss as to what to do. It took a surprising amount of

---

* Or since . . . once was enough to teach me my lesson.

soul-searching to realize an apology was in order. Upon reaching that seemingly obvious conclusion I set out to make amends . . . as best as any 14-year-old could.

I tracked her down to the gymnasium's storeroom. She was sitting alone, huddled on a stack of folded up gym-mats, and refused to look at me. There was only one way to open this conversation. The words "I'm sorry" started things off and before long we were sharing an extended heart to heart. Nothing romantic. I wasn't in a place where that thought even occurred to me. Others, however, grew suspicious of our long isolation. In fact, the principal broke up our little gabfest, no doubt thinking we were engaged in teenage hanky-panky.

Luckily for me, Jane proved kinder than I deserved and forgave me before we found ourselves chased back out onto the dance floor—me to my corner and her to her gathered girlfriends. I, of course, have yet to forgive myself.

• • •

Other disabled people may have grown up with mockery a constant buzzing in their ears but for me, at least, I never felt like an outcast.

In truth, with very few exceptions, my life has been easy. There was no reason for the way my 14-year-old self treated that open-hearted girl. I like to think I've grown since then. That I would never ignore someone else's feelings now, certainly not for cheap laughs. I suspect, however, that there's still a self-centred little jackass lurking inside me just waiting to come out and make others cry.

I needed an embarrassingly long time to learn that everyone has problems. Sitting in a wheelchair doesn't make me special, it just means some of my issues are on display for all to see. If some people choose to treat me differently because of that fact . . . that's their prerogative. My only choice is how to react. And, since I still look back at one unfortunate moment with regret, behaving in a positive manner is my preferred option.

So, I guess thanks are in order to the teary-eyed 14-year-old girl who showed me the error of my words and set me on the path to my best self. Oh, I've had setbacks. Uttered careless words in anger or frustration. I'm not perfect by any means. There's work yet to be done—and many of my finest moments are still to come—but much of the goodness within me comes from her example.*

---

* This incident isn't the sole reason I strive toward courtesy in all things. There are a number of other factors—many of them positive (like various role models)—but few of those involve living with disability.

The Ramp to Hell

Being disabled sucks. There's no getting around that. But using a wheelchair does come with a few perks: no matter where I go, I always have a seat; I save a fortune in footwear, shoes and socks last almost indefinitely; and, so long as the jealous looks don't get me down, I get all the best parking spots. Above all else, however, living with a disability tends to focus the mind.

That's not always a good thing. And in my case, it's downright tragic.

I've been introspective all my life and started taking an interest in religion at an insanely young age. Don't get me wrong, church never meant that much to me. I can count on one hand the times I attended mass of my own free will. But, despite an unhidden distaste for sacred buildings and the holy claptrap foisted therein, faith did play a formative role in my upbringing.

Religious holidays were big in my family, especially Christmas and Easter. Each celebratory get-together necessitated a huge, elaborate potluck dinner.*

Food and faith go hand in hand for immigrants, and my family being proud Canadians of Italian heritage proved no exception. Cooking and Catholicism were handed down generation to generation, almost exclusively by example. We might seldom have talked about religion—that's what Sunday mass was for—but we shared meals with gut-busting gusto. And no one dared stint. Not on contribution or consumption.

My youth spared me from both sanctimony and pot-scrubbing. Most familial duties, both religious and kitchen related, fell to others—older and better suited. I actively avoided church and, thanks to constantly dipping my finger in mixing bowls, got chased away from the cooking. My contributions weren't missed. The majority of my older relatives cooked and prayed with a proficiency I could never hope to match.

These were people who learned cooking as children at their mother's skirts and attended weekly church services with the sort of fanatic devotion I reserve for watching the Maple Leafs struggle during Hockey Night in Canada. My great-aunts and great-uncles (they numbered an even dozen)—first-generation Italian Canadians all—ran the sort of old-world Catholic households where people openly lamented the loss of High Latin mass. Combined with my grandparents and great-grandparents these souls dominated my early religious upbringing.

---

* These meals are the stuff of legends. Decades after the last, I still treasure those savoury memories. Thinking back on all the food—unbelievably delicious and insanely plentiful, with "Enough to feed an army!"—floods my mouth with anticipatory saliva to this day.

It was a point of pride for them, as with all good immigrants, to arrive at church early every Sunday with their cash-stuffed envelopes ready to drop in the donation basket, and to always sit in the same spot on the same pew throughout the majority of their lives.**

By my thirteenth birthday, I had a decade of Catholic school under my belt—complete with compulsory morning prayers and propaganda-like Bible studies—and had reached a turning point in my life: The inevitable crisis of conscience. That not-uncommon moment of religious reckoning normally comes to North Americans later in life. What can I say?

I was a bit of a prodigy. At least when it comes to bucking the church's outdated doctrine.

• • •

Everyone is familiar with the phrase, "The road to Hell is paved with good intentions," right?

What that catchy bit of wisdom means is that even well-intentioned actions can have unexpected, and harmful, consequences. I learned the truth of this when Our Lady of Peace built a ramp—thereby making their facilities wheelchair accessible for the first time in its history—and promptly chased me from the flock.

Arriving at the decision didn't come easy. Nor did it occur in a vacuum. I had been questioning Catholicism's various teachings

---

** The only acceptable excuse for moving was marriage. Newlyweds were expected to join one side of the family or the other—often this seemingly spur-of-the-moment change marked a major shift of power amidst the congregation, with repercussions lasting decades.

for a while when I hit puberty and the proverbial crossroads. The time for my Confirmation ceremony approached and, as it neared, I found myself having very serious doubts about organized religion.

Pressure came from everywhere. Friends and family both urged me to "Just do it," as if personal faith and my relationship with God were some cheap marketing ploy.

"There's presents and a party," they argued, trying to bribe me into taking the plunge. "Think of the food. It'll be great." When that didn't work, the guilting started. And Catholics are experts at guilt—wielding it with the precision of a scalpel while hacking away with the force of a broadsword.

"Do it for your grandparents," almost convinced me. There wasn't much I wouldn't do for those kindest of people. "Your grandma would be so proud," nearly sealed the deal. She'd never been healthy in all the time I knew her and pleasing her in even the most minuscule way seemed a small price for me to pay given all she'd done for me.

Then some helpful busybody tried to push me over the edge with, "They built that ramp just for you, you know."

While it's true that Our Lady of Peace spent a not-so-small fortune refurbishing the church's entrance,* these accommodations were not made solely for my benefit . . . though it sure felt that way at the time. And not just to me. Others commented on the pricey efforts, being sure to do so where I would hear. That bit of emotional blackmail was based on faulty reasoning—there were dozens of parishioners with mobility issues beyond me—and

---

* Ripping out the immense concrete stairway and replacing it with two much smaller sets of stairs (one outside and one inside) and an accompanying ramp was just the start. The elevator, granting access to both the upstairs church and the downstairs reception hall, proved the most expensive addition.

served as the final spur. I abandoned the Catholic Church and embraced a life of sour skepticism.

No one in my family and few of my friends understood my dogmatic stand. My family had a quiet faith. Attending mass with regularity was, we believed, enough to put us sympatico with the man upstairs. As for me and my contemporaries, we didn't exactly sit around arguing theology. Judging from their behaviour, only a handful took their religion seriously and most of those merely parroted their parent's talking points. Prayers seemed just words to them. Something barely remembered and uttered only at prompting, mostly in a mumble.

I thought about those oft-repeated words, weighed their meanings, and wondered about what speaking them meant, especially in context.

The Bible held a power over me long before the Confirmation debacle. I can remember spending lunch hours in my Fourth-Grade class "mending" each individual copy in the classroom's stacks. No one asked me. It just felt "wrong" leaving the "Good News," as they were prominently labelled, with pages dog-eared and covers bent. The damage was all accidental; normal ten-year-old's seldom pay attention to how they treat a book, but my obsessive concern—it seemed to me the Bibles were in pain—was anything but normal.

Smoothing out the onion-skin paper took time, effort, and skill—I used a wooden ruler to get each page just perfect. Only when the book was fully repaired did I set it back on its shelf, aligned right-side up amongst its fellows. That was important. Why? I don't recall. But every day for the entire school year I put them to rights whenever they were stored incorrectly. Not an easy task given that moving each copy required significant effort from my crippled physique.

Those actions didn't go unnoticed. No one questioned me or

my motivations. But I know for a fact that word of my "sensitivity" spread. That no doubt contributed to my often getting picked to say class prayers.*

By the time I reached Confirmation age my attitude toward organized religion had soured. Too many questions went unanswered for my liking.

The pomp and circumstance of the church, which once awed and even comforted me, now seemed the height of hypocrisy. Listening to the priest pompously preach of poverty, humility, and the fraternity of man while conducting service in one of the biggest buildings in town, with casual displays of such garish wealth as could feed multitudes, made me uncomfortable. But it was the ham-handed attempt to emotionally extort me over my disability that made me question the value of church then and still influences my opinion toward Catholicism.

Am I bitter? You're damn right. That ramp might have been built with the best of intentions, but I could never use it without feeling my soul shrink just a little.

---

* Discovering I devoted the same attention to every book in the class put an end to such preferential treatment and helped cement my reputation as "That weird kid."

Parking Lot Blues

Is it just me or do parking lots make people crazy?

Negotiating those rows of parallel lines causes some sort of primitive psychological break; tempers fray, patience evaporates, and drivers—many of them normally law-abiding citizens—become foul-mouthed, bloodthirsty maniacs. And heaven help you if there's any sort of sale (Back-to-School, Black Friday, Christmas, or Boxing Day)—then all of society is reduced to its basest animal behaviour. We circle like hungry sharks, dead-eyed and cold-blooded, hunting desperately for an open space to attack.

Seeing an unoccupied spot triggers some sort of instinctual imperative. Fight or flight becomes fight, fight, fight.

Forget civility, the frustration of not finding a parking space pushes drivers past white-knuckled anger and turns our restraint dial down to zero. I, for one, would run over a box of newborn kittens if it meant completing my never-ending search. Darwin could have skipped his long voyage aboard the Beagle and just set up a lawn chair at the local mall—survival of the fittest is on display every day . . . as in, who can fit their car in that far-too-small a spot. Preferably before someone else steals it.

But for all of that, nothing in the entire vast pantheon of parking lot annoyances—not crowding the line, not leaving half your vehicle hanging out into traffic, not even swooping into a parking space while someone is struggling to back in—elicits a more visceral reaction than those blue-painted spots.* Like a toreador waving a red cape at a bull, just seeing that provocative colour evokes a surge of adrenaline and immediately shuts down higher brain function.

No matter how well-intentioned a driver may be, accessible parking is prime real estate—extra wide and almost always closest to the entrance—and, since supply can never meet demand, that means there's always the temptation to "borrow" one. Seeing a wheelchair-adapted space sitting unused is the sort of real-world psychological test few able-bodied can resist. And it doesn't matter how obvious the spot's label—in fact their status as "reserved" often adds to the temptation.

Most drivers don't intend harm or insult when using blue-painted parking. Their reasoning is as simple as it is innocent: "I'll just zip in and out. If I'm quick, no one will be the wiser."

---

* Apparently, it's no longer acceptable to call them "wheelchair parking." That came as news to me, too. There is no consensus among the PC crowd as to what term is now acceptable. "Handicapped spots" lacks elegance and "parking for people with disabilities" seems a bit cumbersome. "Gimp spaces" sounds cruel even to me. "Accessible Parking" is Ontario's official terminology.

And 95% of the time they're right. It's that other 5% that causes trouble. They come out to either find a ticket on their windshield or a boot clamped around one wheel.

Facing the consequences of their illegal action causes a variety of emotional reactions. I've witnessed the guilty express everything from fear to anger, responding with denial and even attempting to bargain. I've yet to see anyone display acceptance but am holding out hope.

Things go to a whole other level when the guilty parker discovers someone waiting to give them a lecture. Depending on the psychology of the criminal party you get differing responses: there's the rare defiant glare—complete with "what you gonna do about it" stare; the "walk of shame" where the illegal parker refuses to make eye contact as they hurry to move their vehicle; and the most fun, the "parking lot lawyer" who wants to argue legal precedent all while attempting to claim moral authority.

Too often these preferred parking spaces cause nothing but trouble. Maybe that's why those spots are not as popular as most able-bodied think. At least not among their intended users. I, for instance, avoid them whenever I can—like during Northern Ontario's eight-weeks of blink-and-you've-missed-it warm weather—preferring to park away from my destination, out in the lot's far fringes, and "walk" to the door. Leaving my full-sized van on the outskirts reduces the chance anyone will park right next to me and block the side-mounted lift. There is nothing like having to back into traffic to load or unload my wheelchair, a slow and surprisingly intricate process, to annoy the queue of impatiently waiting drivers.

People are protective of their perks. As one Canadian politician so eloquently put it, "I'm entitled to my entitlements." But it is the able-bodied who get most upset when their fellows illegally park on the blue—criticizing and complaining, loudly, about the "thoughtlessness" of such drivers. Me, and most of the disabled people I know, not so much.

The handicapped learn to hold their frustrations inside. Hiding unproductive emotions (negativity, pessimism, and the like) becomes second nature for us. You either control your anger at the world or live angry all the time. And, while there are days when I'd happily start a petition to make public flogging the most lenient punishment for wheelchair parking-spot poachers, I know that justice is seldom so clear cut, even if we can all agree that those illegally using the sapphire-coloured spaces are clearly history's greatest villains.

• • •

Everyone knows, intellectually, that handicaps come in a variety of forms. But, thanks to those cheerfully seated little silhouettes universally designating "wheelchair-adapted parking" signs, we all find ourselves instantly suspicious of anyone walking away from a so-called "disabled" spot. Remind yourself, as I do upon witnessing someone use the reserved space without visible mobility issue, that not all legitimate handicaps are obvious to observers.

And no, despite what your conspiracy theory-spouting uncle says, getting a permit is not easy. At least not anymore.

Sure, once upon a time unscrupulous people could game the system. The days of drivers faking a limp or claiming some far-fetched medical diagnosis as legitimate excuse—"I've got lumbago" seemed particularly popular since few non-doctors knew what that rare disease entailed—are long gone.

The problem is not with the blue-painted spaces but rather with those who take it upon themselves to judge the users. It is not easy to recognize a legitimate handicap. And the convoluted, city by city system long used in Ontario didn't help either. It wasn't until the 1990s that Queen's Park got its act together and organized a province-wide permit.

Prior to that, venturing beyond your home community opened you up for some unpleasant parking surprises. I discovered this the hard way, by falling afoul of the Toronto police. Imagine my shock at returning to my obviously modified van after a nice meal to find a parking ticket stuck under the wiper blade. The issuing officer was still making his way through the lot, writing citations for other miscreants, when I approached—in my large electric wheelchair—and, waving the offending paperwork under his nose, oh-so-politely inquired, "What the hell?!"

To his credit, the policeman apologized. Then he explained his reason for ticketing a clearly handicapped individual for parking his clearly marked handicapped van in a clearly designated handicapped spot: "The city of Toronto doesn't recognize the blue window sticker."

Turns out those decals, which were all I'd ever needed in rural Northern Ontario, didn't cut it in the Big Smoke. The reason? Sophisticated city-dwellers had abused the system so egregiously— taking unwarranted advantage of the "privilege" accorded the disabled—that Toronto had to develop a more fraud-proof strategy.

Remember this special perk was nothing more than being able to park marginally closer to a given destination. People call these spots "preferred" parking. Some able-bodied drivers are even jealous of the perk. Take it from me, given the option, there isn't a disabled man, woman, or child who wouldn't rather walk a marathon of extra steps if it meant they could be able-bodied. But, of course, the handicapped aren't given any option. The specially painted blue parking spots are a rather bitter consolation prize.

Even my being in a wheelchair couldn't get the officer to tear up the citation. I had to go to City Hall and "parade" myself before some petty bureaucrat to have the ticket overturned and avoid paying the ridiculous fine. Needless to say, I did just that. What is pride compared to a few bucks? I've sacrificed the first for the latter before and will probably do so again.

If professional law enforcement can't recognize a genuinely disabled user how can the public? They can't. And still there are people who try to police who should and should not be allowed to use the prime parking real estate. An action that never ends well in my experience.

• • •

I've been the wronged party a time or two—finding someone taking up a handicapped spot without legitimate reason—but parking lot violators only ever anger me on those rare instances where a car blocked me from accessing the curb.

Those cut-outs* might not look like much to you but without them no wheelchair user can climb on or off the sidewalk. At least not safely. I damn near overturned one night back in university when someone left their car in front of the building's only accessible entrance, squeezing into an already taken blue spot. My friends had to roll several small boulders aside so that I could "jump" the curb, a bumpy process that rattled both my spine and my wheelchair.

"We should leave a note," one classmate suggested.

---

* The engineers and designers who put these curb cuts in such poorly planned positions are the real antagonists of this piece. Many of these so-called "experts" need to pay more attention. Take a moment when next walking a city sidewalk and note the extreme detours forced on anyone unable to "step-up" to pedestrian-preferred heights.

Another enthused, "Key his car!"

I overruled both, not needing the hassle, but wonder to this day if anyone ever taught that vehicle's owner the error of their ways. Most illegal parkers don't comprehend their mistake, not even when confronted.

You'd be surprised at how many people misunderstand the relationship between the disabled and accessible parking. Even friends and family fail to realize the number of hoops the handicapped are forced to jump through in order to qualify for a permit. It's not just a matter of renting a wheelchair and rolling into a government office. A doctor's note is required, at the bare minimum. The first time anyway.

If you have a chronic handicap renewing is easy—I just did mine, online, and it only took ten minutes. My new permit arrived in under a month. And I'm good now until 2026. Three more years of favourable parking. Yippee!

In Case of Emergency

What's sadder than a ten-year-old walking home through the rain? A crippled ten-year-old driving his electric wheelchair home through a late autumn deluge and getting intentionally drenched by passing cars. Living through that wet and humiliating bit of childhood misery, I swore never to get caught out unprepared again.

Being born in the latter half of the twentieth century means I've seen my share of technological breakthroughs—microchips, LEDs, even almost cost-effective forms of renewable energy. World-changing developments one and all. But it wasn't ground-breaking surgical techniques, innovative drug therapies, or even the troll-spawning arrival of the Internet that changed my life the most. No, that honour goes to the spring-triggered umbrella.

I carried the same small, collapsible, black push-button umbrella for more than twenty years, keeping it tucked in my wheelchair beside my right thigh. On the first sign of cloud, out it came. People laughed. But they could duck out of the weather or pull a jacket up over their head to avoid getting soaked. Sitting down meant I got wet from head to toe in any sort of rain. The option of changing to something dry was often denied me too, so the cold clamminess would last all day.

If "an ounce of prevention is worth a pound of cure" for the average citizen, then it's got to be equal to ten tonnes or more for the handicapped.

Few able-bodied people give emergencies much thought.* Most grumble through fire drills, anxious to return to their normal routines. When it comes to complaining, disabled people aren't much different. Regarding normalcy we, if anything, find disruptions to our schedules even more annoying. When even the simplest tasks require twice the effort and three times the planning, not to mention taking much longer than seems humanly possible, losing a half-an-hour unexpectedly can throw an entire day out of whack.

Unfortunately, our options in a real emergency are limited. There's no running away for the handicapped. Elevators immediately go on lock down, racing down flights of stairs is unpractical and downright dangerous, and even dropping to the floor isn't always possible—not when strapped into a wheelchair. Should an "active shooter" situation ever develop I am a sitting duck . . . good thing Canadians have sensible gun laws.

---

* This is, of course, hyperbole. A lot of people do nothing *but* think about emergencies: first responders, for instance. And then there are Preppers. Folks who devote enormous amounts of time, energy, and resources to preparing for "inevitable" catastrophes. Rather than digress, just go with my premise.

I sat through four years of high school stressing over every fire drill. Each time the alarm rang the reactions were the same—the teacher looked to me in a panic and I would smile reassurance, mouthing "fire drill" in sincere hope I'd be proven right. The calm I exuded must have been convincing because, with a single exception in first year,* no one ever tried to talk me out of remaining behind. Left alone in the classroom, I would watch through the window as the rest of the student body evacuated the school's premises. My contemporaries laughed and played while waiting for the "all clear" to sound. Me? I sat and sniffed the air, trying to convince myself that any errant odour wasn't smoke.

On my own, with no one to be brave for, fear would run rampant. I never broke down or anything dramatic, but my heart rate skyrocketed as I endured long minutes of solitary uncertainty. Around others, however, I faked resignation. Pretending that emergencies never worried me became second nature. I even laughed off the awkward questions that followed these drills.

With the elevator off-limits there was no escaping the upper floors. (Weirdly, only once in five years of high school did a fire drill ever occur while I was on the ground floor. It happened in winter and I got to rush outside, with no coat, to freeze alongside my similarly ill-prepared classmates. Twenty shivery minutes later we were allowed back into the building to thaw out.)

Someone must have complained because mid-way through my fourth year the principal pulled me out of class—never a

---

* The one attempt came when Mr. F– (my math teacher and the school's assistant football coach) joined five of the strongest of my fellow first year students and tried to pick up me and my wheelchair. The well-meaning effort almost ended in disaster. Not only were the chair and I individually heavy but there weren't any handy gripping points. Plus, my weight kept shifting as they struggled to balance during their lone poorly coordinated half-stride. Sitting me down quickly, the attempt was abandoned.

good sign—to introduce me to a terrifying machine. Basically a seat bolted onto rubber tank treads, this monstrosity was meant to carry me down the stairs. No one mentioned "safely." Strapped in place, I found myself pushed to the edge of the steps and tilted forward for the descent. Hanging there at a precarious angle set me to sweating in terror, with nothing but an untested piece of equipment preventing me from tumbling face-first down three flights. Sitting through a dozen false alarms seemed less stressful than being stuck to that device. Then it got worse . . . we went down to the next floor.

Sedate though our speed might have been—and a gimpy tortoise could have moved faster—it proved a nightmarish ride. Progress came in awkward lurching movements. Each and every one, I felt certain at the time, prefaced the final long fall. It seemed to take forever to reach the next floor. Which was when we realized the machine couldn't go back up. Luckily, the principal fetched my wheelchair using the elevator and I returned to class, shaken by the experience but relieved. Should an evacuation prove necessary I finally had a method of escape. Sure, it wouldn't win me any races, but speed isn't always an asset in an emergency.

I never used that device in an actual emergency. That, some would argue, made it a waste of money. Those people never had to sit through the evacuation of their school while sincerely hoping this unscheduled emergency would prove a false alarm and not the precursor to a fiery death.

• • •

For all the drama experienced during my secondary school tenure, my most terrifying moment came on the way there.

No reasonable person was on the road that winter morning.

Glare ice covered every surface and the bus driver crept along, taking almost a full hour for a trip that usually required just over twenty minutes. Knuckles white from gripping the steering wheel extra tight, she was clearly relieved as we neared the final turn, the one that would take us off the road and onto school ground. Only she forgot that the turn lay at the base of a hill. Pressing the brakes did nothing to slow our descent. The bus slid past our destination and continued straight through the stop sign almost one hundred feet past. Luckily no other cars were crossing then.

Had the road turned at the bottom of the slope we'd have been in the ditch. Not an ideal situation for a small female driver and a large disabled passenger. Instead, we sailed through the intersection until the momentum dissipated. After a long moment where she stared straight ahead and tried to regain her composure, we got turned around and, with much difficulty, drove back up the hill and into the school parking lot.

I arrived at school late, only to find less than a quarter of my classmates had managed the same feat.

Most of the contracted bus-lines had flatly refused to take their vehicles out in such conditions. Few teachers worked that day either, deciding that their safety outweighed their calling. There was a tenseness about the eyes of those few educators dedicated enough to risk life and limb driving to work, like they'd survived some horror.*

The situation could have turned out very different. That thought nettled me for years. How colossally bad it could have been became something of an ongoing nightmare, my overactive imagination spinning out scenarios both awake and asleep.

---

* I think one teacher suffered a small nervous breakdown, he wouldn't—or couldn't—stop giggling that entire day.

Of course, I wasn't brave enough to deal with the emotions directly. That would be off-brand for me. I only exorcised that lingering worry by writing about the experience. It formed the basis of my first (never-to-be-published) novel, Crash Course, where four vehicles travelling along a Northern Ontario highway, none of which were a wheelchair bus, hit a "strange" storm and end up crashing . . . not on our Earth. The victims, none of whom are disabled in any way, must find a way to survive while stranded . . . elsewhere.**

Fictionalizing trauma is a time-honoured literary tradition. Not only can it inspire some truly great stories but the writing functions as a form of therapy. Or, at least, it did for me.

Maybe I'm weird but my mind cannot help but dwell on trauma. I lay awake at night and relive each and every one of my shockingly numerous near-death experiences. That is bad enough, but I cannot stop there. No, I take things further still and spin out worse-case-scenarios with such vividness that they almost feel real. Only introducing an element of fiction to these waking nightmares lessens their impact.

• • •

Being disabled means I have plenty to fear. Those range from the legitimate—amongst a certain less-than-ethical segment of society,

---

** My novel was a "portal fantasy," a very popular sub-genre of science fiction and fantasy. The premise is simple: characters from our world are transported (usually accidentally) to another reality. These can be our past or future but most often is someplace completely different, often with magic. The Chronicles of Narnia is a famous example. So too the Outlander books. My unvoiced elevator pitch was simply: Lord of the Flies meets Lord of the Rings. It wasn't much of a novel but did feature more than fifty named characters.

we're the perfect victim—to things few able-bodied ever need consider. Take the water.

Drowning is a very real concern for anyone venturing out on a boat, that's the reason lifejackets are now required by law (to be carried aboard but not worn). What good is a Personal Floatation Device (PFD) when you're strapped, like I am, to a three hundred pound anchor? You don't even have to leave land very far behind to be at risk. Floating docks have sent one handicapped person (and their wheelchair), that I know of, into the water.

Just crossing the road presents dangers to the disabled. Those signal lights are timed for the average healthy pedestrian, not special needs users—who require significantly longer.

Then there's the visibility question. Commuters are able to see most street-level traffic clearly because their vehicles are low and pedestrians are standing. But what about when there's heavy equipment around. People using assistive devices like walkers, wheelchairs, and scooters generally operate below the hood of those massive machines. And being out of sight of any driver is a recipe for disaster.

I know of several tragedies involving the disabled and industrial machinery, including the time a wheelchair got pinned to the front of a transport truck and pushed along the road at highway speeds for miles before the unknowing driver could be flagged down. That particular cripple got off without serious physical injury (though I imagine he needed to change his pants), but others have been much less lucky.

• • •

Turns out I wasn't delusional, just ahead of my time.

Prepping is now a multi-billion-dollar industry. Chances are there's a home on your street with a basement full of MREs (Meals Ready-to-Eat), bottles of potable water, and a chemical toilet . . . just in case.

Emergencies are no joke. A lifetime of worry has taught me better than to rely on the government in times of crisis. Trusting my health to people elected into power isn't the smartest survival strategy. Given that few politicians can find my hometown on a map during ideal conditions, I have zero confidence they'd come to my rescue during a disaster.

Around the world many forward-thinking citizens are, instead, taking steps on their own. Planning ahead and readying themselves for potential problems. Exactly as one wet cripple did more than three decades ago as he drove his wheelchair home through the rain.

And that is not sad at all.

Cafeteria Fun and Games

At age nineteen I thought I had the world figured. Most young adults do. Naturally, being in a wheelchair, I couldn't match my contemporaries at certain fields. Cocksure, self-involved arrogance proved one such. In that, I exceeded them.

As seniors we ruled the school—leaving me and my friends of the opinion that "life was made." St. Charles College advertised itself as a "good Catholic institution," regaling us with barely heard prayers during morning announcements and peppering us with daily reminders of "proper Christian attitudes" including "appropriate behaviour, dress, and language."

Codes of conduct—duty and discipline dominated—were prominently displayed throughout the school. Every wall and hand-out featured a variation on SCC's unforgiving rules. Even the ridiculously detailed "Student Handbook" harped on the "piety of personal responsibility". But, for those in the know—meaning those who diligently read that annually-updated publication in search of loopholes—there were angles to be played, corners to be cut, and trouble to be found . . . if mostly of a wholesome sort.

Skipping assemblies and dodging masses had become a respected tradition long before my arrival. Since "Honouring tradition" was one of SCC's core principles—when it suited the administration at least*—we were only too happy to carry on that delinquent practice. Sneaking out for "a quick puff" or scarfing down junk food while hiding behind open textbooks, even changing clothes in the halls, were commonplace. Pushing, shoving, and other acts of genteel physical violence established the social pecking order and were routinely categorized as "good, clean fun" for a building full of testosterone-addled teenage boys.

Being of legal age we were able to purchase and consume alcohol outside of school grounds without qualm—best of all, we were all young and fit enough to overindulge without serious consequence. We loved nothing more than spending off-hours planning the future. These included big plans—careers and families—and little plans, like where we were going on the upcoming weekend or how much we intended to drink.

Best of all, however, were the "spares." As Grade 13 students in good standing, meaning soon to graduate, we were allowed to take one period off per day. This "free" time was meant to be spent

---

* Only "traditional" haircuts passed the school's muster. Of course, their definition excluded every culture and time period that fell outside their narrow preferences. "Short" and "neat" were the epitome of style in the administration's eyes. Arguing otherwise, even with empirical proof that mohawks or clubbed tails were "traditional," did nothing to sway the faculty from their steadfast 1950s mindset.

in academic pursuits—preferably readying ourselves for whichever university we'd be attending come the fall. In reality, that hour was filled not with studying but goofing off.

Stress never much affected me, but a lot of my more driven friends felt it. Pressured to get accepted into a good school and make something of themselves by excelling at the right programs, they desperately needed to blow off steam. Mindless pastimes sprung up to distract and entertain. Some gained official approval, like playing chess, while others, like three-card monte, were frowned upon. I had perfect records at both, never winning a single chess match and knowing better than to risk my money at the latter.

Most days sort of drifted into the next. Catching up on homework or analysing the previous night's big game blurred together. One spare period, however, stands out. There were a couple dozen of us sitting around the cafeteria, bored and looking for excitement, when someone decided to question my wheelchair driving skills.

And with that the gauntlet had been thrown.

I don't remember what sparked the challenge or why I became so adamant about defending my abilities but, within moments, we'd moved all the tables—and given the cafeteria's enormous size, it could comfortably sit five hundred rambunctious boys at a time, that meant a lot of tables—to form a crude maze/obstacle course.

It's important to note that, though I broke new ground attending St. Charles College, by Grade 13 I was no longer the only student in a wheelchair. Several of the Life-Skills class had disabilities requiring assistive transportation devices. But since they tended to be better supervised than the rest of us—and so less likely to engage in juvenile mischief—it fell to me to defend the honour of all handicapped people everywhere.

Needless to say, I aced that test—zipping around hair-pin corners at full speed.

More challenging designs followed that first impromptu course as everyone got into the spirit. Well, OK not everyone. One teacher, on seeing what we were doing to the school's large and mostly empty cafeteria, shook her head at our antics. She called us all "idiots" but in an affectionate, if exasperated, tone and then walked, good-naturedly, through all the twists and turns needed to cross the now even-more intricate course. Cheers followed her progress.

A second teacher arrived not long after. This one stopped, glared at us, and climbed over the tables—a neat trick given her skirt and heels. She ignored our good-natured boos. Staring straight ahead in sour-faced fury, she crossed the room and—radiating put-upon outrage in every stilettoed stride—marched, spine stiffened by her embarrassed indignity, directly to the vice-principal's office. There she ratted us out and, with her angry shouts echoing clear across the hall for all to hear, left no doubt as to her low opinion of the "uncouth wretches" tormenting her.

One of those two teachers was beloved by her students. The other? Let me just say that wasn't the first time she got booed, nor was it the first time she set the VP on us for behaviour she deemed "inappropriate and unbecoming of young gentlemen."

To be fair, that woman held us to a high standard for a noble reason. Other teachers called us "animals," "monkeys," and "monsters" too—they couldn't care less what we got up to or where we ended up on graduation. To them we were a job and nothing more. Our prickly persecutor cared. Too bad she had to do it with such open antagonism.

With her complaints ringing in his ears, it took the vice-principle less than a minute to slink into the cafeteria and order us, deferentially, to "put things back." By that point I'd completed a half-dozen variations, proving my skills were more than up to any challenge my friends could concoct. At age nineteen I'd been driving an electric wheelchair for more than a decade and would match my ability to manoeuvre that particular assistive device with anyone. Nothing dreamt up on the spur of the moment could daunt me or my talent steering it.

That triumph didn't go unpunished, of course. No, my comeuppance took place almost immediately, beginning in the cafeteria naturally—the home of most high school hijinks—and almost got me suspended.

Someone, and to this day I have no idea who, hid the mechanical guts of an old clockwork music box in the bookbag hanging off the back of my wheelchair. Its noisome, if off-key, repetition of "Dream an Impossible Dream" proved a subtle torture. Much like the death by a thousand cuts, it slowly wore away at my sanity.

Unbeknownst to me, every one of my "friends" was in on the prank—pretending not to hear the tune all while winding the spring-powered device whenever walking past me.

The inspirational showtune continued. ALL. DAY. LONG. Following me like some inescapable earworm. Only the fact that my teachers heard it too kept me from losing my mind. At least until one unamused educator—having spent almost the entire class searching for the sound's source only to find it buried in my bag—tried to blame me. The song's constant cheerful chorus hadn't left me in the mood for such and my less-than-respectful reply had jaws dropping.

Still, despite its near-disastrous consequences, that good-natured taunting proved a much more inclusive cafeteria experience than first greeted me. My first few semesters at SCC I ate alone, sitting in self-imposed isolation while ploughing through my daily

PB&J sack-lunch. I'd spend the entire forty-five minutes ignoring everyone around me—little cliques huddled together for mutual protections—and instead watch through the second-floor window as the gym class below was put through their paces.

St. Charles couldn't fit every member of its student body into the cafeteria at once, there were more than fifteen hundred of us after all, so we ate in shifts. And somehow none of my few acquaintances shared the same lunch schedule as me.

By third year my circle of friends had expanded enough that there was always someone to share a table with. As I entered senior year, I finally knew every one of my fellows by name—all three-hundred-plus soon-to-be graduates. Many of them took perverse delight in teasing me. And, though I'd long since outgrown the need for an authority figure to intervene on my behalf, the cafeteria's supervision-free status made it the perfect place for teens to torment each other.

Is it any wonder we all loved the big, none-too-clean room?

Jerry Lewis Told Me I Was Going to Die

Believing you're soon going to die is not a healthy way to live. Trust me, I know. I was supposed to be dead a long time ago.

This isn't about when the doctors misdiagnosed me, then in infancy, with the number one genetic killer of children under age two—spinal muscular atrophy Type I (sometimes called Werdnig-Hoffmann disease or infantile-onset SMA). In their defence, the deadliest form of the disease is also, by far, the most common. Luckily for me, I actually had SMA Type II, the survivable and hence much more preferable variation of spinal muscular atrophy. (People with my type of SMA have been known to live almost normal lifespans and, barring accident or illness, I should reach senior status . . . and be able to claim some of that lucrative old-age pension money.)

Neither is this about the 12-hour long, experimental, lifesaving surgery I underwent at the ripe old age of eleven (and three-quarters). That bit of timely medical intervention straightened my spine and prevented a rapidly curving backbone from crushing my lungs . . . not an ideal outcome for a kid already dealing with "diminished" breathing capacity.

No, this is about when I, aged nine, became convinced "my time" was soon to be up. It wasn't a doctor, researcher, or even physiotherapist who warned me of my rapidly approaching death. Those I could ignore. No, Jerry Lewis told me I was going to die and, as a celebrity, he mattered far more than any medical expert to my young and television-saturated mind. Which might explain why I took his offhand comment that "Most kids with muscular dystrophy don't live past their sixteenth birthday" as gospel.

• • •

Venerated for his talent, drawing power, and dedication to his art, Jerry Lewis achieved a whole other level of public appreciation with his decades' long efforts on behalf of the Muscular Dystrophy Association.

As a kid I hadn't seen a single one of his films but, despite appearing to me to be just some old guy in a rumpled tuxedo, I knew he was important because he was on television. And, like most of my generation, television dominated my life.

While my dad and his fellow Baby Boomers can remember those halcyon days prior to TV's ubiquity, Generation X-ers like myself never knew life without the devise's constant company. Detractors might call it "the idiot box" or "the glass teat," but to people of my age TV was, to quote Homer Simpson, "Television! Teacher! Mother! Secret lover."

Jerry Lewis first appealed on MDA's behalf in 1951, while still part of the popular duo Martin and Lewis, but his involvement with the organization became formalized in 1956 when, as a solo movie star, he became the MDA National Chairman. He started hosting regional telethons* that same year but didn't make the variously named telethon** an iconic TV staple until 1966 when it moved to Labour Day.

People tuned in that holiday weekend certain of one thing: that they'd be entertained. Lewis alone guaranteed that. But, of course, the comedy legend was never alone. In addition to co-anchor Ed McMahon from 1973 to 2008, a litany of celebrities joined him. Headlining a veritable who's who of Hollywood elite, he made the job look easy. Not only did Jerry Lewis divide his time between making funny faces, singing inspirational songs, and introducing famous friends but he laid the groundwork for how televised fundraisers should work, pioneering many of the format's most innovative and profitable ploys (like the now-standard "local cutaway").

When I was young, we had a tradition at my house: every September the TV would stay tuned to "The telethon" from the opening song until after the final tally's announcement. No one missed the program's end and Jerry' signature closing number, an aspirational cover of Rodgers & Hammerstein's "You'll Never

---

* There were previous regional telethons between 1952 and 1953. These featured other notable performers of the time and aired in Atlanta GA, Cleveland OH, Grand Rapids MI, Madison WI, and Washington D.C.

** During its decades-long run, the program was called: *The Jerry Lewis Telethon, Jerry Lewis Stars Across America, Jerry Lewis Super Show, The Jerry Lewis MDA Labour Day Telethon,* and *THE TELETHON: Jerry Lewis Extra Special SPECIAL.*

Walk Alone."****

I don't know when I began identifying with Jerry's Kids, that was the term applied to all the MDA's young members—probably around the time I ended up in a wheelchair during the summer of 1982. But, whenever it occurred, the day Jerry Lewis told me I was going to die my life changed—and not for the better.

• • •

Say what you want about the man, and his pitches were undoubtedly crude by twenty-first-century inclusivity standards,**** but Jerry Lewis was effective. Raising an estimated $2.6 billion in donations speaks for itself. Yes, there were more sensitive—and empowering*****—ways to go about appealing to the public for money. However, expecting Lewis—the product of an immigrant stage family (his father was a vaudevillian and his mother played piano on radio)—to embrace today's politically correct attitude toward the disabled is unfair   . . . especially when applied to his earliest efforts. Remember, Jerry Lewis was shilling on behalf of the MDA decades before Canada finalized the Charter of Rights and Freedoms.

**** In 1959, the MDA was given special permission to use the song by Rogers and Hammerstein. The organization made it their official theme that same year and only retired it in 2011 when Lewis stepped down.

**** It has become hip lately, among *progressive* segments of society, to re-evaluate the past and apply modern morals to bygone actions. I'll leave the fairness of that to others—the political crowd needs some controversy to gnaw upon—but the disabled community can stand tall when faced with that self-congratulatory sanctimony. Our members began questioning Jerry Lewis over his fundraising methods as early as the 1990s..

***** The telethon tended to focus on the most piteous MD sufferers and ignore those who "overcame" their disabilities to become functioning members of society.

Doubting Jerry Lewis's dedication to the cause is also patently unfair. His annual performance had him appearing on-screen almost constantly for more than 21 consecutive hours. That still seems superhuman—I grew exhausted just watching the show, and I was a half-century his junior—but somehow he did it for decades.

Understanding the urge to re-evaluate Jerry Lewis is easy, especially given modernity's much-hyped social enlightenment. For many in the disabled community, the last straw came with his 1990 essay, "If I Had Muscular Dystrophy." Appearing in Parade magazine, Lewis writes of himself as if he were an adult with the disease. Explaining of his motivation, "I decided after 41 years of battling this curse that cripples children of all ages, that I would put myself into that chair, that steel imprisonment that has long been deemed the dystrophic child's plight."

That laudable ideal is promptly hamstrung by his central conceit that the disabled are lesser.

To quote his own words, written in character, "I realize my life is half, so I must learn to do things halfway. I just have to learn to try to be good at being half a person . . ." That sentiment was loudly condemned, most notably by the members of "Jerry's Orphans"—a group who, disgusted with the piteous portrayal of the disabled on the MDA telethon, rallied against the 1992 edition. That very public protest galvanized some and offended others—so much so that the issue became a cause célèbre.

In the end, the MDA parted ways with Jerry Lewis. No one, outside the Association's inner circle, knows whether this was an amicable split or if, given the growing controversy attached to the aging star,* he was fired. Regardless, in 2011 the telethon—once proudly named in his honour—went on without Lewis. Three years later, the fundraising juggernaut, now rebranded "The Show of Strength Telethon," ended its nationwide run, and by 2015 was off the air entirely.

Jerry died in 2017 at age 91 having proven the adage "you either die a hero or live long enough to see yourself become the villain." Lewis would have spared himself a lot of headaches in his golden years by talking less about Jerry's Kids and talking to them more.

The majority of the criticism from disabled community members centred on the comedian's habit of portraying MDA's members as, to quote disabled rights activist Mike Ervin, "pitiable victims who want and need nothing more than a big charity to take care of or cure them." Jerry Lewis, the consummate showman who would happily do anything for a laugh, countered with, "If you don't tug at their heartstrings, then you're on the air for nothing."

I'll leave it to others to explain the difference between "identity-first" language and its fundamental contrast with "person-first" language. Nuance, as you can probably tell, is not my thing. To summarize, for those not wanting a deep dive, it comes down to one simple question: Are we "disabled people" or "people living with a disability"?

Some find identity-first naming conventions stigmatizing. To them applying a term defines, even limits, their existence. Lewis bandied about that type of language often, callously labelling Jerry's Kids with such monikers, without ever giving the matter much

---

* A homophobic slur, uttered live on air, combined with some surprisingly old-fashioned misogyny regarding the relevance of female comediennes, was enough to bring down this once beloved star. His 2015 praise of then-presidential candidate Donald Trump didn't help endear Lewis to today's more discerning public either.

thought. His 1968 comment, "God goofed, and it's up to us to correct His mistakes," still rankles among the disabled—many of whom reject such paternalistic patronizing and prefer to proudly proclaim, "We are not mistakes!"

So, what term should be used when addressing someone disabled? The synonyms are varied and ever changing. The "appropriate language" question isn't just limited to the use of "handicapped" (or the cringe-worthy "handi-capable") community. It matters to all visible minorities. Names affect those being labelled and the labeller too. The answer as to what terminology the able-bodied should employ, at least as far as the physically disabled goes, is simple: Ask.

I think the late author Terry Pratchett had the right of it in his novel I Shall Wear Midnight when he wrote, "Evil starts when you begin to treat people as things."

Not even Jerry Lewis's strongest detractors would call him evil but, by using—and reusing—certain terms and phrases for decades, he did categorize and stereotype children, making them little more than props. The fact that it was many of those very same people that ultimately brought his legacy into question is, perhaps, poetic justice.

• • •

Regardless of the controversy surrounding Jerry Lewis, my parents—like a lot of TV viewers—tuned in to the telethon religiously. Me? I quit watching. Not because of the protests. I simply couldn't bear to see the man who told me I was going to die.

The great Samuel Johnson once noted, "when a man knows he is to be hanged in a fortnight, it concentrates his mind wonderfully." That suave turn of phrase might very well be true . . . in adults. I wasn't even ten years old at the time that I was informed of my impending execution. And make no mistake, that is how I took Mr. Lewis's words.

In my defence, my mind had yet to fully form. Somehow, I heard the then-factually correct comment—that muscular dystrophy killed most sufferers at a young age*—and took it to mean I would die on my sixteenth birthday.

The precise mechanics of my demise never made themselves clear. Would a switch be flipped somewhere, turning me off? Would a hit squad burst through the door, guns a-blazing, blowing me to smithereens as I blew out my birthday candles? Or would Jerry himself arrive, mugging for the cameras** and singing one of his signature songs in order to best mark the momentous occasion?

For years, the knowledge—that, February 3, 1990, would be the last day of my life—was foremost in my mind. Far from concentrating my thinking, it weighed upon me. It also impacted every choice I made. Why worry about the future when mine didn't go beyond my sixteenth birthday?

Academics didn't matter. I would never live to attend university. Job prospects and vocational planning didn't matter. I would be dead before needing to find a career. Diet and exercise certainly didn't matter. The condition of my soon-to-be corpse concerned me not at all. Only enjoying myself mattered.

That's right, thanks to Jerry Lewis, I became a juvenile hedonist.

---

* Important note: This figure *was* correct in 1982 for certain types of muscular dystrophy only. The current life expectancy varies depending on the individual disease's severity—Duschene's, for instance, still claims lives at a devastatingly young age. Life expectancy has, however, improved and further positive changes continue to this day . . . thanks in no small part to the money Jerry Lewis raised.

** Weirdly, whatever demented scenario I imagined, there were always cameras there to capture my final breath.

Too young to engage in the more adult carnal pleasures—sex, drugs, booze—I indulged instead in food. By the time I snapped from my snack-filled bacchanal my weight had ballooned into obese territory. The die was set.

My self-destructive "madness" made choosing healthy options anathema. Fruits and vegetables were avoided in favour of junk foods. Sugar, salt, and fat proved my poisons of choice. Potato chips and anything covered in chocolate—the worse for me the better. Lean meats fell out of favour and I focused, like any true carnivore, on the reddest of options. Beef and pork formed the basis of my diet, with pasta* following a close third (though, since I almost always ate it with meat-sauce, it does tie into the first two).

And then, one bright and sunny day, realization dawned: I didn't have Muscular Dystrophy at all! My particular disability was merely categorized alongside the much more well-known disease for convenience's sake. Not my convenience, of course. Otherwise, I wouldn't have spent several years living under a death sentence.

Still, live and learn, eh?

---

* My surname is Del Papa, so Italian food is in my blood.

The Tickle Machine Scam

Anyone got a few spare million? Check the couch cushions, I'll wait. Eighty-six cents and a lint-covered breath-mint isn't going to cover it, sorry. I need Elon Musk-level cash here people. Enough disposable income to influence elections. The sort of vast wealth that guarantees VIP treatment anywhere in the world. So much money that strangers are instantly jealous of its casual display and even friends and family come to hate me.

No, I'm not looking to purchase a Ferrari or fatten up my bank account. Though if you want to buy me a new sports car . . . who am I decline? This money is for medicine. And yes, it really does cost that much.

After a lifetime of waiting, you cannot imagine the electric thrill that went through me when I heard that the first approved drug treatment for SMA was coming out in 2016.* Called nusinersen—but marketed by the much sexier name of Spinraza—it was surprisingly effective, stopping the disease's degenerative progress, and even reversing some muscle weakness. Far less surprising was the drug's ridiculous expense.

The price put it out of reach for most. And that's a damn shame given it is a literal lifesaver.

Not for me. My version of spinal muscular atrophy is not fatal. No, it saves the lives of people with SMA Type I, who are all children under age four.

It is the devastatingly sad truth that those diagnosed with Type I do not live long. Or rather they didn't, until Spinraza came about. This new treatment, a literal life-and-death medication for their disabled children, drove families the world over to desperate lengths. Many resorted to social media and crowdsourced fundraising campaigns rather than wait for the glacial grind of government bureaucracy to authorize the purchase.

Time, unfortunately, is another thing not on these kids' side. How many died while red tape tangled the decision-making process?

Did I mention Spinraza needs to be injected directly into your spine? Under a doctor's supervision (usually at a hospital) no less. In case of side effects. One of which is death. I didn't bother reading past that particular cautionary warning.

As if that wasn't enough, the drug requires annual booster shots. The continuing cost, combined with the eyewatering risks, put me off that particular drug. For now. Luckily for me, my life

---

* The US, where it originated, granted FDA approval in December of that year. The European Medicines Agency (EMA) followed suit in May 2017. Canada got around to approving the drug in July 2017.

doesn't hang in the balance.

There is good news. Since Spinraza's arrival, two other medications have been developed to treat SMA. Onasemnogene abeparvovec-xioi, branded as Zolgensma (a one-time intravenous infusion for patients under age two) received approval in Canada in late 2020 and risdiplam, an "at-home, once daily" oral treatment for anyone over two months and trademarked as Evrysdi found approval by Health Canada in 2021.

And the original's price-tag has become slightly more reasonable. If you consider hundreds of thousands of dollars a dose, reasonable. I don't. Not when it requires the aforementioned booster.** The New York Times described Nusinersen as "among the most expensive drugs in the world."

All three drugs are projected to exceed one billion dollars in sales by 2026.

"But what about Canada's much-vaunted health care system?" you ask. Surely our government is stepping up, right? Well, sort of.

Socialized medicine is great. OHIP has literally saved my life. Better still, it did so without bankrupting me or my extended family. That doesn't mean the system isn't without flaws. Like any multi-billion-dollar bureaucracy, our nation's health care is bloated, top-heavy, and slow to change. Authorizing Spinraza has been "under consideration" in Canada—with each province acting on its own timetable—since almost the day it appeared on the market. So far, in Ontario at least, it has been approved only

---

** Current list price for Spinraza is $125,000 USD per injection—$750,000 for the first year and $375,000 every year after that. Zolgensma is the "the most expensive drug ever" according to NPR, at $2.125US million (but the company offers a five-year payment plan of just $425,000 USD per year). Priced dependent on weight, Evrysdi caps itself at $340,000 per year once a patient reaches 44 pounds but it must be continued to remain effective.

for those with SMA Type I—one of the few government decisions I completely agree with.

No one in their right mind can blame the government for focusing on those kids. Choosing to favour the most-at-risk is basic triage protocol. You may or may not believe me but, at this point in my life, if I was offered the drug at the expense of some soon-to-die two-year-old, I'd have only one choice: to decline. It wouldn't even be a tough decision.

There isn't much doubt that my life would be better with one of these treatments—they stop SMA's progression and even allow many patients to regain some limited strength. Any muscle improvement would be a novel change given I've watched mine weaken for over forty years now.

That said, for me this theoretical exercise boils down to maximum benefit. While I would happily give almost anything to get some long-lost abilities back . . . I'm not about to do so if it meant someone else dying. Especially a toddler. And it's not like I'd leap from my wheelchair and start breakdancing at the first dose. Maybe I'd be able to brush my own hair or drink a cup of tea without needing a straw. Small improvements, sure. But important to me.

Just not nearly as important as someone else's life.

Maybe if I were younger and still retained more functionality the arithmetic would work out differently. Had this drug been around when I was still walking then I might not be so considerate. Perhaps if I maintained the abilities I had as a teen, able to manage most minor physical actions on my own or with some small help, my decision might be more selfish. Who am I kidding? There's no doubt about it. I would leap at the chance and never think twice about the consequences. Thankfully, if only for the sake of my immortal soul at least, the progress of my disease has passed the point of effective treatment.*

And if you think that admission comes easily, well, you probably don't live with a chronic illness.

• • •

I've tried other therapies before, ever hopeful, and—until Spinraza—have always found nothing but disappointment.

Physiotherapy came first. It was never meant to gain me strength—a fact no one bothered to explain to me—but rather to slow my muscular decline and to maintain "flexibility and range of motion." Needless to say, struggling at push-ups and sit-ups didn't much appeal to me—not at age three (when I started) nor years later (when I quit).

Swimming kept me entertained and probably did more for me, both physically and mentally, than any other form of exercise. Being good at something meant a lot to me. Not just good "for a cripple" but good compared to able-bodied friends and family proved a psychological boost to a kid who tended to lag behind in the all-important field of athletics.

The only time I ever felt used, however, involved the professionally marketed "Tickle Machine."

Developed by a private company, the slickly produced pitch revolved around encouraging "the body's own healing abilities." They offered free snacks to prospective patients, decorated their office with poster-sized photos of happy clients, and covered every

---

* If any of you are reading this and thinking of sending me money, please don't. Seriously, I'm fine waiting. Resigned even. Better that you donate to medical research (MDA Canada does good work) or contribute to funding the GoFundMe of some kid seeking treatment. Thank you.

flat surface in artistically arranged brochures. Their hard-sell ended in a thirty-minute Hollywood-quality "promotional" video that, looking back with cynical eyes, was nothing more than glossy propaganda peppered with medical buzzwords.

Basically, I got electro-shock therapy for my muscles.

Remember, this was decades before Dr. Ho infested TV with his infomercials. The idea of using electricity to stimulate muscle growth seemed entirely plausible and even ground-breaking, the device's childish name aside.

Three "easy payments" of $39.95 will get Dr. Ho's device delivered to your door today. Me, I had to travel to Toronto, visit a special "clinic," and then shell out several thousand dollars for mine.

Wearing it while I "slept"—a challenging feat given the periodic jolts of energy sent surging through my skin—meant placing large rubber pads over various muscle groups. There was a trick to holding them in place, we used hockey tape because the "medical grade" sticky surface lost adhesion after repeated use. The important part involved trying not to move. Considering I had electrical wires taped across my body that last wasn't hard. Even the slightest shift felt like a dozen bandages were being ripped off. Slowly.

The constant flow of low-voltage electricity was supposed to "encourage" muscle regeneration.

There was only one problem with this theory: my muscles were fine. Atrophied, sure. But not through any fault of their own. My nerves were the culprit. And this treatment didn't do anything to fix them.

It took me years to discover that this "revolutionary new treatment" basically amounted to a take-home, snake-oil miracle cure. The high-priced Tickle Machine went back into its moulded plastic carrying case and, like every treatment before, was shoved into the back of a closet to gather dust.

• • •

Hope, however, never tarnishes. No matter how often it gets betrayed. My life is now a waiting game. I know there are beneficial options out there, it's just a matter of waiting for them to become widely available. Sooner or later things will get around to me. Until then, I nurture my patience and count my pennies. Who knows how much the next, even better, treatment will cost?

Sneaking Snacks

Who doesn't like going to the movies? This guy (imagine I'm sitting in front of you with both thumbs pointing back at me, smiling in smug fashion).

Many disabled people find crowded public spaces difficult. Modern movie theatres, so-called "megaplexes," might all be designed to be wheelchair accessible—with long-sought accommodations like handicapped restrooms and at least one ticket machine set to a height sufficient for seated patrons to actually reach all the buttons—but these multi-screen theatrical monstrosities come with a downside: a central lobby that is busier than ever. And, for the handicapped, navigating that much foot traffic is a nightmare.

It seems counterintuitive. Bigger buildings should mean more floor space, less crowding among patrons, and a better experience for everyone. In reality, the opposite is true. Going to catch a flick in twenty-first-century Canada is like wading into a raging river of pure chaos, both inside and out.*

Industrializing movie-showing might boost the theatre chain's bottom line, but it does nothing to improve the experience. I, for one, would rather go skinny-dipping in piranha-infested waters while doused in meat-tenderizer aftershave than brave another opening night. No amount of therapy will ever put the popcorn-fuelled stampede behind me.

More room gives the over-excited under-agers added space to run. I've seen hyperactive children, hopped up on sugary snacks, build up some truly impressive rates of speed . . . usually just before running into me. More room allows for rows of arcade games. Their constant stimulation—flashing lights, loud music, not to mention literal bells and whistles—adds to the distracting atmosphere. More room also let theatres expand their concession stands. Thereby creating even more lines of frustrated movie-goers.

Even travelling on level ground with no one around it isn't always easy for people using assistive devices to get around. Spilled drinks and sticky aisles are just the most obvious obstacles. Advertising cut-outs, stacks of merchandise, and crowd control devices all impact our mobility. Adding hundreds of excited theatregoers, milling about in tightly packed groups, only makes manoeuvring safely even more difficult.

I'm lucky. My electric wheelchair is both big and heavy. When

---

* I've already commented on the joy of "handicapped parking" in a previous chapter. Movie theatres, often being a family affair, mean children, and those excited delinquents add a whole new level to parking misery.

it comes to collisions, I almost always come out on top.* The worst that's ever happened to me at the cinema was having half a gallon-sized root beer soak my feet. People using crutches or canes, however, need to be on constant guard. Someone turning suddenly, stepping back unexpectedly, or just rushing around in enthusiasm can easily knock them down. I met one such man at the local cinema not many years ago. He was livid at the way people treated him and, despite never having met me before, decided I was the ideal soul with whom to commiserate. "How do you stand it?!" he demanded. "People are so ignorant. I've only been on crutches for a month and I'm already sick of it." Glaring about the almost full theatre, he added, "Thank goodness I'll be back to normal soon. I don't think I could take much more. And you live like this all the time?" That last was said with utter disbelief.

Smiling, it seemed a less exhausting option than taking offence, I said, "You get used to it."

Unfortunately, he didn't want to hear what I had to say. Our respective lives might be joined by mutual disability but his, being temporary, wasn't giving him the proper perspective.

"Not one person would move for me," he said, gesturing at the full front row before repeating, "Not one! Can you believe it?"

"Really?" I asked, surprised. "In my experience most people are pretty good. Provided you're nice when asking." That last emerged a bit judgemental. I got the feeling this wasn't the kind of guy who did anything "nice."

"Ask?" he demanded. "I shouldn't have to ask. They ought to know to move."

---

* Depending on inertia, angle of impact, and the height of my victim, I've ended up with people landing in my lap—an amusing meet-cute when it's the right girl but a painfully awkward introduction with plus-sized men.

That attitude didn't surprise me. I turned to my friend,** who'd been listening to the whole rant, and raised my eyebrows in a suggestive manner before nodding over my shoulder. He took the cue and, after less than 30 seconds of conversation with a young couple in the front row, had two seats vacated. My new crutch-wielding compatriot took one of those without so much as acknowledging the people who kindly moved for him. I made a point to offer both a grateful smile and an appreciative "Thanks" before going to find my own spot . . . without bothering anyone.

Incidents like that, however annoying, are not what soured me on the movies. That attitude was cemented long ago back when I worked as a mule.

• • •

Concession prices have always been ridiculously high. Snacks are where the theatres make most of their money, after all. That bucket of popcorn certainly doesn't cost them seven dollars. No, those burst kernels drenched in synthetic butter are basically pure profit. Only credit card companies and certain unscrupulous Columbian drug cartels use higher markups. Knowing that, me and my friends never felt guilty about sneaking food into the movies. Or, at least, trying to.

The cinemas have long been on to our oh-so-clever scheme. We were hardly the first to try smuggling cheaper candy bars from home into the darkened theatre. Most chains trained their staff to be on the lookout for obvious signs of sneakiness: bulky coats,

---

** Being unable to drive a vehicle and requiring physical assistance with almost all of life's daily tasks means I seldom travel anywhere without accompaniment—usually family but occasionally a friend—to help out.

overflowing pockets, or suspiciously bulgy purses.

Not even the most litigious usher would call the police on you, not over a package of Raisinets slipped through on the sly, but they made a point to remember faces and banned repeat offenders. Fear of getting blacklisted kept most patrons paying premium prices. Doing otherwise simply wasn't worth the risk. Not when the entertainment options at the time were so slim.*

Being young, broke, and always hungry meant me and my friends didn't have much choice. We could spend our limited funds on one concession stand treat each or hit the nearest convenience store to stretch our bucks. The chance of getting caught only added to our enjoyment in eating those illicit snacks.

Our age combined with our furtive appearance to put us immediately on the theatre's radar. Profiling put us under the eye of every uniformed employee. We had suspicious gazes following every step, from the ticket-taker to the always-moving manager. Such scrutiny left us no choice, we had to get creative.

It didn't take us long to realize that certain movie patrons passed muster more easily than others. The very old and very young skated through the easiest. Adults appearing "responsible" or "upstanding" also avoided second glances. None of us matched those descriptions. In fact, amongst our group of friends only one remotely appeared "legitimate."

For some reason, no one is less suspicious looking than a handicapped youth. I don't know if the able-bodied feel guilty ascribing underhanded motives or if they merely think disability

---

* TV only had thirteen channels, if you had cable, and programming ended at midnight. Atari and Coleco fought for the title of "world's most sophisticated video game system." And cassette tapes marked the pinnacle of the recording industry. There was no internet and other kid-friendly indoor pastimes were few and far between.

makes cripples incapable of committing a crime—most likely they cannot wrap their heads around reality running counter to their ingrained narrative—but, whatever their reasoning, the general consensus regarding disabled kids is: harmless.

And so, the job of carrying our collective contraband past the cinema's vigilant crew fell to me.

One thing you learn using an electric wheelchair is, no matter where you go, your assistive device will draw immediate attention. This proved especially true back in the day, when the design and engineering devoted to these machines' development focused on functionality over comfort and sound reduction. My earliest wheelchairs were less sophisticated and much louder—people could hear me approaching from literally a block away.

You would be hard-pressed to build a mobility aid worse suited for sneaking.

Luckily, smuggling snacks isn't about stealth. Misdirection works too. And, while my wheelchair might be unmissable, no self-respecting adult looked too long at a wheelchair or its occupant. Being caught staring is an embarrassing social faux pas and so most just glance at the handicapped before quickly moving their attention elsewhere.

It didn't take a criminal mastermind to exploit that particular blind spot. Even if someone suspected me, and that was unlikely, what movie theatre employee would dare search a crippled child's wheelchair? Too bad our genius-level planning ended with that question.

Ignorance is the only explanation for our habit of doing all our pre-movie shopping at the only confectionary directly visible from the cinema's windowed ticket booth. Being complete novices at trafficking in treats, we made all sorts of amateurish mistakes.

We might have failed miserably at subterfuge but got to be

pretty good at secreting snacks. My wheelchair's many nooks and crannies aided our efforts. In fact, sneaking bargain-priced food into buildings became something of my specialty. Short of pulling me out of my chair and physically tearing it apart, there was just no way to spot all the hiding places available to a desperate and creative mind.

The back of the seat, when unfastened, left an impressively large gap—a secret compartment as it were—perfect to stuff with bulky foods. Hollow spaces underneath the mechanism's protective plastic casing meant, with the use of a bit of tape, all sorts of goodies could be fastened out of sight. Entire crates of chocolate bars, shelves-worth of chips—there didn't seem to be a sweet we couldn't squeeze in somewhere. Our illicit trade peaked when one of my friends insisted I carry a roast quarter-chicken.

And then there was my person—loose clothing hid more than just a fat belly. Boxes of Smarties, Milk Duds, Maltesers mixed with pouches of M&M's (both peanut and chocolate), Skittles, and Reese's Pieces were up one pantleg. Party-sized versions all. Footlong subs and even litre jugs of name-brand pop went in the other. Long-sleeved shirts housed entire cans of Pringles. We even nestled a quart of ice cream against the small of my back once—a teeth-chattering but effective hiding spot.

It became something of a tradition for my friends to load both me and my machine down with snacks prior to buying our tickets. Licorice, Twizzlers, and Slim Jim's were woven between cables. Jujyfruits and Sno-caps went under my shirt. We even found room for fast food staples like burgers, hotdogs, and French fries. Those last almost gave me away with their distinctive greasy aroma. And it's probably best you don't know how I kept them warm.

No one commented on the fact that it would be just as easy to sneak stuff out of businesses aboard my wheelchair as it was to carry snacks into the cinema. I can't honestly say I never gave the old five-finger discount a try, once or twice.*

One thing became clear: I'd have made a great criminal. Smuggler, bootlegger, or thief . . . no one suspects the cripple.

As much as I'd like to blame peer pressure for prompting me to be party to something so nefarious as sneaking contraband snacks into the cinema, the truth is I chose to do it. Those inflated concession stand prices were an affront to human dignity. And sticking it to the man—even if that "man" was a teenage girl in a paper hat standing behind a glass-fronted display case—smacked of heroism to my then-young mind. Besides, no honestly purchased treat ever tasted half so sweet as those black-market goodies.

All that hard-won skill is now for naught. Movie theatre people no longer much care what sort of foodstuffs you bring in—provided you don't leave a big mess. Where's the challenge for today's crip kids?

---

* Who am I kidding? It was twice. I remember both vividly. The guilt still lingers even though the last was more than thirty years ago.

Good Old Accessible U

Laurentian University was the highlight of my life ... from a purely accessible point of view.

I matriculated at good old LU from 1993 until 1999. For those of you that can't be bothered to do the math, that is longer than needed for a four-year BA. And, yes, I learned "matriculated" there.*

My beloved alma mater has since got itself into some treacherous financial waters—recently revealing a debt big enough to impress even federal government bookkeepers. Local armchair experts and

---

* I needed an extra semester to complete my degree. Not because of any disability-related issues. Pure stubbornness left me half a credit shy of a diploma. Turns out I wasn't "smarter" than my academic advisor, a woman with two PhDs and three decades experience navigating university bureaucracy. Who'd have thunk it?

imported forensic accountants all have their explanations for the institute's precipitous economic collapse. Let me stand up and add my voice to the chorus of tardy suggestions, useless second-guessing, and Monday-morning quarterbacking by admitting, almost two full decades too late, that I am to partly blame for the school's current woes.

Well, me and my crippled ilk.

The university's "Special Needs" office—long-since rebranded as Accessibility Services—might have been small and surprisingly well-hidden** but the department really stood tall for all that. Never once, to my knowledge, did it stint in its assigned duties. Under the steady leadership of Earl Black, himself a disabled Canadian, the small staff worked tirelessly on behalf of all Laurentian's handicapped students, both those with legitimate needs and those happily gaming the system.

You wouldn't think people would fake a disability. Or, at least, I didn't. Until I met some of my fellows. None went so far as to feign blindness or make unneeded use of a wheelchair. But the number of people with other, less obvious (and harder to diagnose) "issues" was staggering.

Most people understand that not all handicaps are visible. Knowing the fact, however, is different from accepting that the guy you just saw bounding up three flights of stairs, the picture of physical health and youthful energy, is now standing in front of you asserting "disabled" privilege. That took some getting used to. I have to applaud Mr. Black—and I always gave him the honorific even though the man, unlike a lot of the university's professors, didn't insist on it—he never once raised an eyebrow or questioned

---

** It sat behind an unremarkable door at the end of an obscure hall in an otherwise forgettable building.

a claim, no matter how far-fetched.

(The cynical might argue that the more students who used the office, the higher his department's budget. I, however, prefer believing the best of his motivations.)

Anxiety issues, learning disabilities, not to mention various psychological disorders all necessitated accommodation. And if no one in the Special Needs department ever commented or criticized, there were plenty of people—students and faculty alike—only too happy to offer judgement. Having no experience with disabilities didn't stop these people from voicing their opinion, nor did common decency.

Come exam time, the traffic through the department grew exponentially, all seeking allowances. Skepticism rose alongside the steadily building academic pressure. One overly suspicious professor even asked me why I couldn't write my exams in the university's gymnasium "like everyone else?" Other students would have happily reported the woman for that or else taken the opportunity to lecture the person who so often lectured them. But not me. Half a lifetime of in a wheelchair had taught me the foolishness of that confrontational attitude. Instead of claiming the moral high ground, I calmly explained the facts as pertained to me and my need for accommodation—for the record, that entailed a desk high enough not to cause backpain.

Shelves full of assistive devices dominated the department. Most mystified me. Every drawer seemed stuffed with adaptive computer software, each expensive program waiting for students in need. In special need. Voice to text. Text to voice. Braille readers. The cost of purchasing just one of those would have beggared most students and the office had them by the dozen—each and every one free to use.

Pre-emptive action seemed the department's overarching

philosophy. Cost didn't matter. Every building on campus had at least one elevator—they'd either been designed or renovated with accommodation in mind—and there were motion-activated door openers on all important entrances. Inside, the school exceeded code. The place was tricked out.

Unfortunately, the construction of the school's grounds predated the Special Needs department, and this made travelling across campus a nightmare for anyone with mobility issues, especially in winter.

Given LU is located in Sudbury, Ontario—where winter can start as early as October and routinely stretches into April—it wasn't just the school's disabled students who suffered from this rather glaring design flaw. As winter's cold wind blew off the lake, with nowhere to hide from the freezing blast, co-eds and faculty took to joking about the campus's layout. Bitter, teeth-chattering jokes.

Let me state that the grounds were gorgeous . . . in summer. Lush greenery, natural wild-spaces, and the pristine waters of Lake Ramsay sparkling under the sun, all warm and inviting. Students lounged on the expansive lawns and lunched on the spacious paved patios. Crossing the campus was like walking through an especially well-kept park—only this one was full of healthy young people living life to the fullest while away from home for the first time and eagerly sowing their proverbial oats. There was even the occasional bit of wildlife living nearby, in the undeveloped green space fringing the campus or along the neighbouring golf course's private fairway. The entire multi-acre footprint stood as a testament to the beauty of Northern Ontario.

I discovered Laurentian's seasonal splendour in my final year. Foolishly, I had kept to the traditional September start and never once considered "summer school." That dreaded term, to my mind, only applied to those academic reprobates who failed during regular semester. Come the end of April's exams I was, invariably, out the door, missing the time when LU shone.

Clearly the design was meant for the more congenial clime of Toronto. No true northerner would put buildings so far apart or create "scenic" walkways with no protection from gale-force gusts or blizzard-driven snow. Very little at Laurentian, during my time anyway, acknowledged the north—its realities, its sensibilities, or its weather. Rather than embracing its uniqueness, LU tried to recreate the congenial college atmosphere familiar to campuses the world over. Stonework and stately brick dominated. Towering architecture and large imposing buildings, clearly meant to impress, dotted the landscape. The place might have lacked ivy-covered walls but not for lack of trying.

Still, despite Laurentian's failings—or perhaps because of them—I found the place wormed its way into my heart. When graduation day finally arrived, after a long but enjoyable tenure, a surprising feeling of sadness came over me as I drove away for, presumably, the last time.

Then, barely even a year later, my life took an unexpected turn. I didn't end up back at LU, that would be too perfect, instead I applied for a job at Sudbury's other longstanding post-secondary educational institute, Cambrian College. The advertised position of "Research Assistant" fit my interest and I managed to land an interview.

My resume was then (and remains) fairly standard. It doesn't list "Expert wheelchair driver," "Professional special needs advocate," or "More than thirty-five years sitting experience" under Skills. The first time that prospective employers learn of my disability is seeing me roll into the room. That surprise introduction is often awkward. Shock gives way to pity, then the panic sets in as they all think the same thing: How do we tell this guy "No" without making it about his disability? Luckily, even those who plan on passing me over feel obliged to go through the motions and, once the questions start, I invariably win them to my side.*

That day, in the too-small and inadequately ventilated former storage closet hastily converted into an interview room, I must have really impressed because the two women—both, I later learned, from HR—turned me down for the Research Assistant job in record time.

Reaching across the battered conference table, or as far as my limited range-of-motion allowed, I was automatically thanking them (politeness often hides my true feelings) for the pro forma rejection when they looked to each other and conducted some sort of unspoken dialogue.

The blonde, a tall woman even seated, dressed expensively. Impeccably, even severely, groomed—she pulled her hair back into a braid so tight that even an ounce more pressure would surely result in a scalping—she didn't crack a smile the entire interview. She nodded once, decisively.

That gesture was hurriedly and repeatedly returned by the rapidly greying brunette positioned to the side. Enthusiasm leaked from her wide-open pores but in a charmingly endearing way. Her all-natural "hippie" look eschewed cosmetics but she looked happier, and far more comfortable, in loose garments of natural woven fibre** than her pristine co-worker.

Their agreement, instantaneous, set the first to moving. She stood abruptly and, towering like some avenging Valkyrie, advised

---

* This has little to do with my inherit charm and everything to do with the absolute brutal honesty I employ when being interviewed. There is no prevarication or obfuscation. I lay everything on the table and, usually, leave my interrogator baffled by my forthrightness.

** Probably hemp given her whole vibe.

me to, "Remain a moment," before striding from the room, her painfully high heels clacking with each step. Moving at a more deliberate pace, the second woman smiled and added a warm, "Give us a moment, please. We'll be right back." On realizing the other hadn't waited, she scurried out as if her very life depended on following the other's wake.

Twenty minutes later, the women were back, sitting across from me, both smiling. "How would you like to head our Special Needs Department?" the shorter asked. She hadn't even finished her question before the other leapt up, announcing, "Come on. We'll give you the tour."

Construction was still ongoing but even with unfinished walls and open ceilings I couldn't hide my amazement. Back at LU, I watched Mr. Black and his team operate out of an insanely cramped office. If more than two people in wheelchairs wanted to use the space, they had to take turns. All too often I found myself waiting in the hall for someone to vacate the premises before stepping inside. Meanwhile, Cambrian was erecting an entire wing.

"Vast" didn't do the facilities credit. "Huge" came closer. But ultimately, I discovered "palatial" fit best. Every step of the tour revealed further opulence.

"That," the shorter and more talkative of the two began, pointing to a wide, partially framed opening, "is where the main entrance is going. Automatic double-doors. Triple-paned, smoke-tinted glass. With a temperature-controlled airlock to create a mitigating micro-climate—keep the cold air out in winter and the hot air out in summer. There is reserved parking out front, with spots set aside especially for faculty."

Spacious, elegant, and clearly designed with room to expand, the place didn't have to try to impress. "We're installing fibre-optic cables throughout," gushed the blonde, her earlier reserve giving way to surprising enthusiasm. "Much more responsible than traditional wiring," she added.

"Fifteen hundred square feet on the main floor," the other continued as if never interrupted. "Open concept throughout, with a dozen multipurpose rooms spread around the upper balcony. All the finishing is to be done in natural wood."

"Locally sourced and sustainably harvested, of course," assured the taller woman, before adding, "In-floor, geo-thermal heating and eco-friendly central air conditioning complete with an industry leading microfibre filtration system. Special attention is being given to livability—everything is designed to be harmonious and pleasing to both the eye and the spirit."

"Your starting salary would be comparable to industry standard but there's a generous expense package to see things started. And you'd oversee all decisions—hiring, spending, and the like," her recruiting partner explained, focussing on the practical despite appearances to the contrary. "We would seek input from you on any issue pertaining to the department and would expect you take a leading role in all accessibility issues."

I didn't need to ask a question. The two women laid the sales pitch on thick, taking turns tag-teaming me with facts and flattery.

"A staff of four would be working for you. With a couple of student interns each semester. And the biggest office would be yours."

"It's on the south corner, with large windows along both exterior walls, so expect plenty of natural light and a great view of the quad," the blonde said, leading to the unfinished space and waving dramatically like a game-show spokesmodel indicating: All this could be yours! "There's a private bathroom too. Fully functional, including a roll-in handicapped-shower. Every part fully compliant with responsible water usage."

I didn't question why I'd need to shower at work, just nodded acknowledgement.

"You'd have a private secretary," the shorter said, indicating the space out front of the office door where a large desk would sit, guarding my private sanctum from would-be intruders. "And the department would have the latest in equipment. Are you a Mac or PC guy? We'll make sure your computer is top of the line. No expense is being spared."

"The facilities here are meant to be a showcase. Environmentalism combined with practical functionality . . . built in accordance with traditional practices, all harmoniously incorporating native Northern Ontario materials. Nature and nurture, if you will."

I don't know what was more overwhelming, the facilities, the promises, or the women's enthusiasm. On leading me back to the interview office, they sat and beamed.

It never occurred that they were waiting on me until, finally, one prompted, "Well?"

"It's impressive," I answered, hedging with the truth. Then added, "Very impressive," with enough admiration in my voice that no one could doubt my sincerity. Then, after a long moment of silence, hit them with, "But . . ."

That one word almost set the two flinching in horror. Not wanting to stretch the discomfort, I ripped off the proverbial bandage and spoke the blunt truth: "But . . . are you sure I'm the person for the job?" Adding hurriedly, "I have zero experience and never took a single course in education, let alone dealing in special needs."

"You'll figure it out as you go," the blonde assured.

"That's why there are books and seminars," the other smiled as if there were no obstacles we couldn't overcome together.

Realization struck then. They want a cripple. I'm a token hire.

It was a red-letter moment.

• • •

Six and half years. That's how long I attended good old LU. Mr. Black was the first person I met, even before I registered. He took over an hour out of his busy schedule to give a me, some anonymous prospective disabled student, the grand tour. And made a point, after guiding me through the campus's byzantine back halls and showing me the location of every elevator, to say, "The department is here . . . whatever you need."

He even sounded like he meant it.

Thinking back on his steadying presence left me in awe. Under his leadership, the Special Needs department fought on my behalf, helping in myriad behind-the-scenes ways, to ensure I could stand on my own merit and claim an education without prejudice or impediment. Hundreds of handicapped students, both before and after my time, benefited from Mr. Black's constant uphill efforts. The man changed lives. Mine for certain.

Realization struck. That could be me. I could be like him and help people. Make a difference. All of which appealed immensely.

Only, of course, I couldn't do any of that.

I have my strengths and weaknesses the same as anyone else. Lacking confidence has never been a fault of mine. But, somehow, risking others' futures just isn't in me. Knowing that the success or failure of hundreds of future Cambrian College students rested on my scrawny, inexperienced shoulders proved too much.

Not even a cushy corner office complete with generous expense account could tempt me. Though it came close.

A more experienced man would have said, "Could I have a couple days to think about it?" Someone with more confidence or even a realistic understanding of the world and the brutally harsh job market, especially as relates to people with disabilities, would have leapt at the offer. But I looked at the two women and offered a straightforward, "No, thanks."

My answer didn't seem to penetrate. Perhaps they couldn't believe someone would turn down this once-in-a-lifetime opportunity—no doubt every member of the faculty was busily positioning themselves to take charge of the new department. The mountain of resumes must have rivalled Everest. Whatever their thinking, they weren't prepared to take "No" for an answer.

Everyone who knows me has learned, much to their frustration, that making me see reason when my mind is made up is akin to repeatedly bashing your head into a concrete wall. I pride myself on being stubborn and the more I'm pushed the harder I dig in my feet to fight.

The two HR ladies tried every trick in the book . . . to no avail. Logic, emotion, even bribery—none of it worked. I left the office and that life-changing job behind . . . only to regret the decision more with every passing year.

What could they have said to get me to sign on? Probably nothing. But the truth might have been a good start. Of course, at the time I was sure careers of that calibre lurked around every corner. Worse, I felt confident that I would soon be churning out bestselling novels by the bucketful. Neither delusion panned out.

Three months later, I began to realize my mistake. Writing proved much harder and far less lucrative than I'd imagined. The job market, at least for disabled Canadians, failed to live up to my expectations. Even my fall-back job, clerking at a bookstore, fell through. Chapters wouldn't even grant me an interview—neither my overqualified resume nor the staggering amount of money I'd shovelled into the store's tills over the years mattered.

In fact, the only place that deigned to give me a shot was the government. Sudbury's Data Taxation Centre offered me a schedule I couldn't make work but at least they wanted me.

And that, above all, is what Earl Black did . . . made me, and my crippled ilk, feel welcome. He made good old LU accessible.

Drunk Driving is No Joke

Everybody's a comedian. That's one thing you discover when sitting in a wheelchair minding your own God damn business and trying to enjoy a quiet beer. Not good comedians, mind, but that doesn't stop these (often drunk) people from trying.

You cannot imagine how many drunk driving "jokes" I've had lobbed at me. The same handful of tired chestnuts are trotted out every time I set foot in a bar. Rather than dignify these sorry attempts at humour—even repeating them in mockery provides too much credit—let me offer this advice: Just stop.

The only funny part in those sad one-liners is the ironic fact that I have never actually been drunk.

The indignity of drink turned me off long ago. Sure, you may feel ten-feet-tall and bulletproof after a few vodka martinis but there's nothing suave about slurred speech or stumbling steps. All those beer commercials lied. Neither Spuds Mackenzie nor the Swedish Bikini Team are appearing at your party—no matter what brand of domestic brew you buy. Drunkenness is not attractive. Chances are the cooler you think you're acting the bigger a fool you appear to anyone not pickled to a similar level.

Having been cornered by my share of drunks—a disproportionate number of whom were weirdly "affectionate"—let me state that your sloppy kisses and desperate embraces are not reciprocated. Trust me, if I could run away from your clinging hugs and desperately groping fingers I would.

• • •

Alcohol and I have, historically, not been the best of friends. It didn't help that, growing up, no bar in my hometown was wheelchair accessible.

Drinking at home, alone, struck me as tragic in the extreme. Socializing was the part I most looked forward to—imagining the day I'd walk into the local watering hole and everyone would know my name. (Yes, most of what I knew about bar-life came from the TV sitcom Cheers.)

Inappropriate teasing aside—and the drunk driving comments started long before I could legally imbibe—nothing about consuming intoxicants ever appealed to me. Certainly not the idea of climbing behind the wheel while impaired.

I reached legal drinking age while still in high school* but I had, of course, "sampled" a few choice beverages prior to turning

---

* Back in my day, that required five years—Grade Thirteen was standard for anyone planning to attend university.

nineteen. Like many kids growing up in the 1980s I was given the odd sip of beer and even got a taste of scotch (it reminded me of rancid apple juice mixed with turpentine). Becoming a teen changed that from a game to a challenge.

In Capreol, we called them "Pit Parties" even though most of the time they took place in the bush. This was long before social media or cell phones, so organizing things required time and effort. Dozens, sometimes hundreds, of kids would show up at the agreed upon time and place. Each bringing whatever booze they'd managed to get their underage hands on. I won't go into the various tricks we used to get our "wobbly pops"—no point incriminating anyone else in my youthful indiscretions—but most of the attendees begged, borrowed, or stole a bottle or two.

My first Pit Party was also my last.

Some bad things went down that night. I witnessed several fights, and numerous acts of casual vandalism, not to mention some light arson. There was indiscriminate making out and what struck me, an admittedly sheltered teen, as "inappropriate behaviour." Acts that now would border on sexual assault were perpetrated on several of the more intoxicated young women. I left disgusted, both at my contemporaries for their idea of "fun" and myself for not denouncing the whole affair.

It wasn't until university that my opinion of drinking would change. The on-campus pub (called, logically enough, "The Pub Down Under" in honour of its basement location) was the first bar I'd ever encountered that was wheelchair accessible. It had a tiny little elevator hidden at the back of the kitchen to aid with deliveries. Unfortunately, before I could enter the establishment and order my first draft, I had to pass through the mazelike cooking facilities. Unused stainless steel preparation stations gathered dust and industrial grade appliances rusted around me as I ran, what I took to calling, "The Kitchen Gauntlet." The place was just storage by that point. It hadn't put out a hot meal since butterfly collars and bellbottoms dominated undergrad fashions. But rules were rules. So, every time I joined my friends in the pub for a drink, I had to don the dreaded hairnet. Perhaps I should say hairnets, plural, since I was forced to wear one on my head and another over my beard.* It proved a humiliating experience. Hairnets don't do much for your appearance or your dignity. Luckily, I didn't need to keep them on the entire time. Just long enough to pass through the kitchen and enter the pub proper.

Today it wouldn't bother me. There isn't much hair left, to be honest, and I'm much less sensitive in middle age than I was as an insecure twenty-something-year-old. Truth be told, now I'd just laugh off the embarrassment but back then it bothered me. None of which ever stopped me from imbibing . . . only socially appropriate amounts, of course.

So, how did I become a teetotaller? It has nothing to do with my disability. A lot of people in situations similar to mine drink. Some even to excess. There's no medical reason preventing me. It's not as if enjoying a few scotches would make me more crippled. I could get "legless" any time . . . but I don't. Instead, I avoid social situations where drinking dominates. The reason is simple: fear.

It would be easier to claim some high-minded moral justification. And I often cite the example of my grandfather, who gave up drinking (and smoking) cold turkey, as just such a reason. Emulating the example of a much-admired family member makes sense to people—especially those fortunate enough to have known the man in question. But there is no denying that it is, in fact, cowardice that has kept me stone-cold sober the entirety of my life.

---

* I should mention that these protective garments weren't always clean.

I live in terror of losing control. There may be nothing I can do to slow the degenerative aspects of SMA—the disease's progress is beyond me, something to be endured with grace . . . or as much good grace as possible—but that doesn't make me helpless. Sure, my body is failing, but that sorry truth only makes me cling to the parts of my life I can control (emotions, attitudes, and intellect) all the more tightly. Why, then, would I willingly decrease my faculties . . . even temporarily?

Let me lay it out in the most pretentious way possible, In Vino Veritas. That bit of Latin translates to "In wine, truth." We've all seen people who, thanks to copious amounts of drink, have no filter. Sometimes this is amusing. Other times it proves embarrassing. In my case I'm afraid such honesty would be devastating.

What kind of drunk would I be? My suspicion is: unpleasant. There is an anger in me and a maudlin streak too. Keeping the negative emotions under control takes effort. And that doesn't count many of my more "extreme" opinions. There are topics I tend to avoid and consuming alcohol would open the proverbial floodgates. As the saying goes, "Better to remain silent and be thought ignorant than to open one's mouth and remove all doubt."

And that is why I avoid alcohol to this day.

The closest I've ever come to being drunk was the night of my high school graduation when a group of us rented one of Sudbury's seedier nightclubs for the evening and just sort of hung out. I smoked more than drank, trading most of my drink tickets for my friends unwanted cigars. One beer* and half a beach-bucket of mixed alcohol—the exact ingredients were indeterminate beneath the cloying cover of cheap pineapple and peach juice—had me

---

* Drunk through a straw since even then, almost thirty years ago, I couldn't lift a bottle to my lips.

feeling no pain. Other than becoming even more talkative than usual, which is hard to imagine, I remained mostly in control.

Even if I were interested in what bars served, and I'm not, few drinking establishments are wheelchair friendly—especially in small towns. It wasn't until I was twenty-one, at a wedding in the United States,** that I stepped into my first off-campus bar. That sorry establishment proved a letdown on a number of levels. First, it lacked décor. I expected one of two extremes: either tired old walls dripping with ambiance, tables full of memorable characters, and a worn, lived-in, and much-loved vibe; or else new and clean, with a cold corporately mandated kitsch. Instead, there was the worst of both worlds—sadness and despair seemed the dominant vibe.

And, naturally, the drunk driving lines were waiting for me. In fact, the waitress hit me up with one before even taking my order. I pounded back a draft beer and returned to my hotel room to watch gameshow reruns until the rehearsal dinner.

• • •

Bad jokes are one thing. There are few groups—especially among visible minorities—that haven't been the source of some questionable humour. Being the brunt of drunk driving jokes is nothing to get excited about. Most disabled develop thick skins.

No, the frustrating part of is the amount of time, effort, and money spent trying to educate the public as to the habit's dangers. Mothers Against Drunk Driving (MADD) alone has dedicated

---

** The Americans with Disabilities Act (ADA) mandated accommodations for handicapped patrons in a number of wide-ranging businesses decades ago. Why Canada hasn't passed a similarly vigorous set of laws remains a mystery to me and hundreds of thousands of other disabled citizens.

decades to informing people of the horrifying statistics. All, it seems, to no avail.

Seriously, try it. Go rent a wheelchair, roll into some cheap bar, and have a drink. In moments you'll discover that everyone's a comedian and suddenly it's a Night at the Improv. No matter your beverage of choice, it will quickly sour.

Spitting on Shakespeare

Me and the Bard are tight. Or at least we were ... once. Before our falling out. Over a woman, naturally.

I knew a bit about Shakespeare heading into university. It's hard not to at least learn the basics growing up in modern Western society. The man's influence is everywhere—film, stage, literature, you name it. No secondary school experience would be complete without at least one traumatized PE teacher struggling to hold an English class's bored attention while explaining, in exasperated monosyllables, why a long-dead playwright is still venerated as the language's greatest author, a challenge greater than navigating the toughest "confidence" course—even the dreaded vertical rope climb.

Back in my day, teachers pushed Shakespeare like they were

on commission. I remember two specific plays from high school, Julius Caesar and Hamlet. The first sticks in mind because everyone had to memorize the entire "Friends, Romans, countrymen . . . " speech, which went over like a lead balloon with most of my teenage classmates. The second's iconic graveyard scene, with the "Alas, poor Yorick! I knew him, Horatio . . . " soliloquy, fared slightly better with my contemporaries—skulls spoke to the Heavy Metal crowd far more than togas—but few students enjoyed either play.

I, unlike most, found Shakespeare fascinating enough that I bought a cheap edition of his Collected Works only to discover the ridiculously small type and onion-skin paper made it unreadable. (I still have that book—throwing away any form of literature is anathema to me and literally pains my soul.)

Once enrolled at an institute of higher learning, I leapt at the chance to take a course entirely dedicated to the famed Bard of Avon. Not only were his plays short but there were dozens of televised versions available for rent. Best of all, almost every bookstore stocked the Coles Notes. Academically speaking, there probably wasn't a better author in the entire history of written English to compose essays about. The resources and analysis are practically unending. I know because I cribbed from them all.

That class marked the high water mark of my academic career. It was the first and only time I managed a grade higher than my much smarter friend, Paul,* a fact I still oh-so-randomly bring up in casual conversation.

Our friendship began in Introduction to Shakespeare. I arrived

---

* I beat him by 1%.

early to find a suitable spot** and Paul strode in late. As he went to climb around me and my aisle-blocking wheelchair, I uttered an apology, saying, "Excuse me for not standing." That off-hand comment might have launched our acquaintance, but it was surviving the class that cemented our friendship.

Together, Paul, me, and our new accomplice, Biker John, mercilessly mocked the professor from our back row seats. I know that sounds cruel, but he deserved ridicule. While the man knew his stuff, inside-out and upside-down, he somehow managed to suck all the joy out of the sharing. To this day I'm baffled at how a tenured professor could turn some of the most riveting tales in English from enthralling epics into something so utilitarian and, dare I say, boring?

Then I discovered the Stratford Festival and learned, much to my surprise, that live theatre breathed new life into Shakespeare's plays. Far from the stuffy, stilted words dissected in the classroom— in the professor's dry-voiced monotone—on stage those centuries-old lines sang.

For those of you unfamiliar with Canada's preeminent Shakespeare theatre, all you really need to know is that there's no barrier between the action and the audience. Love and betrayal, murder and mischief, petty jealousies and nation-shaking turmoil— all of it belonged on the boards. And in Stratford I found those fierce passions played out in front of hushed crowds. The moment the lights went down . . . magic.

** Though Laurentian University prided itself on "accessibility," the school fell a bit short when it came to "accommodations." No classroom, at least none I ever found, had wheelchair seating. Luckily for me, I could make due with regular desks—provided an aisle seat was available. Staking claim to the prime real estate was just one reason I always tried to be first into a room. I hated having to ask someone to move and managed to avoid it for almost the entirety of my academic career.

Each play enthralled me. Imaginatively interpreted and professionally produced, these individual tours de force amazed. Taken together the experience overwhelmed, helped, in no small part, by the ground-breaking "thrust stage" design. The innovative set-up allows for unrivalled intimacy. Actors amble amidst the aisles, duel through the entranceways, and, during one memorable (and extremely wet) occasion, leaned on my wheelchair to declaim dialogue.

That proved a most unwelcome creative choice. At least from where I sat.

I've had my wheelchair put to a number of unintended uses over the years. It's been a coatrack and a stepping stool, purses and baggage have been hung from its various protuberances like I'm some sort of pack-mule, I've blocked doors with my wheelchair, and it's even been coopted for nefarious purposes—assisting in five-finger discounts. But never before Stratford had the assistive device been incorporated into a Shakespearian comedy. Far from its original purpose, to nobly haul my fat arse about in some semblance of mobility, each inappropriate repurposing grated on my very soul.

The casual assumption people take when "borrowing" my wheelchair is what I found the most frustrating. Even insulting.

As You Like It was, prior to arriving in Stratford, one of my favourite plays. I found myself liking it significantly less as actor after actor made the questionable artistic decision to use me and my wheelchair as an impromptu prop. Getting closer to the action than I ever wanted almost ruined the entire experience for me.

Technology may have changed the theatre immensely in the centuries since the Elizabethan era but, no matter how sensitive the microphones, actors still need to both project and enunciate their lines. Spittle often emerges as dialogue is spoken and, that fateful day, I found myself sitting squarely in the splash zone.

It was my first ever live theatre experience and no one had warned me to avoid sitting in the front row.

Being shown to the select seating spot proved a surprise to me. I didn't pay extra for the privilege. Ordering the tickets by phone I only specified, "One wheelchair and one companion." Discovering that the theatre's handicapped space sat front and centre made me smile. The VIP treatment accorded to me didn't hurt either—a uniformed usherette guided my cousin Kathy and me to our places first and then, once certain we were "comfortably settled," went to attend the rest of the still waiting crowd.

We sat so close to the stage that I could almost reach out and touch it.

Strange expressions were directed my way as people filed past, making the long trek to their far more distant seats. At first, I thought it mere envy. Our proximity to the impending action eliciting jealous looks. The first sibilant syllable spoken sank my enthusiasm and revealed the truth—that the veteran theatre-goers were looking on me with pity.

I quickly learned that phlegm flies far. Each uttered line, exhaled in Iambic Pentameter, was accompanied by the warm sputter of saliva raining down upon my head. Every actor-inhaled breath caused me to wince in watery anticipation. Drops of drool drenched me starting with the first line . . . and the play stretched on for hours! I sat there, being soaked by spittle and regretting ever setting foot in Stratford, until the lights dimmed. Then I made my escape, leaving the theatre in search of a towel and a change of clothes.

Never before or since have I more longed for hair. Having started balding as a young man, there wasn't much up top to protect me from the rain of moist particulates. I felt the precipitation plop on bare scalp. Each and every minute bit of mucus mocking me.

You'd think that such a tragic experience would have soured me on live performances. Far from it. The play was salvaged by Rosalind's arrival. A stunningly beautiful actress played the lead and she could have used me as scenery forever. I wouldn't have cared had she hoicked one directly on my head. Her gold-trimmed, low-cut dress and the evocative aroma of her come-hither perfume mixed with fragrantly florid shampoo to overwhelm and enthral one virgin theatregoer.

That's right, my lifelong love of Shakespeare came about (in part) because I had the hots for a woman—one whose name I never did learn.*

I went back the next summer and continued that tradition for half a decade, searching in vain for my lady love Rosalind; knowing better thereafter, thanks to sputum-scarred experience, than to sit anywhere near the front. But love, it seems, really is blind because without the hideous blond wig and leeringly trimmed bodice I never recognized the actress again.

Four consecutive summers my family and I journeyed to the charming town of Stratford, Ontario, there to spend three days and two nights immersed in theatrical wonder and loosely themed Shakespearian propaganda. We arrived in town expecting the bucolic serenity of Avon, England—a green and pleasant land—but found instead a gimmicky tourist trap. Oh, Stratford, Ontario, disguised its crass commercialism behind a veneer of civility but,

---

* Acting can be a lucrative, glamourous, and even respected profession today but for much of Western history this wasn't the case. In fact, those performing on stage were often viewed as just a step above prostitutes in the social hierarchy—a very short step. I include this fact, not as excuse for objectifying the individual, but rather to note how far theatre performers have risen. Now professionals are lauded and applauded, honoured and feted, and even, occasionally, paid.

coming from Capreol, I know a jumped-up railroad town when I see one.

The much-lauded, world-famous Stratford Festival had been founded by a community not much different from my hometown—the truth was merely hidden behind Shakespeare's skirt of respectability. Big name actors graced the theatre's playbills over the years, each lending added legitimacy to the town's thespian aspirations. Many celebrated Hollywood stars served their apprenticeship in Stratford, learning their craft in small-town Canada before finding fame and fortune elsewhere. Others took valuable time from lucrative careers to rejuvenate themselves in front of a live audience.

Some of the more prominent performers to visit the town include Dame Maggie Smith, Jessica Tandy, Hume Cronyn, Sir Peter Ustinov, Christopher Walken, Christopher Plummer, Sarah Polley, William Shatner, Lorne Greene, Sir Alec Guinness, Brian Dennehy, Andrea Martin, and Eric McCormack.

Despite the thin Shakespearian façade, I thoroughly enjoyed my time in Stratford. Our traditional stay involved three days and two nights. We'd arrive mid-afternoon and have a nice meal and catch a play that evening. The next morning would be breakfast, a touristy walk through the downtown, lunch, then a matinee, followed by a high-end supper and the third play of the trip. The final morning would be a lazy breakfast then the trip home.

Three plays became our tradition. After the first year, I reluctantly agreed to limit my choices—since I bought the tickets, I also selected our shows—to two classics penned by the bard and one more modern piece.* My various guests and relatives drew straws to see who "won" accompanying duties—that way none of them had to sit through more than one Shakespeare performance at my side. (They still complained—despite my footing the bill.**)

In between showtimes we wandered the picturesque streets, listened to buskers in the park, fled the maliciously beautiful but evil-tempered swans—like fowl ninjas, they lay in wait before striking with shocking ferocity and feathered grace—and sampled the town's various restaurants while guessing the servers' assumed accent (most were actors earning a crust while honing their improv skills on gullible tourists).

Those visits are long behind me now, but the community left me convinced of one thing: If I were to ever relocate within the province, Stratford would be the place. Sign me up for VIP season passes—to the festival and the local Junior B hockey team too. It doesn't get more Canadian than cheering the Bard one day and a good open-ice bodycheck the next.

(Note to self: If sitting near the stage, bring an umbrella.)

---

* I still get chills remembering the *tour de force* performance Al Waxman gave as Willy Loman in *Death of a Salesman*. The entire audience was putty in the veteran actor's hand as he put his character, and us, through the emotional wringer. Stunned silence dominated the crowd's reaction—a feat I've never seen repeated.

** For compulsively curious theatre geeks, we saw the following. 1996: *As You Like It*, *Merchant of Venice*, and *King Lear*. 1997: *Taming of the Shrew*, *Romeo and Juliet*, and *Death of a Salesman*. 1998: *Julius Caesar*, *Much Ado About Nothing*, and *Man of La Mancha*. 1999: *The Tempest*, *Macbeth*, and *West Side Story*.

Big Brother, Don't Bother

Siblings are hard. For every child whose brother or sister is their first, best, and most trusted friend there's another who found a lifelong rival, if not outright enemy, in the arrival of another so-called "mouth to feed." Fights for attention and the splitting of parental affection—once the sole domain of the firstborn—are common. It takes time for families to establish a pecking order and there are plenty of tears as children work out dominance. Jealousies, naturally, abound.

And that doesn't even consider the stress added by bringing a special needs child into the mix.

• • •

Try as I might to put a humorous spin on my memories, and believe me I'm trying hard, a lot of this book still comes off as me whinging about how hard my life is. Don't get me wrong, I have my daily trials. But for the most part I've resigned myself to the situation. I long ago realized how ridiculously lucky I am—born in a great country in an enlightened time to a close-knit middle-class family—and that things could be so much worse for me.

Seeking out happiness and appreciating my good fortune doesn't mean that I live regret free. Everyone has moments they wish to do over and actions they would love to mulligan. For me, most revolve around me and my brother.

We were close when little but gradually grew apart. Most of the blame is mine. Selfishness dominated my younger self. I wasn't mean but didn't put much effort into being kind either. Looking back, pushing him down the stairs probably didn't help build trust between us. Nor hitting him with a baseball bat—sure, it was plastic but the material doesn't much matter when you strike a male where I did.

Big brothers are supposed to look out for their younger siblings, protect them, and do anything and everything in their power to help them grow up healthy and happy. In this, like so much, I failed miserably.

It doesn't help that one of my family's most repeated anecdotes involved the surprising lengths my uncle, Dave, went to protect my dad, his younger brother, Bob. The two have an enviably close relationship to this day, talking over the phone once a week for anywhere from twenty minutes to an hour. The incident occurred more than sixty years ago, back when both attended Capreol Public School. A teacher decided to physically reprimand Bob for some schoolyard infraction or other. My father would have been 10 or 11 at the time and, like most of the men in our family prior to puberty, scrawny in the extreme. Before that educator knew what was happening, he found himself being manhandled by a very unhappy Dave, who, at 14, grabbed the fully grown adult by the collar, picked him from the ground, and held that teacher against the fence to rethink the error of his ways.

Knowing there's someone who has your back, that regardless of the situation or consequences you have someone in your corner, is a powerful feeling. My dad had it with his brother but mine never got that from me.

It boils down to the "Dead Hooker Hypothesis." Let me explain this entirely imaginary scenario for those unfamiliar. Suppose that, for whatever reason, you did something truly bad—grossly illegal even—like accidentally killing a prostitute. Now, who would you call? I'm not talking about phoning for legal advice or moral solace. No, which person could you count on to help make the problem go away (meaning cover the crime and dispose of the body)? You need someone utterly reliable and loyal to the extreme. This is a "no questions asked, pretend this never happened" type scenario. Do you even have someone in your life that shares such trust and understanding?

Should such an ethically dubious situation, or anything of similar importance, ever crop up in my brother's life there is zero chance I'd be his first choice. Given our very different lives I might not even rank in his top ten. He has friends, one in particular, who'd aid in that nefarious deed without hesitation.

My dad could call his brother and know that help would be coming. His brother is in the same position. Able to count on his sibling for support regardless of the situation. Without hesitation.

Admittedly, their childhood differed from mine in important ways. Predating me by twenty-five-plus years meant they grew up in a cruder, less sheltered era. Life was rough and tumble during their formative years. They fought and annoyed each other, like most brothers do, but looked out for one another, too. And continue to do so to this day.

I envy them and their relationship.

• • •

The very first time I failed my brother that I can remember took place at the local hockey arena. He was insanely young, aged maybe three but definitely no more than five. I was in the stands sitting with my parents and waiting for the game to start when the worried-looking coach climbed halfway up the stairs and signalled that something wasn't right. My dad went to see what caused the problem. I'm not sure what prompted him to bring me along as he went to investigate but he carried me down to the dressing room. Inside, my little brother sat crying. "I don't wanna be goalie," Scottie managed between sobs. "It hurts." He wasn't making a lot of sense. Upset children seldom do.

The truth came out; several of the older kids on the team had been teasing my brother and feeding him lies about how painful stopping the puck would be. This was Scottie's first year of organized hockey. Tyke or Squirt-level, I forget the name used at the time. A good belch contained more force than these entry-level kids' hardest shot. Most players at that age can't even lift the puck off the ice, let alone inflict injury. But Scottie didn't know that. He'd been lied to by his teammates and nothing the coach or my dad could say would convince him different.

A good big brother would have thrown an arm over his shoulder, whispered something encouraging, and got him out on the ice. Of course, a good brother—in ideal circumstances—would have been playing on the team with him.

Still, able-bodied or not, looking out for Scottie was my job. And seeing him huddled there, his confidence bled out from dozens of vicious little lies, I knew the truth: I'd failed. Instead of being a protector, sitting in the locker room by his side (or at least within shouting distance) to prevent any bullying, I spent the games in the stands drinking hot cocoa. That wasn't a choice, of course. Okay, the beverages might have been. But I'd have given anything to lace up my skates alongside my brother, then or even now. Fate, or more accurately genetics, prevented my participating, which meant my naïve baby brother was left to the not-so-tender mercies of the locker room. You wouldn't know it now—my brother stands six-foot-three and is an avid outdoorsman who's more than once stood up for himself, me, and any number of other underdogs—but as a youngster he was quiet and sensitive. Easy prey for mean-spirited brats.

Eventually the coach issued an ultimatum. "Either you play goalie or you quit."

Scottie chose the latter and we went home.

Was that the turning point in his burgeoning hockey career? I would argue, "Yes." He stayed away from the game for several years and, when he did get back, found himself playing catch-up with the other kids. Eventually, he made up the ground and, by the time he reached 16, became one of the better players of his age in town. But if he'd just gone into the net . . . who knows what might have happened?

He had the right goal-tending build (tall, long, and lanky) and developed the perfect mentality to be successful in that pivotal position, able to focus on a task to the exclusion of all else, unflinching in the face of danger, and just a little bit crazy. Could he have become a pro? Hard to say. Hockey, especially in Northern Ontario, is ultra-competitive. But those few missing years sure didn't help his development.

To this day I regret not contributing to that long-ago locker room conversation. It wouldn't have taken much to pull a pad on and challenge Scottie to whack at it with a stick. Goalie pads, even back in the late 1970s, were big and bulky. The chances of someone my brother's size hurting me through the leather and horsehair were miniscule. If that didn't convince him, I could have asked my dad to perform the same action. That would have been riskier. My dad played some pretty high-level hockey and would have still been in his physical prime at the time, meaning he could have swung a stick pretty hard. Even suffering a bruise or two would have been worth it if it proved to Scottie that hockey didn't hurt.

Instead, however, I sat in silence—something I'm ashamed to say I've done far too much of in my life*—and left him to suffer alone.

• • •

The only time I remember ever standing up for my brother came at another local sporting facility. This took place in the height of summer at the ball field. And it didn't go like you might expect. I ran away crying.

Okay, rolled. But you get the point.

In my defence, we were all children—I might have been 12 or 13, my brother 10 or 11.

Some friends and I had organized a game of pick-up softball

---

* This line, no doubt, has my friends and family laughing. Not shouting "Shut up!" at me is a daily trial for anyone in my social circle. Nonetheless, it is my belief that all too often, I remain quiet when I should be speaking. But that would involve causing a stir or making a scene—both things I try to avoid.

when Scottie showed up, glove in hand, and asked to join in. That was when the shit hit the fan. My "friends," guys I'd grown up with and palled around with almost daily for nearly a decade—some of who were blood relatives—huddled together, whispering secretively, and then announced, "He can't play."

"What?!" I remember my surprise and hurt. "Why not?"

"Too young," came the reply.

That, of course, was a load of garbage. Scottie might be my "little" brother, eighteen months separated us chronologically, but even as kids he towered over me and all my friends. Besides being blessed with a surfeit of height (passing the six-foot marker before his 13th birthday), he was a pretty talented athlete, as good as most of the guys I chummed around with. None of that appeared to matter, though.

Rather than argue I merely pointed to the outfield where another guy's brother, who was even younger, stood waiting for the game to resume and demanded, "What about him?"

"The game's full," they tried then. "There's not a spot on the field for him."

"Then he can have mine." I stormed off, announcing, "I quit . . . and you guys all suck!"

Unsurprisingly, the same little shits from the arena locker room were involved in this incident. It might have been almost a decade later but those particular kids, troublemakers of the worst sort, hadn't changed.**

In the end, my leaving worked and, after much grumbling, the self-appointed gatekeepers allowed my brother to join. I didn't find

---

** Eventually they all grew up and became decent, functioning members of society but I'll always remember the joy they garnered tormenting people younger and more naïve than themselves.

that out until hours later, though. My churning emotions drove me far from human company and I spent most of the afternoon alone. I like to pretend that my temper tantrum convinced my friends that given the choice between them and family I'd choose my brother over their company. Scottie was never excluded from our events again. Though, in retrospect, I suspect his on-field performance did more toward that feat than me.

• • •

As my SMA has progressed, our roles have reversed. He more often takes care of me. And has for years.

Being a burden on my brother is not something I relish. I've got to give him credit though, he's never once complained. If our roles were reversed, and he lived with "special needs" and I was expected to care for him, I'm not certain I could show such restraint. But that's family for you, complicated.

I think it's safe to say mine is fairly typical. Our dynamics may be different than most but we deal with them as best we can. So far, it's worked out. Scottie might not be my best friend, and I might be ready to throttle him on occasion, but it's pretty clear that I'm the luckiest sibling.

The Best Medicine

I laugh easy. Especially at myself. I don't particularly like being the butt of a joke or the centre of attention but I am willing, on occasion, to put myself out there and mock my own mistakes. And there are lots of those, let me assure you.

The flipside of humour—making fun of others—seldom works out well for me. Especially in print. Words written in black and white often come across as harsh and accusatory, not an ideal combination when attempting to be funny. It's taken me years but I learned to keep two points front and centre when writing: firstly, the long-standing comedy tenet "Never punch down" and, secondly, the much more modern axiom, "The failure mode of clever is asshole."

Both of these "rules" were driven home in the most humiliating way possible. It happened back when I was still an undergrad attending university. Luckily for my much-bruised ego, the lesson occurred at someone else's expense—not that he even noticed.

None of us studying "Introduction to Rhetoric" knew what we were in for when our regular professor left on maternity leave, but we certainly didn't expect the class to almost immediately turn into a disaster. Our replacement instructor marched into the room and announced that we'd "had things too easy" and ordered each of us to prepare a speech. The orations would start the next day. Neither topic nor tone mattered. This professor couldn't care less about the details. His sole goal was to put each of us on the spot and make us sweat.

While the rest of the class was still angrily grumbling over the surprise assignment, I volunteered to go first.

It's important to know that speechifying is not my thing. The formality and rigid structure don't appeal to my more conversational style. Nonetheless, when it came my turn to perform, I was ready and spent the entirety pretending to struggle, giving the impression that the entire speech was ad-libbed on the spot. The performance, entitled "The Dangers of Being Unprepared When Making a Public Presentation," went off the rails immediately . . . as intended.

The gag was simple: I lived through each danger as if it were happening to me in real time. My "difficulties" started with me looking nervous as I left the safety of the crowd, then sighing audibly once hidden behind the podium—tall enough for the able-bodied to stand at, it blocked me entirely—and it degenerated from there. Each failure, and the increasingly panicked lengths I went through trying to cover that more and more obvious incompetence from view, created the humour. I was, in short, the butt of my own joke. And it worked. Everyone laughed.

The exaggerated antics even amused the professor—especially

when, at the end of class, I dropped the typed, double-spaced, and professionally formatted script onto his desk to prove that I was, in fact, prepared.

At week's end, the last of my classmates strutted to the podium. The calibre of speeches had varied but we were all looking forward to this final performer. That guy, let's call him Mick, had been bragging for days about how smart and funny his upcoming speech would be. He stood there before us all stretching out the moment before proceeding to insult everyone else's effort in a truly painful attempt at humour. His constant smirk and cocksure attitude rubbed everyone the wrong way. No one laughed. In fact, most frowned at his demeaning opening and grew angrier from there. Not one single previous speech escaped mockery. Mick tried to follow in the footsteps of insult comics but lacked both their charm and wit. Worse, he thought he killed. Laughing at his own "jokes" with the sort of smug self-satisfaction guaranteed to turn off even the most receptive audience, he marched arrogantly back to his seat and gloated.

I topped the list when the marks came out while Mick sat at the absolute bottom. The professor, who seemed so hostile toward us that first day, even sought me out to personally congratulate my success. Making a point to say, "You were funny. Your friend . . . not so much."

While it's true that laughing at others' suffering has been a comedy staple for millennia, timing is everything, and Mick failed to recognize that fact. I tried to explain his failure to him—citing the longstanding aphorism: "Tragedy is when I slip on a banana peel. Comedy is when you slip on a banana peel,"—but Mick refused to listen.

Self-awareness is another much-ignored comedy staple. Few are more aware of that fact than legendary funny-man Mel Brooks.

He put his own unique spin on the tragedy/comedy difference with unique pithiness, saying, "Tragedy is when I cut my finger. Comedy is when you fall into an open sewer and die."

Far be it from me to disagree with a giant like Mr. Brooks but, in my experience, the exact opposite is true. People happily laugh at stories of my failure but often react less favourably to me telling tales of others' misadventures. The secret, for me at least, is to be in on the joke. By laughing at my own misfortunes, I signal that I'm okay with others doing the same. In essence I give them permission to find humour in my humiliation.

Comedy is a highly subjective art form, and growing up it didn't take me long to learn that not everyone shares my take on a given subject. My unconventional sense of humour has gotten me in trouble a time or two.* Put simply: I'd rather laugh at life's ridiculousness than fight against its unfairness.

I am not the sort to protest or march, and the day I donate money to a worthwhile cause will be the first. I do, however, tell pointlessly long-winded anecdotes, work tirelessly to lighten the mood whenever things get tense, and I've even been known to amuse myself for hours on end—laughing aloud for no apparent reason—just by letting my ridiculously vivid imagination range through a single insanely elaborate daydream.

That said, I am not an especially funny guy. Jokes sound forced when I tell them—mostly because I can never remember the punchline correctly—and physical humour, except for a bit of facial mugging, is beyond me and my crippled range of motion.

---

* Most notably the time I substituted "seniors" for "teens" in a piece I wrote about hooliganism and society's growing lack of respect. Turns out making pensioners play the fool offended quite a few of those same folk. Who knew old folk could be so thin-skinned or that they could pack so much vitriol into their hate mail?

Sure, I can make people laugh. Sarcasm and one-liners roll from my tongue with ease. Off-the-cuff humour is my real forte. Those unexpected witticisms that catch the listener just right are where I shine. I've even caused one friend to literally soil himself in a bout of uncontrolled amusement. But, for all that, setting out to be funny is not my thing. Neither are crowds. Nor being the centre of attention.

So, it seems weird that I once contemplated becoming a stand-up comedian.

The impulse, like many of my wilder fancies, proved fleeting.** And yet, unlike my dreams of playing professional hockey or working as an archaeologist deep in the dark Peruvian jungle, this fantasy ultimately resulted in something useful—a tight five-minute set.

• • •

Comedians live and die by routine. Their careers flourish or fail based on the ability to deliver a reliably funny act. Historically, a top-quality bit could keep a stand-up touring for years. Performing in a different city for a different crowd every night meant they could recycle material without fear of losing the audience. Old jokes grow tired and become stale—which is why the best stand-ups work to constantly reinvent themselves.

I remember reading how the late Canadian stand-up Mike MacDonald wowed his contemporaries while first breaking onto the scene by launching into a fresh set every night. The then-young

---

** Even my slipshod research skills quickly uncovered the difficulties faced by those making a living in comedy: fierce competition, constant travel, fickle crowds, and an ever-changing market are just the tip of the iceberg.

newcomer didn't know an act could be repeated. Luckily the man was talented enough to compose a new routine while travelling between gigs. That book's author credited Canada's constantly evolving crop of top-tier talent to our nation's vast geography. So many of our comedians succeed in the United States because of the hours needed to cross the vast landscape. That travel weeds out the undetermined early.

MacDonald, to his credit, broke a lot of ground in Canadian comedy, including being the first stand-up ever given a dedicated one-hour special on the CBC. His phenomenal success on the small screen allowed many others to follow his snowshoe tracks.

Of course, there are plenty of hilarious stand-ups operating outside of our borders. One of my favourites is Emo Phillips. The epitome of the "weird-guy" persona, Emo had his routine down to a science when I caught his first special. The one bit that resonated most was a simple joke: "They say laughter is the best medicine . . . unless you're diabetic . . . in which case Insulin is really the best medicine."

Inspired by their polished examples, I gathered up my courage and put pen to paper to try to create an act. Unfortunately, my career in stand-up never got much beyond the idea stage. The oh-so-clever tagline "The Sit-Down Stand-Up" didn't test well, not even among friends or family, and neither did most of my material.

Making excuses would be easy. I was ahead of my time; my stuff was too high-concept; I was out on comedy's cutting edge. But the truth is much simpler: I didn't have it—"it" being the magic spark needed to grab hold of the mic and own a room. There's a charisma needed to command an audience. You have to believe in yourself and every aspect of your persona. Even those comics that act neurotic on stage have a confidence I can never emulate.

Even worse, prolonged momentum has never been my strength.

Not in person and not on the page.* So, while a full fifteen-minute set may be beyond me, I did manage a much shorter stand-up routine. Without further ado, here is a selection of my never-before-seen act, Matthew Del Papa—On a Roll:

My cousin bought a used car the other day and won't shut up about it. Not the car, though that would be bad enough since I know jack about them and care even less. No she's obsessed with the "ordeal."

That's what she calls it . . . "The Ordeal." You can hear the capitals when she says it.

It might have been the most miserable experience of her life—according to her it combined a root canal with sitting next to a screaming baby on an eight-hour transatlantic flight—but it's not like someone held a gun to her head. She could have up and left that car lot anytime she wanted. There are only a hundred more car dealerships in the city. Each worse than the last.

The same isn't true when looking for a wheelchair. The options there are severely limited. And let's just say, if you think buying a used car is hard try shopping for a used wheelchair!

I was all of 12, not even dreaming about shaving yet, when introduced to the painfully pushy world of wheelchair sales. Needing to replace my then-current wheelchair put me in a weak bargaining position. But it was not knowing what to expect that made the purchase so painful. Every agonizing step along the retail road came as an unpleasant surprise.

And don't think being disabled spares wheelchair shoppers from the usual shenanigans. I faced them all—the bait and switch, the upsell, the exaggerated promises. Being little more than a kid

---

* There's a reason I've written more than a dozen "collections" and never, yet, finished a novel.

meant I bought into every oily-ingratiating word. For a moment, at least.

Young, naïve, and ignorant of salespeople's well-earned reputation meant I was primed to fall hard for the smooth pitches and polished charm. Smarmily desperate to please, pathologically cheerful, and always with one beady eye on closing the deal my introduction to the professional wheelchair salesman soured me forever.

Rolling into the showroom—they have wheelchair showrooms by-the-way and they're as demented as you imagine—it took me all of three seconds to recognize a universal truth: used wheelchair salesman are the worst human beings on Earth.

The salesman, straight out of central casting, leapt upon me before I'd even cleared the door. Everything about the guy screamed "salesman." In fact, you could tattoo "salesman" across his forehead in big neon letters and it would only add to his unctuous personality.

Am I being a bit hard on him? You decide. He slicked his hair back with three-quarters of a tube of stale Brill Cream, pasting his rapidly receding hairline in place with damp, glistening glue. This wasn't the 1950s, mind. When such "style" dominated. No, I went shopping for a wheelchair in the early 1980s. And this man was an anachronism.

Fashion-wise he embraced polyester with perverse loyalty. Pants, shirt, suit-jacket, even his tie—all were comprised of this space-age, stain-resistant fabric. Loud colours and clashing prints fought in eye-searing intensity.

Pumping my hand up and down, pretending not to notice my desperate attempts to reclaim the limb, he announced, "Welcome, welcome, welcome," in a rapid-fire staccato that left no room for me, the prospective customer, to get a word in.

Turns out there's no place like a wheelchair showroom to

experience the hard sell. Having an audience incapable of running away removes all subtlety from the pitch. He opened with "Looking for a new chair, are we?"

Continuing without ever pausing for breath, he said, "You've come to the right place. If you look over here, I'll show you our luxury model. You look like a discerning sort of customer . . . a man of substance."

That was patently untrue on many levels. My clothing consisted of a stained tee-shirt, jogging pants stretched almost beyond recognition, and a pair of Sears-special running shoes of no identifiable make. I looked like a typical pre-teen . . . except for the too-small wheelchair beneath me. And even that didn't exactly scream "Affluenza." Being battered, dirty, and in obvious need of replacement.

"This is the Deluxe package," he enthused before launching into a lovingly detailed chronicle. "It features nickel-plated grillwork and three coats of deep black paint—flecked with metallic particles to give it that lustrous shine." Caressing the seat he added, "Custom, hand-stitched upholstery. Made of only the finest Corinthian leather," the last phrase rolled off his tongue with the sort of breathless ecstasy normal reserved for bad adult films.

"What," I asked, "no heated seat?"

That butt-warming innovation had been introduced in high-end vehicles two decades earlier, however, the thought of including such a convenient feature on a wheelchair would take years to become reality. Foam padding marked the new "in" thing—though rumour had the R&D crew tantalizingly close to cracking "recline." That much-anticipated breakthrough would mean wheelchair users would soon experience the sort of laid-back comfort previously reserved for Lazy-Boy owners.

"Wheelchair Fancier magazine called it 'the Cadillac of

wheelchairs," he said, ignoring the smart-mouth reply and instead expounding, "No expense has been spared. In fact, some of the world's foremost engineers were consulted in its design, and the manufacturer even brought in Enzo Ferrari's grandson to–"

"How much are we talking?" I asked, interrupting the unending sales pitch. "Ball-park," I added on seeing his sudden frown.

It didn't take a cynic to recognize the suddenly suspicious once-over directed my way and realize I'd fallen short of some byzantine tax-bracket judgement.

"Let me just go speak to my manager," he said before excusing himself for the briefest of moments and slipping through a door I hadn't even noticed was there. Nothing happened for a few seconds, then the curtain on its window twitched—as if someone were peeking out—and he returned with a smile. "Perhaps something from our Economy line would be more your speed," he offered directing me away from the priciest model and toward the other side of the showroom.

We didn't get far before the ugliest monstrosity I'd ever seen caused me to stop. The thing—all army camouflage where it wasn't draped in patriotic flags—dripped testosterone.

"I see our resident bad boy caught your attention. Look at those tires, eh? They wouldn't be out of place on an off-road vehicle. This is what we call the 'All-Terrain' option."

"Really . . . how's it do on stairs?"

"It goes down like stink," he answered with practised smoothness.

Unwilling to let that slick comment slide, I asked, "And up?"

"Not so good," came the admission. He smiled a big crocodile grin and added, "But they're working on that." Some salesman sense told him this fish was slipping off the hook and he pivoted, "We offer a wide range of flexible payment options, including instalments. All major credit cards are accepted. And, of course, we stand behind our products, offering the best warranty in the business."

I hated myself for even bringing it up, but knowing the question needed to be voiced, I asked straight out, "Do you accept trade ins?"

"No," came his immediate reply. "But if you buy now, we'll include this complementary set of steak knives!"

A more observant person would have noted that not one person working required an assistive device. No salesmen leaned on canes, no secretaries sat in wheelchairs, everyone working appeared healthy and able-bodied. Which didn't bode well. How could they know the products they sold and serviced without first-hand experience?

A handicapped salesman would have known that neither function nor form were a wheelchair's main selling points. Features and options are nice but comfort is king. Anyone sitting for 14 hours (or more) a day recognizes that the smallest discomfort associated with their mobile throne grows to epic proportions over time. The glutinous maximus is a surprisingly sensitive area, even when amply padded like mine.

The direction of my thoughts must have been visible because he hastened to add, "There are a variety of different seat cushions available. All are attractive and comfortable but most of our customers like the beaded bamboo—very stylish. There is also a special medical option for people with sitting issues." Seeing I wasn't following, he stage-whispered, "Haemorrhoids," loud enough that passing cars could have heard.

Embarrassed and hoping to change the topic I blurted out the only phrase sure to distract him, "I'll take it."

The issue had never really been in doubt. If I wanted a wheelchair this store was the only option in town. But he smiled anyway.

• • •

Next time you pass a used car lot and laugh at the suckers browsing the barely roadworthy stock know that somewhere there's some poor little crippled kid being fleeced by a used wheelchair salesman ... probably of your hard-earned tax dollars.

The Storyteller

"I can make shit up all day long!" That particular boast emerged a lot louder than I intended and had every head in the room snapping around to stare. Appreciative smiles met my claim and it seemed, for one heady moment, as if the announcement might almost win me a standing ovation.

"You ought to put that on a tee-shirt," came one enthusiastic comment.

Another voice helpfully offered, "That should be your motto."

Of course, that opening bit of braggadocio was made to a receptive audience: writers. And writers, for those who don't know, are a supportive and easily impressed lot. Discovering that fact back in 2009 changed my life.

Joining the Sudbury Writers' Guild introduced me to some

weird and wonderfully creative people. I am proud to call almost all of them my friends.* It was the SWG who convinced me that admitting my passion for writing—to myself and others—didn't make me a pretentious twit.

Getting to know some of the local writers marked a turning point in my "career." For the better, though that probably goes without saying. This book wouldn't exist if I hadn't been so warmly embraced by the group. They welcomed me into their world and encouraged me to mine my life for material and convinced me that doing so wasn't cheating but rather "recognizing my truth." The first few tentative forays I took writing what I insist on calling "my crippled stories" were all exercises and prompts for and from the Guild. All my earliest successes can be laid at their collective feet, if not always directly.

It took me a while to find my place amongst my fellow writers**— there are lots of personalities in the writing community—but their kindness and encouragement pushed me to try new things. Like writing my stories. The good, the bad, and the ugly.

Sharing the first two is easy. Humour has always been a shield for me (the same goes for politeness and courtesy), but admitting to the last has proven much harder. I share a few ugly truths in this book for the very first time—"Keeping it real," as the kids might say—even though a lot of those darker stories will come as a shock to those who think they know me. We are all complex, disabled people no less than the rest of you.

---

* Don't expect me to name names, this isn't that kind of book. Just know that "beefs" occur in any artistic environment and my nemesis knows exactly what she did . . . if not how I intend to exact my revenge.

** Even now, with a dozen self-published books to my name, I still hesitate to apply that word to myself.

• • •

Simply put, stories fascinate me. They always have. Whether it's a classic fairy tale, the simple good versus evil of the Saturday morning cartoons I consumed alongside too many heaping bowls of sugary cereal, or the long, rambling, and often disjointed reminisces**** shared by various elderly relatives during elaborate family meals— the mere memory of whose deliciousness still brings a nostalgic tear to my eye and a barely remembered ecstasy to my tongue—is of no matter. I love them all.

Stories are the reason I adored comic books and still watch almost every animated Disney movie immediately upon home release. My favourite author is British fantasist Terry Pratchett, mostly for his sense of story. As he once wrote, "There's always a story. It's all stories, really. The sun coming up every day is a story. Everything's got a story in it. Change the story, change the world."

Unwilling to digest accepted wisdom on humanity, P Terry***** argued, convincingly, that "The anthropologists got it wrong when they named our species Homo sapiens ('wise man'). In any case, it's an arrogant and bigheaded thing to say, wisdom being one of our least evident features. In reality, we are Pan narrans, the storytelling chimpanzee."

"A natural storyteller." That's how people describe me. Kind people, anyway. The rest mutter something more like, "Matthew? He's so full of shit." Both are technically true. I learned long ago not

---

**** Being incapable of running away taught me to endure these meandering yarns and, having sat through them with grudging good humour, to appreciate—even enjoy—these enthusiastically-told tales.

***** That is Terry Pratchett's nickname among his most devoted fans, whom he referred to collectively as "A bunch of bloody loonies"—with the utmost affection, of course.

to let inconvenient things like facts get in the way of a good tale.

Regardless of how the words are meant, as compliment or criticism, I take pride in them. Story, so lauded by Terry Pratchett, is often dismissed by less imaginative minds. My first visit to Laurentian University brought this home.

"Storytime," the goateed undergrad announced, shaking his long-haired head in disbelief while storming past us on his way out of the classroom. No doubt off to save the world given the slogans written, graffiti-like, across the back of his faded jean jacket.

Not sure what to make of that opinion, I approached another student and asked, "Is it always like this?"

Seeing her confusion I gestured about the room—rows of desks, a blackboard at the front, relieved students making haste toward the exit—not any different than a high school as far as I could tell.

"No," she answered after getting my meaning. "I think the professor was playing to the crowd."

And what a crowd we were! The entirety of St. Charles' College graduating History class—all ninety-three of us. We lined the walls, squeezed between desks, and almost infringed on that most sacred space, the area surrounding the instructor like some sort of inviable forcefield.

My big wheelchair and I took up one entire corner, blocking an aisle and forcing everyone to go around the long way. Everyone did, most without audible grumbling. Normally that sort of conspicuous presence would make me self-conscious. There's a reason I tend to stay in the back, "out of the way," when attending public events. But that day, excitement blinded me.

Touring Laurentian University and sitting in on a real post-secondary lecture was supposed to be a reward. In reality, it proved overwhelming. I was one of five SCC students who had applied to study History at Laurentian the following fall but that visit convinced me to go with my safety school—also Laurentian but to read English Literature—instead.

Disappointment overwhelmed me on hearing the news. "Are his lectures normally different?"

"Much different. He seemed to be in story mode today. Probably because of you and your gang. It was a nice change to be honest."

• • •

I can take or leave people, but I love stories. Listening to someone relate an adventure or debacle is one of my favourite things. And like all of my favourite things, stories have led me both into and out of trouble. Luckily for me, everyone enjoys a good story. That fact has saved my fat behind on numerous occasions.

Spinning an entertaining yarn has gotten me out of a truly surprising number of predicaments. It's a talent I've relied on almost my entire life. At home, at school, and even in the workplace. The ability to tell a convincing story has let me slide through difficult projects and important presentations without fail. My motto has long been: If you can't dazzle them with brilliance, baffle them with bullshit. What does it matter if each devolves into me rambling? My obvious enthusiasm has let me get away with a criminal lack of focus.

As you'll no doubt discovered reading this book, I've continued that haphazard strategy. Not only do my thoughts meander, sometimes wandering entirely off-topic, but I often drift onto tangents completely unrelated to the issue at hand, sometimes never to return. Oh, points do get made, occasionally. Usually in the most roundabout way. Which leads me to wonder: Am

I actually skilled with words or are people merely being kind? Anecdotal evidence has convinced me of the former . . . three separate times. Twice I've helped others with schoolwork—both times when I was still a student myself—and both "good deeds" backfired. The story I wrote for a desperate group of friends earned them a failing grade. It got returned with the comment, "I know you three didn't write this. Which book did you copy it from?" in red ink across the front. And the other story, which I wrote for a project my brother was struggling with—only to discover he, in turn, sold it to another student for fifty bucks—went on to win a prize. I got no credit for the writing, nor did I see any of the money.

The third comment on my writing prowess came from the Sudbury Star's Short Story Contest. It happened more than a decade after the others and occurred when I was still debating the whole "writing profession" thing. The fact that my silly story about an octogenarian psychic winning the lottery was judged worthy of third prize—fifty dollars coincidentally—gave me the final, much-needed push.

• • •

I come from a long tradition of storytelling. Not only does my family have its share of storytellers but so does my hometown. Railroaders excel at spinning yarns. Trains hold a certain romanticism about them, especially for writers. At once familiar and yet exotic, forever coming and going, bringing news of the outside world to isolated communities, and thereby providing a small taste of the excitement residing beyond the horizon. Adventure, the railroad promised, lies just a train ride away.

There are stories all around us. Capreol has more than its share, which makes the fact that I often exaggerate—purely for effect—so ironic.

My supposedly "true" tales have raised a few eyebrows over the years. I cannot help myself. My imagination is just so damn fertile that, at times, I misremember a fact or event. No one, so far, has accused me of lying. At least not to my face. Which is good, considering I almost never lie in print. At least not intentionally.

Telling how I wish something happened instead of how things actually transpired isn't technically a lie, is it?

If it is, then enjoy this book of fiction. Otherwise, know that this is a work of creative non-fiction. I took some liberties but, on the whole, what you're reading is what happened. Give or take.

The Obligatory Sex Chapter

Every disabled person experiences the awkward sex conversation.

This isn't the birds and the bees as explained by red-faced parents or even the most awkward of all gym class lectures with your embarrassed teacher visibly regretting their life choices while ham-handedly demonstrating how to apply a condom to a banana. No, this is worse than watching a once-sane educator meltdown in front of a classroom full of giggling, barely pubescent teens.

I'm talking about random strangers—both men and women—who, minutes after making your acquaintance, ask, "How do you . . . ah . . . you know?" The intensely personal question is always accompanied by a raised eyebrow or comradely shoulder punch, complete with grinning bonhomie . . . like any gesture could make it less invasive.

What is it with able-bodied people? Why are you so fascinated by how us cripples "get off"?

I think it's the same motivation that makes drivers slow down when passing an especially gruesome car wreck—there's a visceral, almost primal thrill to witnessing something horrific. And most "normal" people cannot imagine anything more horrifying than having sex with a disabled person. Speaking as a disabled person, I can honestly say: you're not wrong.

So, let's just get this unpleasantness over with.

All sex is awkward and weird. Physical limitations just magnify that. Take me: thanks to a set of genetic quirks certain parts of my anatomy simply don't work* and others, though functional, are severely limited in what they can and cannot do. My hips, for instance, have fused from sitting more than 14 hours a day for 36-plus years; my back won't bend thanks to the stainless-steel rods lining the both sides of my entire spinal column; and my atrophy-weakened muscles mean I can only lay there in flagrante delicto and make encouraging faces. Not the most enticing partner—and that doesn't count the non-disability issues (balding, fat, and pale in the extreme). Truth be told, I even find myself somewhat repulsive—I more resemble the wormlike Star Wars villain, Jabba the Hutt, than any lion-maned romance novel cover hunk.

Not every disabled person is the same, of course. Individualism means that even if we suffer identical medical diagnosis, we each cope with it differently. Now is neither the time nor place to rehash the old nature vs nurture debate. Just know that there is as broad a spectrum of personality type in the disabled community as you find in everyday life. I've handicapped friends who get angry,

---

* NO, not that part ... get your mind out of the gutter! This is a classy publication not some crude bodice-ripper.

offended, or otherwise upset when talk inappropriately turns intimate. Others ignore invasive and prying queries with stoic indifference. By far the healthiest long-term approach is using humour to defuse the situation.

I know one man—let's call him Roddy—who, when asked about his sexual abilities, has an effective comeback for too-curious interrogators, "Let's go back to your place and find out!"

I cannot imagine ever using that line, not even on a stranger. Calling people out on their lack of couth, sexual or otherwise, just isn't how I roll—quiet brooding and silent judgement is more my speed. Appearing calm in the face of such obvious provocation has earned me a reputation for serenity. Friends and family marvel at my meditative calm, never realizing that I am like the swimming swan—all the furiousness is hidden beneath the surface.

The same stony-faced restraint is true for me with regards to human sexuality. I act indifferent when talk turns "naughty," but it is all a front. Like most disabled people, I'm as obsessed with sex as the rest of you horn-balls. Some of us just hide it better—not being able to stand means, in my case, that certain prominent male physical reactions remain hidden from view.*

Let me admit one thing up front: I am a prude. That isn't due to being wheelchair-bound, but it is important to know. I wince at public displays of affection and despise crude "locker room" talk—even when it's just with the boys.

Not to overanalyse my baser motivations, but the root cause

---

* I can remember being a typical randy teen and wheeling out of high school math unconcerned and unembarrassed while all the rest of the guys in my class avoided looking at the young tight-skirted sub, instead fiddling diligently with their pencils or notebooks, waiting for the errant blood to flow back into their brains.

of this behaviour is as obvious as the nose on my face.** Living life sitting down gives the physically disabled a unique outlook on things—I'm not talking philosophy here but rather the literal way we view the world: always looking up. All but the shortest of people tower over someone in a wheelchair. Try as we might, and believe me I try hard, it is impossible when looking up at someone not to notice what's in their noses. But nasal passage cleanliness, or the lack thereof, is not the worst daily distraction. Imagine having your eyes stuck at chest height. Everyone who's ever been a teenage boy knows how hard it is to look a woman in the eyes, especially when all your hormone-powered gaze wants to do is stare at their cleavage—it is eight-hundred times more difficult when staring straight ahead means you're constantly at breast level. Not looking is a full-time job. And then some women lean down to talk, meaning their blouses hang open, giving a clean view straight to the navel, talk about distracting. Is it any wonder that as a youth I become a gibbering idiot whenever conversing with a woman?

Having confessed that wheelchair life is rife with pendulous preoccupations, it should come as no surprise that my romantic interactions have been few and, almost universally, unsuccessful. It took me an embarrassingly long time to learn the hard truth: having an obviously crippling disease is the ultimate form of birth control.

In my admittedly limited experience, even women open-minded enough to look beyond glaring physical disabilities (and there are a few of those around, believe it or not) get turned off on hearing, "It's genetic." Forget cold showers, if you want to ruin the mood instantly just mention the prospect of passing on flawed DNA. No sane person wants a special needs kid. They involve a lifetime of work—trust me, I've watched my parents sacrifice

---

** Being of predominantly Italian descent means that nose is rather *prominent*.

themselves time and again on my behalf.

Not that there weren't a few benefits in my condition—for them and me. I was a perfect, ready-made excuse for avoiding awkward or unwanted social obligations. "We can't make it, sorry. Matthew..." they would say, trailing off to let the other half of the conversation fill in the blank. The few times they couldn't escape, familial obligations like weddings and funerals mostly, I'd catch them checking their watches well before midnight, muttering for all to hear, "We should be going. Matthew's getting tired." It didn't matter if I was rocking out to the music or putting the moves on a boozy bridesmaid, home we went.

To our collective relief, my wheelchair-bound status spared us the traditional parental sit-down discussions: there were no lectures regarding missed curfews, responsible drinking, or safe sex. There was simply no need. Opportunities for mischief were limited by my disability.

With very few exceptions my hometown had a distinct lack of wheelchair accessible buildings. My liver and libido were willing but circumstances conspired against patronizing bars, picking up willing partners, or practicing any promiscuity. Until university. And, even then, casual sex proved hard to come by for a shy teen like me... especially given my inability to get in or out of bed without substantial aid. It took a strong man to move me or several average women working in well-rehearsed concert, neither of which ever added to the "mood."

Exempted from high school gym class due to my disability, I was left to pick up the basics of human sexuality second-hand.* And

---

* This was well before the Internet, back when "dirty" magazines still came in plain brown wrappers and were kept out of reach behind store counters—it was easier to buy beer or bullets than a *Playboy* when I was young.

let me tell you, the schoolyard is not the place to learn anything. Thank goodness I met a few patient women while matriculating who kindly put me to rights on "the facts of life." Not that I became any kind of expert. Far from it. University just showed me how much I didn't know about sex.

I did learn one lesson well while at post-secondary school, though: that being in a wheelchair meant I was doomed to be forever a wingman.

Dating is tough enough for most people but for the disabled it's worse. Being in a wheelchair means dancing isn't my "thing." Combine that with the fact that bars—and I can count the number with ramps on one hand—are crowded and loud and my limited pick-up "moves," all conversation based, become useless. The few times I hit the club with my friends, I found myself relegated to being their prop, like a puppy. Not even the "less-attractive friend" went for me.

The most action I ever got at a bar was when one woman, more than a little drunk and feeling sorry for "the poor dear,"** leaned down to whisper something no-doubt inspirational in my ear and found her low-cut, thin-strapped, very sexy top unfit at holding back her impressive bosom, accidentally flashing the entire place. I don't know who was more humiliated by the incident, her or me. Somehow, I doubt her friends took to calling her "boob-face" like mine did me.

Needless to say, I gave up on the bar scene. In fact, I abandoned dating entirely not long after. A lifetime of near-constant failure convinced me that finding a healthy physical relationship was just not in the cards.

** Those were her exact words, recorded here in all their emasculating glory. They weren't even addressed to me.

Many of society's so-called "rites of passage" have proven painful for me*—going back to my very first humiliating dating experience. I still remember it vividly: the stress of being a 14-year-old bundle of acne-wracked awkwardness and being pressured to "make a move." At the time I was terrified of the prospect of even talking to a girl let alone daring to ask one on a date. Having other things on my mind** meant I was the only boy in my Grade Eight class not to have landed a girlfriend, even just a temporary one.

My big chance came while touring prospective high schools. My friends tried to set me up, sight unseen, with a nineteen-year-old high-school senior. It made perfect sense to them, the young woman and I had an obvious connection: we were both in wheelchairs.

It hit me then that everyone, including the people I'd grown up with, would always think of my disability first. That played havoc with my psyche for a long time. I never trusted anyone expressing any kind of romantic interest, always wondering: What's wrong with this person that they'd be willing to go out with someone like me? A paraphrase of Groucho Marx's famous line danced through my head every time someone asked me out: I don't want any part of a woman that would have me as a date.

It wasn't until years later, on another failed field trip, that I got my "groove" back.

The teacher in charge of making the arrangements had forgotten to check that the venue was wheelchair accessible and so I, arriving

---

* Missing out on road trips, sleepovers, and camping adventures, turning sixteen and being unable to drive, reaching my age of majority and not going to the local "downstairs" bar—all hurt. I'll save the specific tales of woe and regret for another day.

** I had just discovered that, contrary to what Jerry Lewis told me during one of his famed MDA Telethons, I wasn't going to drop dead on my sixteenth birthday like some pubescent-version of the sci-fi classic *Logan's Run*.

to find a flight of stairs barred me entry, stayed on the bus. I didn't mind missing out on the museum's afternoon tour. In truth, the teacher's fawning apologies, especially the teary-eyed, "I forgot you were in a wheelchair!" struck me as strangely liberating.

Even now, in the age of computer dating, I had resigned myself to living a life of celibate sadness when I heard that there was supposed to be a disabled-only orgy taking place in Toronto. The news covered the story with such horrified shock that local authorities, ultimately, put a stop to it. Turns out "civic-minded" busy-bodies and religious groups combined to oppose the idea. Citing "moral grounds" they argued that the "poor unfortunates" were "being corrupted and taken advantage of." City politicians, obviously not knowing any actual disabled people, bought into that ableist garbage and my carnal dreams died unfulfilled. The drive from Northern Ontario to Toronto might be long and uncomfortable but I'd have gladly faced all the travel difficulties in the world (and more!) for a chance at a little of that corruption.

I mentioned that story in passing to a writer friend of mine and she used it as an opening to ask for help with her latest project—a series of lewd horror stories featuring disabled protagonists having gratuitous amounts of graphic sex before dying gruesomely ironic deaths. What she wanted was a blanket pass, like I speak on behalf of all disabled people or something. Instead of agreeing to read her work-in-progress and providing feedback on the kink, I borrowed some of my friend Roddy's courage and told her, "If you hire the hookers, I'll happily 'field test' the action." Awkward laughter emerged from her end of the phone and, sadly, I never heard another word about the endeavour.

Human sexuality isn't something people think applies to the handicapped. Most able-bodied prefer to think of us as desexualized neuters or, worse, too "pure" to think about such carnal drives.

It's like having a disability automatically puts you in the friend category. Plenty of campaigns have fought the stigma—the one I liked best featured a climaxing silhouette astride the familiar person-in-wheelchair parking logo, all above the tagline: Sex in a wheelchair; it's electric! Needless to say, the promotion never really sparked with the general public.

All I have to say is, "Thank God for the pornographers." That most-broadminded industry, at least, doesn't judge the admirers of their "art."

Did you know there are entire sub-genres of porn featuring the physically disabled? This isn't "Inspiration Porn," a term coined by Stella Young, that encapsulates the fetishization of disabled people's "achievements" by desperate media—always as symbols of hope and inspiration. No, I'm talking real porn—sweat-soaked bodies slapping together on cheap sets to cheaper production standards. Thankfully, because even porn-makers have to draw the line somewhere, these are usually able-bodied actors mimicking disability. Hollywood might spout inclusive claptrap, no doubt prompted by guilty consciences and forward-thinking marketing firms, but mainstream adult entertainers know better than to feature real cripples.*

I've watched a broad selection of contemporary adult fare— for research purposes only, I assure you—and blindness seems the most commonly featured disability. You don't need to sit through freshman Psychology to get the power dynamics at play or the appeal to a certain desperate personality type. I'll leave it to professionals to get into the deep-rooted anxieties involved in

---

* Though, to be fair, there is a very small niche market for disabled performers—talk about "handi-capable"—Google "gimp porn" or don't . . . you can't unsee those images, believe me.

disability kink or the unconscious longings driving these people to take advantage of "lesser" individuals—even if only in fantasies.

For those of you unwilling to sit through hundreds of hours of "authentic" disabled porn let me sum up the difference between such mainstream cinematic classics as Debbie Does Dallas, The Devil in Miss Jones, or Pirates 2: Stagnetti's Revenge and the more specialized niche market featuring those labelled handicapped: there is none. All these so-called "adult movies" lie.

In the end, it's just sex. Dress it up however you want, add in first-rate production values, A-list talent in front of or behind the camera, and even top-tier storytelling—and there's nothing magic or special on screen. Intercourse with the disabled is merely sex stripped of the mystique. You know what you're getting, and it is neither provocative nor erotic.

Just remember, when the lights go out, we're all the same . . . some of us merely need an assistive device or two to get our kicks.

"Lame" Claims to Fame

Push the button again. That'll help. Dumbass!

Those unkind thoughts, and worse, run through my head whenever I'm forced to share an elevator with idiots—which, given society's growing anti-intellectual attitude and the baffling trend to devalue education, is always.

Tackling stairs is beyond me thanks to my wheelchair. That means I've spent a lot of time riding aboard (and waiting for) what the Brit's perversely insist on calling "lifts." That has made me something of an expert on the vertical conveyance, including the development, weight limits, and recommended safety procedures. Upon boarding any elevator, I immediately consult the service ticket, then confirm that the combined weight of my wheelchair and me do no exceed the manufacturer's listed capacity, and finally I check the emergency phone—not that it's functional, one affronted lecture in a lifetime was enough thank you, but that it exists undamaged.

And yet, even with paranoid levels of precaution, entering the enclosed confines of an elevator car never fails to put me on edge. It's not claustrophobia or agoraphobia or even fear of getting stuck inside that elevator for a protracted period of time, but rather terror of having to interact with able-bodied passengers.

Maybe I'm overstepping but someone needs to re-establish the rules of elevator etiquette and call out the woeful behaviour all-too-commonly found while aboard that popular step-saving mode of transport. Luckily for everyone I have the time and the anger to tackle that task.

Being in a wheelchair means I have a natural enemy: stairs. Whether I need go up or down doesn't matter. Nothing ruins my day like finding myself faced with a set of insurmountable stairs. So, naturally, I spend a lot of time in elevators. Big ones, little ones, clean ones, and dirty ones. I've ridden in elevators so old they should be in a museum and others so new they could have fit in on the Starship Enterprise (sadly none have ever been voice activated, but fingers crossed!). Hell, I've even rolled onto an elevator just after a particularly amorous couple "got off"—seriously people that is so not sanitary. And the one thing all these elevators have had in common is my inherent dislike.

Elevators are ridiculously safe. They have been since a man named Elisha Otis perfected his "safety elevator" way back in 1852. But that doesn't mean things can't go wrong. I've been stuck in malfunctioning elevators more times than I care to think about. And yet, for all my many ordeals, I count myself lucky. I've never had to spend more than a couple hours in an elevator at any one time. Other people have faced whole days. Some have even been trapped with—shudder—children. Perhaps worst of all are those poor saps forced to deliver a baby while stuck in an elevator (fear of that messy fate is why I refuse to ride with pregnant women).

The thing about elevators no one ever tells you is how to behave while on one. Proper elevator etiquette has become just another of those things you're supposed to "pick up."

Well, let me tell you something: a lot of people aren't too sharp. There are millions out there who never learned the basic social niceties needed to share a confined environment with random stranger. So, I'm offering a little refresher. Three vital rules, please take a moment to memorize them:

1. Stare at the little numbers above the door
2. Remain quiet
3. Do not pass gas

Seems simple enough, I know. But you'd be surprised how many elevator boarders fail to follow the trifecta of politeness. Trust me, I've ridden with all sorts of annoying people at one point or another. You know the types: the people who sing along with the elevator music (and always get the lyrics wrong), the ones who can't stand still, the impatient type always poking at the buttons, the natural-born conversationalists who want to "get to know you" between floors, and, of course, the sweaty, deodorant-averse who always seem to stand way too close.

It's not just the people that annoy either. I've had elevator doors close on me. Been forced to exit even though the floors weren't properly aligned (one time navigating a drop of nearly a foot), and, on more than one occasion, ridden with a large and grossly overflowing garbage can shoved forgotten in the elevator's corner (it kept getting riper throughout the day, too). I've had unidentifiable "stuff" drip from the ceiling onto me and discovered all sorts of "other stuff" smeared on the buttons.*

I could easily spend pages listing the disgusting, humiliating, and/or horrifying things that I have experienced while riding on elevators—waiting for a corpse to vacate the car only to discover the lingering odour of death sour me on church funerals, learning that laziness trumps shame when fellow students crowded in ahead of me, none meeting my eyes when I announced "Never mind, I'll take the stairs," and reading decades worth of obscene graffiti written (between wads of petrified chewing gum) on dusty cinder-block walls, their crude witticisms recorded for all posterity or at least the eyes of anyone aboard that antique "gated" elevator. Those are just the merest taste, and they don't even begin to touch on the frustration of malfunctions. "Out of Order" signs might as well say "Go Home" to those of us in wheelchairs.

Stairs may be my mortal enemy but at least they never betray me. Elevators can . . . and have. Still, until science perfects something better,** I'm stuck with the elevator.

You know who else sticks with the elevator? Celebrities. I'm not sure if they fear being photographed using the stairway like some sweat-soaked commoner, hate the idea of cardiovascular exercise conducted outside of their high-priced personal trainer's supervision, or just like the power of having their private security wave off regular citizens but, whatever their reasoning, I've ridden with a few celebrities in my time.

And yes, they too insist on repeatedly pressing the button.

---

* I learned better than to look too closely at these substances for fear I might actually identify them—ignorance being eminently preferable to knowing what "fluid" wouldn't wipe off of my finger.

** Where the hell's my jetpack?!

I've never been much impressed by fame. Following the gossip rags or tuning into TMZ has never been my thing, but I don't live in a bubble either. Recognizing people and giving them a nod of acknowledgement isn't the same as fawning over them at the grocery store or interrupting them at dinner to beg for an autograph. Weirdly, my most memorable run-ins with society's rich and famous were the unpleasant ones. They say never meet your heroes and I can testify to the disappointing truth to that warning.

Twice while attending Blue Jays games in Toronto, I met prominent baseball figures. Both encounters took place at old Exhibition Stadium. Known and loathed by locals as "the mistake by the lake," that ball field served as the team's home from their founding in 1978 to their move to the ground-breaking SkyDome in 1989. The first recognizable sports celebrity I rode an elevator with was the organization's "star" catcher Ernie Witt, and that day poor Ernie was in a foul mood. Not only had the Jays lost the game but he stepped off the field to discover his kids had been robbed while in the stands. Justifiably angry at hearing the news, Mr. Witt didn't even bother to change out of his jersey (he still wore spiked running shoes and had burnt cork under his eyes), he just grabbed the first elevator and rode down to, as he put it, "have a talk with" security. It was not an ideal time to meet a young fan, but he tried to be kind. I may or may not have offered my battered second-hand baseball glove for his sons, having no idea at the time that he had the money for much better or that he probably had a trunkful gifted to him by the manufacturer's rep. The incident took place long ago and reality blurs with time.

The second encounter involved former ballplayer turned Milwaukee Brewers broadcaster Bob Uecker. My uncle had to point the loudly dressed "celebrity" out to me, despite it just being the three of us in the elevator at the time. The radio play-by-play man—nicknamed "Mr. Baseball" by Johnny Carson—made a point of being nice to the know-nothing kid in the wheelchair. At the time, he was working as colour commentator for network television (ABC), wearing his iconic garish plaid sports coat, and breaking into broader fame thanks to his just-starting five-season run as the harried father on the ABC hit sitcom Mr. Belvedere. And that doesn't touch on Bob's scene-stealing work in the Major League films. (There were three in the series, each a paler imitation of the one before.) Many of his lines have gone on to film, and baseball, immortality. "Juuuuust a bit outside!" being one. Bob Uecker's career isn't what it once was but I'd sure like to meet him again, now that I know who he is.

Not all sports celebrity encounters went so pleasantly, like the time I met Eddie Shack in Toronto. The Royal York elevator wasn't exactly crowded with just me, my father, and my grandfather aboard—though my electric wheelchair did take up a lot of space—but, when it stopped, we all squeezed tight to make room for the waiting men to board. Imagine our surprise when some of the NHL's most recognizable "elder statesmen" joined us. Once again, I was at a loss. Most of these guys were retired before my birth, some a decade or more before. Putting names to faces proved beyond me. But my grandfather knew them all and, being an affable sort, attempted to engage them. Unbeknownst to us, the group had just emerged from a turbulent meeting with the National Hockey League Player Association (NHLPA, essentially the union for all current and former NHL players), where they learned some not good news regarding their pensions.

So, not in the mood to talk.

My grandfather's openness must not have sat well with Sudbury's own Shack because he just, sort of, glared at the introductory, "I'm Silvio . . . from Northern Ontario." Then, after clearly thinking about not replying to the friendly overture for a long insulting moment, said, "Oh, you can always tell the people from Northern Ontario" in a superior and dismissive tone.

Never have I ever seen my grandfather at a loss for words or unable to summon enthusiasm when conversing with anyone—be it stranger or child—but he grew quiet after that. When the elevator reached the lobby, he didn't offer the group a goodbye or wish them a good day. He just waited for them to leave. I don't know who said it first, my dad or me, but we shared the same sentiment, voiced under our breath: "What an asshole."

Mr. Shack was, of course, right. You can always tell the people from Northern Ontario. We're invariably polite, which is why none of us called him out for his rudeness. Instead of making a scene we offered excuses for his behaviour. "Probably trying to be funny," ended up our best explanation for the discourteous comment. Needless to say, that's one elevator ride I could have done without.

The good thing, for me, about meeting people on an elevator is that they can't get away. That gives me time to say "Hi" and start up a conversation. The bad thing is I'm usually in a hurry, having a scheduled meeting or appointment to get to, and so can't sit around chatting for long. That was the case when I almost ran over Weird Al Yankovic while emerging from the elevator one winter afternoon at Laurentian University. I smiled on seeing the musician, recognizing him instantly in his signature Hawaiian shirt, and shouted "Al!" in a volume more suitable to a stadium concert than the halls of an institution of higher learning. He must have been used to such overreactions because he didn't freak at the inappropriately enthusiastic greeting. No, Weird Al just nodded casually—his long, curly hair making even that gesture look amusing—and got out of the way of my wheelchair with the sort of rock star panache only a lifetime of dodgy groupies can give.

Looking back, I wish I'd blown the class off and stopped to talk. Instead, I left him to board the elevator in my wake—no doubt off to visit CKLU, the campus radio station, to record some promos and sign some swag—and rushed about my way.

Weird Al's music has always been a favourite of mine, going back childhood—the first, and only, cassette tapes I've ever played to destruction were both by him, Weird Al Yankovic in 3-D (1984) and Dare to Be Stupid (1985)—and merely meeting him proved a thrill. Sharing a few words would have made my year. As it was, I practically walked on air the rest of the day and told everyone about the all-too-brief encounter, leaving out the part where I just missed squashing the musical genius.

If almost turning my musical hero into roadkill wasn't bad enough, there was always the time I boarded another elevator, turned around, and found a wall of heavily-armed Klingons clambering in after me. These weren't real Klingons, of course. Merely convention guests cosplaying as the iconic Star Trek species. Nor were their weapons meant as any sort of threat. Most were foam rubber. Those made of steel had been blunted as per World-Con policy. For all that, the costumes looked genuine. Worse, they smelled like the real thing too. Sweat-soaked armour, rank furs, and genuine, poorly tanned leather gave the elevator an aroma that none of us commented on but could practically taste.

At the time, 2003, I was an avid Trekker. There wasn't an episode of Star Trek, or its various spin offs, that I didn't diligently watch and then watch again in reruns. Like many fans of the 1989 series reboot, I found myself drawn to the redesigned Klingons (needing to be talked out of spending two hundred dollars on a replica dagger). The race, once little more than some bad forehead prosthesis on Shakespearian actors, now looked amazing. Makeup effects had advanced substantially in twenty years and the one-time bad guys finally appeared intimidating.

This new portrayal attracted a lot of fan appreciation. During the original Star Trek series (abbreviated TOS), the Klingons were rather generic villains—essentially a stand-in for the Soviet Union during the show's Cold War-era run. Star Trek: The Next Generation (TNG) changed all that. Filmed after Mikhail Gorbachev introduced the world to a concept called "glasnost," TNG pivoted in an unexpected way. Rather than continue portraying the Klingons as invariably hostile and insanely aggressive, the rebooted Trek—set a generation later as per the title—imagined the entire race as tentative allies of the program's heroes. The series' creator, Gene Roddenberry, made this shocking decision for a lazy reason: he grew tired of reading scripts with the good-guy United Federation of Planets fighting the bad-guy Klingon Empire. TNG even included a Klingon, Lieutenant Worf, as part of the new Enterprise's (NCC-1701-D) soon-to-be iconic bridge crew.

Still, it proved the longest and worst smelling elevator ride of my life. It didn't help that after the looming warriors left and I followed them out of the car, I almost knocked Vampirella on her picture-perfect behind.

Again, not the real Vampirella—who's a comic book creation that, thanks to some incredibly suggestive pin-up type cover art, is pretty much every teenage nerd's fantasy female. This was a very real, very beautiful young woman. Like many of the highly attractive characters paid to pose for pictures around the convention floor, she was a professional model. And right then she was wearing the heck out of a costume consisting of two ridiculously thin strips of blood-red cloth positioned strategically—they tapered from each shoulder, barely covering her nipples, before meeting at the groin in a bare nod to decency.*

To this day I wish I'd spent time in the elevator with her—I bet she didn't reek of stale Axe Body Spray, industrial strength theatrical prosthesis glue, and would-be Klingon flop-sweat.

Now I reconnoiter carefully before entering any elevator platform. Planning ahead, with plenty of time allowed for various unexpected delays, means I can be choosier about who I share a confined space with. Better to pass on an uncomfortable ride rather than allow myself to be hoisted alongside another clan of Trekkie cosplayers.

And if no one wants to ride with a man in a wheelchair . . . well, that's their problem.

* Needless to say, she proved highly popular with a certain segment of con-goers . . . the male contingent.

Not My Finest Moment, Part Two

"It's a good thing I'm good natured." My dad trots out that deadpan phrase often. Usually when my mom or I are ready to strangle him. I'm not sure if he's being ironic, sarcastic, or facetious. Regardless of his intentions, the ridiculous inaccuracy of the statement only adds to our frustration . . . as is his goal.

My dad may be many things but "good natured" is not one of them. He is, in fact, an inveterate tease. There is little in life that thrills him as much as getting a reaction out of people. And it doesn't much matter what that reaction is. A laugh, a scream, or a groan—it's all the same to him. There hasn't been a single day of my life where he didn't poke, prod, joke, josh, taunt, tickle, and otherwise torment me until I could no longer take it. Annoying me is both his goal and his reward. This is a grown man who, all too often, acts like a mischievous toddler—complete with shit-eating grin and a twinkle in his eye.

Sure, small doses of this juvenile behaviour can come across as charming. But as I age I'm finding it harder and harder not to snap at his antics.

It's not just me; everyone's fuse grows shorter with age. Perhaps our well of patience dries up or, more likely, we stop worrying about what others think and just speak our minds more freely. One of my great-aunts, whose attitude became more forthright with every passing year until her frankness grew shocking, once said, "I'm too old to bother with being polite and too old to care if someone takes offence."

While I'm not at that point in my life—courtesy still matters to me, a great deal—the once inexhaustible depth of almost saint-like patience is no more. My dad is finding it increasingly easy to get under my skin. Politics is my weak point and so has become one of his favourite targets. He starts with his smart-assery early, usually at six a.m., twisting the news of the day to get my proverbial goat. Needless to say, I do not react well to teasing at that time of day. Who would? Certainly, none of my relatives. We may excel at dishing it out—and yes, I can be as much of a pain as my father—but fare much more poorly at taking it.

My family is known for several prominent characteristics, both good and bad—friendliness, athleticism, are some of the good, while the bad ledger lists diabetes and heart disease. But it is our stubbornness and our temper that often get the better of us. I know I've lost mine a time or twenty.

Only once, however, did I ever scare myself. I became enraged, beyond control even. It was one of the few occasions I've been grateful for my disability. Had I been physically able there is a high probability I might have hurt someone. Admittedly, it would most likely have been myself—punching a wall or kicking a table would have vented most of the debilitating anger. Things being what they were, and me denied that much-needed outlet, I spent a truly disturbing amount of time screaming, swearing, and crying.

What prompted this uncharacteristic outburst? Underwear. Well, that and Tom Cruise.

Relax, it was nothing sexual.

Cruise had a new movie in theatres, a military sci-fi/time travel blockbuster called Edge of Tomorrow. Its trailer looked promising, and the reviews were positively glowing. I'd mentioned my interest and my folks decided that the next "nice" day we'd go.

I wasn't feeling quite myself that morning—minor stomach issues—but, rather than say anything, I decided to remain quiet. The drive from Capreol to New Sudbury did nothing to help. No matter how slow your speed, the city's lousy roads provide a rough ride. Our old full-size accessible van amplified each bump, rattling my spine and jostling the already questionable gastro-intestinal contents. Regretting lunch, three-day old chilli eaten hastily just before leaving home, I arrived at the theatre with a sore back, a rebelling stomach, and a burgeoning headache. That was when my dad, who had lost the coin toss to accompany me into the film, saw the poster outside the door and announced, "If I knew Tom Cruise was in this I'd have stayed home."

We took our seats and he spent the entire two-plus hours shaking his head and otherwise looking miserable. One half-hour stretch saw him sitting with his eyes covered. All through the drive home he complained about the movie—forty-eight long minutes. It only stopped when I got inside the house and he took the dog for a walk. Which is when my bladder decided it had had enough. The bouncing ride to and from the city combined with the theatre's overactive air conditioner, and what might have been an incipient infection, to force me onto the toilet.

Requiring assistance to relieve myself is one of life's more humiliating moments. I've spent decades training to resist the urge. Normally 14 hours between bathroom breaks is no problem for me. But that day, circumstances—the weather, the road conditions, and my own body—conspired against me and I asked for help. My parents are that help. They are always around and willing. Most times my dad does the duty but since he was out it fell to my mom. And she'd be the first to admit she hasn't much patience, especially when tired. After the day we'd already had, she seemed exhausted. Her short-tempered reaction didn't thrill me, but we managed the intricate dance needed to get me out of my chair and onto the porcelain throne.

Then, together, we moved on to the next step—lifting me onto the bed to get me redressed before dumping me back in the wheelchair. Only, for some unknown reason, she decided to change the routine. And nobody messes with my routines! Deciding, unilaterally, that I didn't need underwear wasn't her choice to make. I tried to explain that logically. When that failed to convince, I grew angry. Which is when she did the cruelest thing possible: she laughed.

I get it. Lots of men go commando. What's the big deal?

Well, for one, those free-swingers made that decision on their own. They weren't forced into it. I, meanwhile, was laying on my bed as helpless as a newborn baby. Though capable of making my own informed choices, I found my opinion being ignored. Worse, by dismissing my words and laughing at me, a much-denied though long-suspected truth overwhelmed me: nothing I do, say, or think ever matters.

And so, I blew my fuse.

To say this was not my finest moment would be a colossal

understatement. Tears of rage and frustration overwhelmed me. I spat the vilest curses imaginable and hurled the most foul-mouthed insults with the speed of a coked-up auctioneer. Barely pausing between one hurtful, hateful word and the next, I tore myself apart in tearing my imagined tormentor—my mom—down. There didn't seem to be any end to the anger inside me, a lifetime of bottled-up frustrations came boiling out, and I threw it all at my biggest, most loyal supporters: my parents.

They genuinely feared for my sanity. And, to be honest, so did I. It took me an embarrassingly long time to get my faculties back under control. But, after demanding to be left alone (only with much more swearing), my normally sunny disposition returned ... if forever marred.

We never discussed the incident. Talking things out is not something I'm comfortable doing. Instead, everyone just pretended it didn't happen. The fact that I've managed to maintain my composure (more or less) since then helped to put the outburst behind us and move on.

To be honest, just knowing I am capable of that sort of raw emotion changed me. Prior to that moment I thought rather highly of myself. Sure, I lived with a disability but I would have argued that my condition didn't impact me ... other than physically. Turns out I was wrong.

The sad truth is none of us know what will push us to the breaking point, at least not until something does it. Chronic illnesses, like SMA, are insidious. Gnawing away at our psyches with invisible teeth. Too often the obvious physical drawbacks of disease distract us from the subtler affects. Mental health gets pushed to the back burner by the more pressing day-to-day concerns. Or at least they did in my case. And a person can only ignore life's frustrations for so long before something gives way. Explosively.

Still, considering this was only the second lingering moment of regret out of almost five-decades of living, that's nothing to complain about.

Re-evaluating my self-image has not been a fun process. It is, however, making me a better person. Moving forward, I will continue trying to be the man I once imagined myself.

No doubt there is a third none-too-fine a moment lurking in my future. Some unseen trigger waiting to set me off. But so long as these incidents remain the exception rather than the rule, I will remain able to look myself in the mirror. Should that ever change, and the bad begins to outnumber the good, then it will become time for a change.

I may need to take a page out of my dad's book and become more "good natured."

Aim High/Straight Shooter

There's no feeling like squeezing a trigger. It's like jamming a hypodermic full of adrenaline straight into your heart—the call of the Old West rattles your over-civilized bones and the virile spirit of Teddy Roosevelt's Roughriders sings through your veins. Critics say guns offer a false sense of security, but those people have clearly never fired off a few dozen rounds. Shooting a gun is a thrill unmatched.

From the smell of burning propellent to the ear-ringing BOOM! of an exploding shell, the comforting weight of even the smallest firearm is addictively reassuring. I love the power conveyed by simply wrapping my fingers around a pistol grip; chequered walnut or grooved steel, it doesn't matter. Heading to the range, or more often (given my rural upbringing) into the bush, meant visiting my happy place.

Let me pre-empt all the anti-gun naysayers and admit that I'm compensating for certain masculine shortcomings. So what? Knowing there was a deadly force held in the palm of my hand conveyed a God-like boost to my fragile ego. Let me have my moment of machismo.* And that's with nothing more than a .22 calibre target pistol clenched, two-handed, between my sweat-soaked fingers.

Few sports are as accommodating to the disabled as shooting. Most ranges are one-level and easily wheelchair accessible. Firing a gun doesn't require much in terms of physical fitness, strength, or dexterity. As far as hobbies go, there are few cheaper or more rewarding. Plus, there's the potential "fringe" benefits, like being able to hit where you aim which could, theoretically, save your life—provided you're quick with the gun case and trigger locks and can load with super-human proficiency.

"The only way to stop a bad guy with a gun is with a good guy with a gun." Or so pro-gun activists would have us believe.** I spent more afternoons than I care to count imagining myself as that "good guy" and the line of empty pop bottles my iron sights centred on were "bad guys" in need of stopping.

Shooting is an honoured tradition in my family. Back in the day, "target practice" meant tromping off north of town and spending half a day with my brother, my dad, my grandfather, and our loyal dog, Copper, taking turns plinking at some homemade bullseyes.

---

* If it makes you feel any better, know that my gun-toting days are long behind me. Our federal government's ever-changing position on gun control proved too much trouble for even a certified "gun-nut" like yours truly.

** Conveniently ignoring the much-more-reasonable option of NOT allowing the bad guys a gun in the first place.

In between, we ate cold beans, drank warm pops, and choked down half-raw/half-burnt hotdogs. Good times and great memories . . . even that time the recoil punched me square in the nose.

In Northern Ontario, hunting is more than a sport. It is a rite of passage, a mark of manliness, and one of the few pastimes that bring generations together. More than one house in Capreol still supplies their larder with wild game or brings in some much-needed income through ancillary occupations (outfitting, guiding, taxidermy work, etc.).

According to only slightly exaggerated family stories, my grandparent's generation lived through the Great Depression and faced more than a few times when the only meat they ate came from skilled shooting (fishing and trapping played important roles, too). Rabbits and partridge formed a big part of their diet during those tough years. Me? Living generations removed from the "dirty thirties" leaves me spoiled in the extreme. I only eat the prime-est of "Grade AAA" meat now, preferably free-range and grass-fed cuts, with no artificial hormones or GMOs.

Soft though I may be, I know that guns are not toys, even if some modern Canadians view them that way. Regardless of your position on gun rights versus gun control, most people in this country agree they should be highly restricted. That fact has elected governments and divided our nation along rural versus urban lines. Successive federal governments have targeted our nation's gun laws, figuring to score easy political points on this hot-button issue. In reality, they've hit legal gun owners with increasingly minute rules and penny-ante fines. One of Canada's more humiliating "Billion-Dollar Boondoggles"—a term now applied with frightening frequency to governmental incompetence—was the poorly thought out and much maligned long-gun registry. That bit of federal overreach helped bring one party down and elevated several others to unprecedented heights. Speaking as a gun-owner, I know how I felt during those uncertain days: like a criminal.

Which explains the siren-like call of the Crean Hill Gun Show.

Every spring for almost a decade, me and some outdoorsy friends/family made the drive to Copper Cliff, anxious to attend that town's annual firearms display. Dozens of tables and thousands of weapons made the arena floor Shangri-la for gun enthusiasts like us. Familiar faces awaited, including the mandatory police presence at the front entrance.* In all those years, I never bought a gun, wasn't even tempted, but that didn't mean I left empty-handed. Every visit, regular as clockwork, I purchased at least one knife. Most years I splurged and bought two.

During my third year of attendance, however, I took "the test."

In Canada, at least in the twenty-first century, you need a license to own firearms. Abbreviated PAL, the Possession and Acquisition License** requires you to pass the Canadian Firearms Safety Course. Back then, the people at gun shows made everything easy by offering both the course and test to anyone attending their event for free.

My decision wasn't spur of the moment. No, I planned ahead. Memorizing the CFSC (aka Long-Gun) manual in the week prior. After scoring a perfect one hundred percent on that test, the instructor offered to run me through the Canadians Restricted Firearms Safety Course (aka Hand-Gun) portion. Not having read

---

* You might be able to pay cash and walk out of gun shows, your purchase loaded with complementary ammo, in the second-amendment loving U, S, of A. but Canada has saner laws. A licence, complete with background check, is just the start of the process.

** There are, in fact, three licences available: PAL (for adults 18 or older), POL, the Possession Only License (again adults only), and the Minors Firearms License (for those under age 18).

that particular manual, I had some trouble but still passed easily enough. Neither proved especially difficult—caution and common sense were what was needed. Very few questions involved anything technical. The goal was simply to prove that I, as a disabled person, could complete the course and qualify for a licence. Sure, some accommodations had to be made—I was physically incapable of lifting the demonstration weapons, let alone loading or unloading the dummy cartridges—but, with a friend acting as my hands and me talking him through every step of the process, the deed was done.

Once I had the papers in hand, testament to my passing the two courses, there was no need to move further. It took money (for fees) and time to finish the application process, including submitting a passport-style photo and undergoing a criminal record check. That photo proved the deal-breaker. There was no way I'd willingly pose for such. Getting my picture taken is one of my least favourite things. Volunteering for that particular form of torture convinced me to abandon the quest.

I still have the documents certifying to my achievement. It doesn't matter that they've long since expired.

• • •

Did you know Disney World once sold toy guns by the truckload?

Their phenomenally successful TV miniseries following the adventures of Davy Crockett did more than just supercharge the coon-skin cap market. Though it only aired five movie-length episodes from 1954 to 1955, it inspired legions of young fans—helped in no small part by the catchy theme song "The Ballad of Davy Crockett"—to emulate the titular hero. Boys across America wanted the frontiersman's trusty rifle and toy replicas flew off the shelves.

Knowing a good thing when they saw it, executives at Disney began selling simulated weapons based on many of their properties. Even theme park rides like Pirates of the Caribbean offered such to children. I still own a gun purchased from that swashbuckling-themed spectacle, a wood and plastic flintlock pistol.

Of course, Walt Disney was just following corporate examples. Both the Sears and Eaton's catalogues advertised real firearms for sale—delivered through the mail with no questions asked. Those were simpler times. The Boy Scouts of America even promoted firearms as part of their moral code. You could find advertisements for rifles and shotguns right in their famed handbook. If you come across any of the group's promotional posters from prior to the 1960s, chances are the scout featured is carrying a weapon. All red-blooded American males did . . . or so pop culture would have us believe.

My relatives in Michigan all kept guns, mostly for hunting but also to protect the homestead, eliminate varmints*, and, occasionally, cull the livestock. Firearms weren't quite a part of their daily lives. They were, however, considered commonplace. Everyone knew their neighbours owned a gun and nobody cared.

Contrast that with the treatment given to gun culture today. There isn't much respect for this once-honourable tradition anymore. The face of guns in America has been hijacked by macho Rambo fetishists and extreme right-wing fringe elements like the National Rifle Association (NRA)—a group more interested in lobbying the government than competently managing its

---

* That isn't artistic embellishment. My maternal grandfather ran the family farm for most of his life, selling it in his twilight years. The new owner, a man named Jed, almost immediately discovered oil while hunting rabbits on the property and moved to Beverly Hills with his mother-in-law, daughter, and nephew . . . just like in the TV show.

own affairs—to the point where many legitimate gun owners no longer want to be associated with those spouting more "out there" opinions.

I still hold a soft spot for firearms and always will. Sure, I squeezed my last trigger years ago, discovering that my finger muscles were no longer up to the job. Standing around watching someone else shoot took a lot of the fun out of the pastime. Not even seeing my friend fire a ten-gauge shotgun, and get knocked on his butt only to come up grinning, could compensate.

Turns out, even guns require a minimum level of strength. In the end, I couldn't fire. Not even blanks. Talk about an emasculating development.

Hard to Swallow

If we were ever to meet, as the kids say, IRL (In Real Life) it would take you a single glance to deduce one important fact about me: I like to eat.

Don't let the XXXL waistband fool you, I'm no glutton. In fact, people often comment in surprise at how little a man of my more-than-ample girth actually consumes. Part of that is me being on "best behaviour" when dining in public and part is pure stubborn bullheaded fickleness. I've always been something of a picky eater.* If something wasn't prepared to my exact specifications, there would be hell to pay. Dignified pouting and a well-mannered tantrum

---

* Those who knew me as a child—or know me now for that matter—are no doubt rolling their eyes at that prodigious understatement.

would be just the beginning. The venue didn't matter, I could be in the fanciest restaurant or at the home of a friend and "I won't eat that!" would be my outspoken response to any offerings not meeting my standards. That sentiment might be spiced up with reactions along the lines of, "This doesn't taste right" or the ever popular, "I don't like it!"

At no point in my overly opinionated childhood did it ever occur to me that this all-too-brutal honesty might offend. Though, thinking back, my constant forthright criticism does explain why few homes ever invited me back for seconds.

No doubt other youngsters might have faltered when given the traditional threat, "You don't leave that table until that plate is clean." I, however, was made of sterner stuff. Replying in all seriousness, at age five mind, "Fine. I'll die here." My conviction must have been clear because, even then, I meant every word.

When it came to stubbornness, especially around food, no mere human can match me. Hunger might be the best sauce but I've found indignant righteousness to be a tastier condiment.

Besides, who can resist this face?

The particularity of my palate became the stuff of legends. My family learned, much to their regret, to always offer one of my favourites. Whole food groups found themselves excised entirely from the menu at my behest. Fish and seafood of any sort were complete non-starters. Chicken could, occasionally, be acceptable—if it were KFC—and, even then, only the leg. Sandwiches came in two choices: baloney or peanut butter and jam, always on white bread (those specifics have since been codified and expanded—I have added both ham and whole wheat to those ingredients deemed "acceptable"). "Ethnic" food other than Italian was off-limits. An exception could be made for Chinese (provided it came from Capreol's Peking Palace and, even then, I usually preferred the cook's world-famous "Fay-burger").

Above all, I loathed anything labelled as "Ready-to-Eat" or "Instant." Even as a child I recognized that quality nourishment could not be "pre-packaged" (certain "name brand" canned goods were allowed. Campbell's Tomato Soup, for instance). Good food to my thinking requires hours of kitchen-bound effort. And shortcuts cannot, no will not, be tolerated.

Should the fare somehow meet my exacting approval then, in my carefree youth at least, that meant pigging out. Gorging on beloved favourites and turning my nose up at anything else, especially anything described as "good for you," became my modus operandi.

Chocolate of almost any sort ranked high on my list, and while I made short work of some sweets—I'd easily eat five or six good-sized brownies in one sitting—I wouldn't dream of touching others. Pie never did it for me, except chocolate and then only the filling. I could plough through an entire box of Timbits, provided they were chocolate, but refused homemade creampuffs. In short, I was awash in contradictions.

Back then Jello and pudding, ice cream and cookies combined to wreck my waistline. No PSA or parental warning could scare me off. The siren call of sugary treats pierced my consciousness like a hook through an eye—holding tight.

Not that I was alone in my bad behaviour. Breakfast cereals of dubious nutritional value, complete with "Prize Inside," started generations of children off with questionable understandings of "a well-balanced diet." What chance did impressionable youth have? Brainwashed by slick marketing campaigns masquerading as Saturday morning cartoons, they were led to believe that overly-sweetened bits of coloured cardboard comprised the "most important meal of the day."

As I grew, both up and out, my dining habits matured . . . slightly. The term "portion control" found its way into my vocabulary and I finally clued into the dieter's mantra, "A moment on the lips, a lifetime on the hips." Vanity didn't enter into the discussion. But, when I could no longer even see my toes, it soon became obvious that something needed to be done about my growing obesity.

Changing how I ate proved hard. It didn't help that my grandmother, a phenomenally gifted home cook, proved only too happy to indulge my spoiled appetite. I challenge anyone with elderly Italian relatives to eat responsibly. Not a week went by that some great-aunt wasn't putting on a huge, elaborate meal. And there's always room for family at an Italian table.

Holidays were the worst. Feasts don't do those meals justice. Lovingly prepared, with no effort spared, each house put out a spread fit for Caesar. Deliciousness was guaranteed—generations of cumulative experience backed up every well-practiced dish—and despite the mandating of certain staples (like turkey on thanksgiving or ham at Easter) the menus always surprised and astounded. That doesn't even touch on the appetizers, the wines, or the glorious array of desserts. The most critical culinary connoisseur would weep at the foods we consumed celebrating routine milestones like birthdays, anniversaries, and various religious ceremonies. Everything was homemade. From scratch.

Gradually my gluttony gave way to more nuanced considerations. Stuffing my face by the fistful changed to careful deliberation and weighing of consequences. For the past three decades the more that is on offer the less I consume.

My friends still fight over who sits beside me at weddings—to the extent it's become something of a running joke—to see who could scavenge my uncleaned plate or steal entire courses I'd left untouched.*

Moderating caloric intake might be an effective part of a healthy diet but, since I could never pair it with exercise, the weight never really went away. The fatter I grew, however, the smaller my appetite became. When I reached my most rotund things changed. Being diagnosed as diabetic brought a desperate discipline to my dietary choices. Growing up to horror stories of my paternal great-grandfather and his amputated leg brought home the disease's seriousness in a way no doctor's warning ever could. And the thought of needing to inject insulin terrified me.

For all that, I still like what I like the way I like it. Now I just eat a bit less of everything. Reducing my sugar intake proved a monumental challenge given my innate hatred of change and lifelong antagonism toward healthy living but cutting down my six-daily cups of tea—each with three tablespoons full of that sweet white poison—helped do the trick.

Finding someone has changed a recipe, even the tiniest little bit, still drives me insane. Entire dishes have been ruined by using a different grind of pepper or substituting a healthy "alternative." "Why fix something that ain't broken?" is my theory. Give me the same-old meals prepared in exactly the same ways—don't swap ingredients, don't switch brands, and don't ever try anything new.

Food is, as you can probably guess, my one vice. Not high-end fare, mind. No lobster, foie gras, or caviar for this guy. "Refined" does not describe my palate. I'm more of a meat and potatoes guy. Red meat and fried potatoes, preferably. Mock my pedestrian taste if you must but know that I am a connoisseur of such foods.

---

* Dessert caused the most trouble. People took to calling "dibs" before we even entered the reception hall. Breaking the news that the sweets were "already spoken for"—usually by my mom—resulted in betrayed expressions and faces full of disappointment.

Keep your fancy chefs and haute cuisine, give me a plate piled high with homemade pasta (and don't forget the traditionally prepared tomato sauce!). Spare me the delicate delectables diced to tiny bite sizes and bring out the heaped platter of BBQ. Sugary, salty, and fatty are my flavours of choice—seriously, do not get between me and a bag of potato chips unless you want to lose a hand. And don't even think of interrupting me while I'm devouring some of my family's gnocchi.

So, imagine how my stomach sank on learning that SMA was going to affect my eating?! Turns out chewing and swallowing, besides being things few of us ever think about, involve using a lot of muscles—voluntary muscles in the mouth, throat, and oesophagus. And mine, thanks to this disease, are wearing out. Or are destined to . . . eventually.

Only they're not. It's complicated.

I discovered all this at the impressionable young age of forty-seven. How is it that I only stumbled upon my stomach's sad fate so late in life? Simple, I live in a state of constant denial. And not just in regards to my disability. It strikes me as stupid now but growing up I refused to read about SMA. Eschewing slick glossy brochures and badly photocopied information packages with equal disdain. "I'd rather be surprised," was my glib go-to explanation. Other, more mature, people would have sought out the facts no matter how unpleasant their diagnoses. It didn't exactly take a genius to figure out that life with spinal muscular atrophy meant some unforeseen difficulties lay in my future. A few simple mental preparations, taken when young, could have made a world of difference. Planning ahead and otherwise readying myself for the forthcoming physical failures would have been the smart decision. But did I go that route? Of course not.

No, I buried my head deep in the sand and plugged my ears

whenever talk turned "real." Eventually, people gave up trying to help and left me to wallow in my blissfully happy ignorance. Then I read Laughing at My Nightmare by Shane Burcaw and found this kid half my age managed to not only face his reality, head on, but turned it—through the power of humour and some awesome mental kung fu—until his disability became his superpower. When I grow up, I want to be like this guy, I remember thinking as I read Shane's book.

I won't get into all the gory details of how those who can't swallow eat. Not out of sensitivity but because it turns out those invasive options may not be in my future after all. The thing about SMA is that it affects everyone differently. If you're lucky enough to have Type II, then the severity of the disease depends upon one factor: How long you remained "ambulatory." The longer you were able to walk, generally, means the slower the onset of muscle degeneration. I managed to maintain my mobility until the summer of 1982. Aged eight and a half (give or take a few days) is when I stopped walking.

Those seven and a half years made a world of difference.

I've yet to experience difficulty swallowing and, given my current age and surprisingly robust health, probably won't have to deal with the more disturbing aspects of the disease before old age claims me.

Or at least that's what I tell myself. I still refuse to read up on the subject of SMA.

Better to swallow my worries. I'll keep living in ignorance, thank you kindly. For me, life boils down to a simple but satisfying philosophy: Eat, drink, and be merry.

Where's My Hover-chair?!

Picking out a new electric wheelchair is a chore. I've gone through it too many times to count and, despite the best intentions of all involved, have never enjoyed the process. Not that the experience hasn't improved over the years, because it has. Immensely.

The involvement of government marked the biggest turning point, believe it or not. Prior to that, it fell to wheelchair users—and their families—to purchase and pay for all their assistive devices. That proved a complicated and costly effort. While some funding was available from various charitable organizations—Easter Seals and MDA Canada helped me out—those resources were stretched pretty thin and so could never cover everything or everyone adequately.

Since health care has long been a provincial jurisdiction, it fell to Ontario to step up. Which they did . . . in their own sweet time. Experts convinced our elected officials of the important role wheelchairs play in the daily lives of many citizens and, miraculously, our MPPs actually listened. Queen's Park accepted outside advice and the government agreed to fund 75% of qualifying citizens equipment through the Assistive Devices Program.* (The ADP isn't limited to power wheelchairs. They contribute to the cost of manual wheelchairs, specialized positioning supports for wheelchairs, forearm crutches, paediatric standing forms, and wheeled walkers.)

Of course, it isn't that straightforward. Those, like me, applying for funding assistance for a "high technology" power chair—meaning one that includes "power dynamic tilt and/or recline"— have to go through a different program called the Central Equipment Pool. The good news is 100% of the cost is covered, including maintenance and repairs. The bad is we don't "own" those devices (the CEP "loans" them to us) and have limited control of their purchasing, including no choice of retailer. Both the ADP and CEP are managed by the Ontario Ministry of Health and Long-Term Care and allow replacing of parts that wear out fastest—padding for instance—every two years. Expensive "big-ticket" items, like drivetrains and custom-fitted seats, are eligible after five years (for adults—children can apply whenever they "outgrow" theirs).

You'd think wheelchair users would be anxious to upgrade. Most people, if the government offered them a new car every half-decade, would jump at the chance. But that's not the case with me or most assistive device users. Comfort and familiarity play a

---

* ADP is just the latest in the long line of acronym-inspired agencies tasked with assisting disabled Ontarians.

big role in our lives. A wheelchair we know and like is preferable to change. In fact, I generally try to keep my mobility aids rolling for as long as possible—meaning I often go seven, eight, or even ten years between purchases (my current chair arrived in 2013). Distrust of change outweighs the thrill of purchasing new.

Not that buying a wheelchair is especially exciting. Take all the tedious parts of shopping, add extra pressure—this assistive device is going to be used daily for years so you better get it right—and you end up with a stress-filled ordeal. One I put off as long as possible.

Imagine my surprise on learning that, while in the midst of writing this book, my current wheelchair needed replacing. That machine was, like its predecessor, an Invacare Storm Series Arrow. Custom-made to my exact specifications, with a tilt motor alone worth in excess of $5,000, it had been used constantly for almost nine years and that showed. Much of the upholstery was worn, rips let padding leak through, and entire pieces had broken off. Nothing essential but, taken together, these "issues" pointed to the inevitable truth: I needed to schedule a visit to the "Seating Clinic."

This process, for those who don't know, is rather involved. Entire teams of highly trained professionals ensure that every wheelchair purchased through the ADP/CEP is custom-fitted. Individualizing for each client leads to an exhaustingly exacting process, one that involves weeks, or even months, until the final product is complete. I began the process early with a phone call in the summer of 2021. That led to an appointment in mid-September. "Be prepared for the initial assessment to last several hours," was the warning I received, in between a long and terrifying list of COVID-19 restrictions. Given that there are a limited number of certified technicians on the government payroll and every one of these is overworked, I felt fortunate to be scheduled in the same calendar year.

They were almost right. That first meeting took four full hours. Only the fact that I arrived at the hospital with a list of demands—changes I wanted incorporated into my new wheelchair and several firm ideas as to what needed to remain the same—kept things that brief.

Unbeknownst to me, the "Seating Clinic" had changed its routine since my last fitting. Oh, they started off in familiar fashion—with a series of meticulous measurements—before moving on to the expected questions. Out came the few "samples" kept on site. But that's where things veered wildly from my expectations.

Since 2013, "customizable" has become the refrain among retailers. Wheelchair designs are now modular, allowing users to meet their needs in a mix and match approach before the manufacturer ships a single component. Off-the-shelf parts cover most requirements, freeing up specialist to address the truly unique cases. This approach is faster, cheaper, and less time consuming for all involved. Unless you're used to the old system and hate change.

It took me a while to wrap my head around this "new and improved" procedure. Every part required lengthy explanations and monotonous comparisons. Even the most basic wheelchair building block—the number and configuration of available wheels—comes in a bewildering variety of forms. Four-wheel rear drive still dominates but four-wheel front drive and six-wheel mid-drive are making inroads. Each, naturally, comes with their own pros and cons—which we had to discuss in detail.

Modern assistive devices come loaded. The power wheelchairs presented to me during our initial meeting proved a far cry from those first sold in 1950. George Klein, the Canadian most often credited as inventor of the electric wheelchair, would be hard pressed to recognize today's fully tricked out examples.

Companies realized the upsell potential of options a decade or so back. There are "functional" choices like the "stand" mechanism (just add $10,000 to the bill), Push-Rim Activated Power Assistance Wheelchair (chairs able to sense when the weakened user is pushing on the wheels and can amplify their strength with electric motors), or even Brain-Computer Interface (and yes, modern wheelchairs can be controlled by thoughts—if you can afford the tech), and comfort choices such as heated massage seats.* Standard features now include LED lights and shock absorbers. It sometimes seems manufacturers are trying to outdo each other—sure, programmable controllers are useful, being able to cancel out tremors or other medical impairments that affect driving are good—but do these devices need to synch to your personal computer and double as a mouse?

Of course, these elaborately endowed rides don't come cheap**. Every "available upgrade"—and there are new ones appearing on the market every day—adds to the cost. That fact keeps me sticking with what I know works. Tried and true. There's little benefit to experimenting in my mind—why risk your primary mode of mobility on some untested technology when there are well-established alternatives that do the job perfectly adequately?

I carried that reluctant attitude into the Seating Clinic with me as an almost visible prejudice. Fittings are not fun, be it for a tuxedo or a new, much-needed, electric wheelchair. Discovering that the reliably arduous process had changed did nothing to improve my mood. But somehow, at the end of four hours, we

---

* For my most recent wheelchair I had to choose between more than thirty types and styles of seat cushion—that's not counting cover materials or colours!

** The final cost of my new chair came in just under $20,000.00—a bargain really.

had everything arranged. My new wheelchair was built-to-order. Once the funding approval came back, we could move forward.***

• • •

Nobody wants to be in a wheelchair. I don't care how soft the leather, fancy the suspension, or even what colours it comes in—I was surprised to learn pink and purple are both popular—wheelchairs are a poor substitute for walking. But when these expensive assistive devices are needed, there are some things that users should expect, like functionality and reliability. That first trait is often hit and miss. For every function I use daily, like the ache-alleviating power dynamic tilt mechanism, there is another no sane person would want...namely the horn. This long-standard feature comes built-in and is too anaemically quiet to cut through any serious noise. The weeny little button produces a warning so embarrassingly tiny that I flatly refused to use it. Too bad everyone I knew kept asking to hear it. Some of the younger ones didn't even bother with asking, pushing the button for their own amusement. It got so bad I now have the sound deactivated. It served no practical purpose as far as I could see...except to annoy me.

Modern wheelchairs may be pretty bullet-proof, but that wasn't always the case. Fuses and flat tires were once the bane of my existence. I'll never forget blowing a fuse while visiting relatives in Michigan and discovering a shocking shortage of wheelchair supply stores in the most rural part of the Wolverine state. We drove to every auto repair shop within a 200-mile radius trying to find one with a 50-amp fuse in stock, crisscrossing half the state,

*** I submitted this manuscript before the orders were completed and so can only hope there are no problems.

only for my youthfully keen eyes to notice that my uncle had that exact size sitting in an old jam jar on a shelf in his garage.

My first power chair was chosen for me, dropped (literally) off at my house from the back of a delivery truck one 1980s summer afternoon. I should have known I was in trouble then. All the signs were against me: it arrived in a Canadian Pacific branded truck, it had blue-cloth covering all the padding, and it featured a truly alarming amount of plastic in its manufacture. And yet, despite my doubts, I took what was given with gratitude.

That "electric" wheelchair allowed me to move without requiring aid, a welcome experience after being pushed around for months. Even the eye-searing safety features—there was a big orange flag, more suited to an airport emergency vehicle than a wheelchair, stuck atop an eight-foot pole sticking out the back— couldn't dissuade me . . . though the flag came off immediately, broken "accidentally."

Built by industry leader Everest & Jennings, the chair sported some questionable design choices. Lethally sharp edges dominated. There were corners everywhere, none of which were rounded, blunted, or capped—one part even stuck out of the side like some sort of medieval spearpoint. Combine that with a dangerously difficult-to-engage manual brake system, large but weirdly narrow back wheels,* and you can see why that machine didn't exactly endear itself to me. . The stone-wheeled, foot-propulsion car on The Flintstones made that wheelchair look primitive by comparison. And don't get me started on the drive system. Rubber belts provided the motive power The elastic band-like mechanism was prone to

---

* Being big, those wheels let my wheelchair spin on the proverbial dime—unfortunately the narrowness meant it got stuck a lot. Mud, snow, loose gravel, thick grass, you name the surface and, if it wasn't perfectly paved bone-dry concrete, I found myself immobilized.

slipping on any incline or during the mildest of weather. It once failed at the top of a hill, almost sending me to a watery grave. So, it's no surprise that, after a couple of years and several more near-death experiences, I wanted out of that E&J deathtrap.

My current, slowly degrading model is lightyears ahead of that introductory effort. It still features all the basics, four wheels, electric motors, a battery, a controller, and a seat but that's where the similarities end. No doubt thirty years from now I'll look back on this wheelchair and scoff at how primitive it seems in retrospect. Hopefully by the time 2050 rolls around I won't be rolling any more. If I turn 76 and the future hasn't perfected cheap wheel-less assistive devices—flying would be nice, but I'd settle for some sort of hovercraft-hybrid—there's going to be one very angry septuagenarian rolling around Capreol. Heck, I'd even accept tank treads. Just give me some method of tackling stairs.

Why Media Matters

By all rights I ought to be a villain. But not just any average villain. No, being disabled means I'm destined for super villainy. I should be in my lair right now, lurking high atop some ominously named landmark—Skull-crusher Mountain!—scheming world domination. Needless to say, all of my overcomplicated plans would revolve around a preposterous series of nefarious tasks, each with an obvious failure point, probably involving Freeze Rays or giant robots.

That, at least, is what film and TV would have you (and me) believe.

Most cultures harbour some kind of ableist prejudice. That's not just some poor cripple complaining, it's categorically true. History is full of examples—even if most are conveniently left out of the curriculum. Sparta, memorably, used to "expose" (meaning they were abandoned in the wild to die alone and forgotten) any baby born with physical deformity or any other obvious sign of weakness. The belief that physical imperfections reflect some sort of inner failing was terrifyingly common. Read any fairy tale and you'll find a shocking portrayal of handicaps (even the saccharine Disney versions, G-rated one and all, fell into the same old traps), "evil" characters tend to be crippled or old (and almost always ugly to boot).

A lot of Western society is still influenced by the Medieval church and its cruel argument that those suffering disease and physical defects were victims of God's judgement "made manifest." Of course, according to official doctrine at the time, anything including impure thoughts, moral failings, lustful urges, along with any other sort of "deviant behaviour"—from impiety to wilfulness—would be punished. (Is it any wonder the majority of people living with disabilities have trouble accepting mainstream religions?)

But that was hundreds of years ago. Surely humanity has evolved beyond that sort of senseless superstition, right?

Unfortunately, no. Society still buys into prejudice. Modernity just hides it better. Mass media has replaced religion as the dominant force in most peoples' lives and, though the source has changed, the same tired old lies continue to be spread. And the disabled, though relieved not to be called sinners, still find themselves vilified. Portraying people with handicaps as the bad guy in film and on TV is so common there's even a name for the trend: The Evil Cripple Trope. (Often combined with The Crippled Genius Trope, whereby physical weakness is balanced by an ominously brilliant intellect.)

Speaking on behalf of all handicapped people everywhere,

I have just one thing to say: Bring it on. Better to be the villain than the victim.

●●●

You are what you watch. That truth became undeniable with the rise of right-wing media bubbles and the violent hypocrisy of the MAGA movement. Discovering that the priorities of the U.S. government could be swayed by what aired the previous night on Fox News proved an alarming wake-up call for many Americans. But minorities, like those people comprising the disabled community, have long known the power mass media holds over public perception. Positive portrayals can build people up while negative ones serve to tear them down. Nothing is as devastating to a struggling community, though, as being ignored.

It's important people with handicaps are seen, period. Overcoming that is the first obstacle. From there, representation needs to be shaped so that the handicapped are shown for the things they can do instead of lingering over that which they cannot. How society views the disabled influences how we are valued—including how we value ourselves. Portraying us as pitiable, pathetic, or perpetually vulnerable is cheap Hollywood gimmickry. I've yet to meet a single handicapped person like entertainment's most cliched cripple, Tiny Tim. That helpless English waif always seems happy waiting to die—conveniently off-screen. There is a certain soul-crushing humiliation in seeing people like yourself being used to elicit sympathy. It reinforces the notion all disabled are incapable.

TV and movies may be immensely popular but they are hardly the most sophisticated of mediums. Limited running times and budget constraints mean simpler is usually better for plot and characterization. Contrasting brawn with brain or pitting handsome wholesomeness against lame and broken badness is easy. Lazy writers fall back on tired clichés and none is more popular than blaming the conflict on the so-called "bad guy"—often someone disabled.

The fact that those same writers use handicaps as hackneyed shorthand to tell audiences the character is intimidating, suspicious, or downright sinister is something of a tradition. Anti-social behaviour can be ascribed to "psychological issues," but the root cause almost always boils down to being "different."

Me, I like the idea of being the villain. Villains do stuff. They plan, they act, they monologue at inopportune moments—conveniently laying out their ridiculously complex strategies in digestible bite-sized chunks—and never fail to provide the hero that desperately needed chance to escape. Antagonists get a bad rap in fiction but they are needed—without darkness there can be no light.

• • •

Despite the fact that 15-25% of the planet's population live with a disability (more than six million people in Canada alone), we only feature in 3% of media.* Growing up I saw plenty of handicapped people on TV. Almost always on telethons. It wasn't until The Facts of Life debuted "Cousin Geri" that I witnessed an actual character with a chronic disability. Portrayed by an actress, Geri Jewel, who actually had cerebral palsy, this was my generation's introduction to

---

* 2021 marked a record for American television. 3.5% of scripted broadcasts featured a series regular with a disability—an eleven-year high. Impressive until you learn that one in five people in the U.S. have a handicap of some sort. Meaning there is a large disparity between the reality and what gets portrayed on TV.

handicap not being played solely for sympathy. Geri only appeared 12 times—not a lot given the show ran nine seasons and aired over two hundred episodes—but she made an impact. Some might argue that Geri was merely comic relief and to a certain extent they are right. That criticism overlooks three important facts. First, the show was a sitcom, eliciting audience laughter is an essential component of the genre; second, Geri's backstory included her aspiration towards stand-up comedy, meaning being funny was central to her character; and third, they cast a disabled actress for the part.* All of which helped the series address some real issues in between the humour.

Did Cousin Geri change TV? Hardly. Long after her final appearance people with handicaps are still underrepresented. But she opened the door and other performers followed. None, however, had the same impact on me.

• • •

A lifetime of dedicated TV obsession means I've watched more than my share of "the boob tube." It wasn't uncommon for me, during my viewing pinnacle, to watch 10 to 12 hours of TV a day. If I'd spent a fraction of that time learning an instrument or studying for a degree I'd have long since become a virtuoso performer or earned several PhDs. Instead, I grew fat and cynical about the greatest art form of the past millennium.

Long before our current "Golden Age of television," I was addicted to the so-called "idiot box". It didn't matter what was

---

* It is estimated that more than 95% of all "special needs" characters are portrayed by actors *without* any disability. This casting choice is often derided, among the disabled community at least, as "cripping up."

on—quality educational programming, ham-handed government propaganda, or the crassest cross-promotional dreck designed only to sell video games, toys, or even sugary breakfast cereal—I watched, mouth-open but not quite drooling. I am, in short, a "TV nut". Always have been and always will be.

One of my parents' favourite stories to tell—meaning humiliating in the extreme—involves me, then very young (not much more than 14-months old) and not having yet spoken my first word, waking them in the middle of the night and, using only gestures, getting them to turn on the TV so all three of us could sit on the floor and watch the test pattern.

For a time in my childhood, I became a living version of that venerable periodical TV Guide. Admittedly, the dial only went from two to thirteen at the time** and a couple of channels (10 and 12) were French and didn't matter except when the Expos, Habs, or Nordiques were playing. Television played such a pivotal role in my early life that I determined the day of the week based on what was airing that night. This presented something of a problem in August of 1985 when I came out from under 12-plus hours of anaesthesia just before eight p.m. and, remembering that it was Thursday, demanded a television be rolled into the recovery room. Even waking from surgery, I knew it was vitally important not to miss "Must See TV." Three different nurses and their supervisor all tried to overrule me with, "That's never been done before!" But even at the tender age of eleven there was no making me see reason—not when four of my favourite shows, The Cosby Show, Family Ties, Cheers and Night Court, were due to come on.

** Remote controls might be ubiquitous now but were once reserved for the rich. My family didn't get its first flipper until the early 1980s. Purchased so that I could change channels from bed—an uncommon luxury at the time.

There is, however, one type of show that never clicked for me: medical dramas.

I haven't spent any prolonged time in hospital but even a cursory stay proved enough to sour me on the facilities. It doesn't take much imagination to find exciting stories in a building where people are born, suffer, and are either cured or die. With few exceptions—M*A*S*H, Doogie Howser, Northern Exposure, and Scrubs, all what are now categorized as "dramadies" (meaning part drama and part comedy)—I avoid emotionally manipulative "doctor" shows.

Still, I somehow got sucked into House starring Hugh Laurie. What can I say? I liked him in Jeeves and Wooster. Imagine my surprise when the first patient our titular misanthropic genius proves unable to treat, besides himself of course, was a man with SMA.* Worse, that character died! Not from SMA, fortunately. Instead, spoiler alert (for an episode that aired in 2007), his helper dog ate the lifesaving medicine and promptly overdosed. Yes . . . the dog died too. The part that hit closest to home wasn't the untimely death of the patient, a thirty-seven-year-old not too dissimilar from me, but rather when Gregory House—himself one of the few TV cripples of note—challenged his team to save the young man's life and preserve the " . . . twenty or more miserable years he's got left with SMA."

Did the show mean that all people with SMA live in misery? Because, if that's the case, the episode's writer and I need to have a chat. Sure, some people with the disease are miserable but so are plenty of healthy individuals. Happiness is not guaranteed to any of us. Being born with a chronic health condition doesn't

---

* This character was, in fact, the fifth to die under House's care. It, for reasons, struck me the hardest and stuck with me the longest.

automatically destine a person to suffering. Perpetuating the myth that all handicaps are life-ruining tragedies ignores the truth: That humans are resilient and can find moments of joy in the most tragic of circumstances.

I finished watching that episode convinced of one thing . . . that nothing good comes from a helper dog.

• • •

Representation is a popular buzzword lately, at least among visible minorities, their army of advocates, and those do-gooding enablers who insist on sticking their noses in other people's business. When I was growing up no one gave the notion much thought. We all knew the characters on TV and in movies weren't real—even "true" stories played fast and loose with the facts. And no one was fooled by those "based on real events."

Maybe we were wrong to be so accepting. Media matters in how people see themselves and, by accepting the mainstream pap of comforting "family friendly" entertainments, we ate up the popular but blandly palatable lies like good little consumers. Oblivious to life's iniquities, the majority of the viewing public fell under the powerful influence of network TV and never blinked at harmfully stereotyped portrayals or prejudiced hiring practices. Laugh-tracks overrode our better judgement.

Living in television's new "golden age" has changed our view of entertainment. We expect more of our media. Holding the multi-billion-dollar film and TV industry to a higher standard is a good start. Nothing, though, can replace an educated and aware viewership.

But I still miss the days when you could enjoy a random cartoon mouse violently disembowel an innocent cartoon cat for no apparent reason without worrying about the sociological consequences.

Balancing on a Soapbox

Some people get off on telling others what to do. Issuing orders, making demands, and otherwise flaunting their—usually ill-gotten—power. No self-important display is too petty, no pompous utterance too belittling, and no indulgence too juvenile ... provided it impresses. This sort of megalomania is reserved for petty tyrants and tinpot would-be dictators mostly. Oh, and me.

How is it I count myself among that notoriously ill-mannered ilk? It's not because I share their bloated egos and vastly inflated senses of worth. I am not especially proud to include myself amidst that clownishly monomaniacal and paranoidly unpopular crowd. But honesty demands I admit my complicity with that controlling cohort.

The simple truth is, since I'm unable to do much of anything physical unaided, I've mastered the art of instruction. Learning to tell others exactly how to best accomplish my wishes wasn't a conscious choice but rather a survival mechanism. Unfortunately, this simple "expressing of preferences" can sometimes be misconstrued.

Sounding pushy or imperious is never my intent.

I take perverse pride in the fact that frustration seldom gets the better of me. That said, even my legendarily prodigious patience wears down on occasion. And repeating the same requirements—in excruciatingly minute detail—day after day does begin to grate.

My occasionally high-handed tone works better with professionals—people paid to help me—than with family and friends. Those poor souls are forced to put up with me and my often overbearing behaviour merely from affection. To say I make it difficult is an understatement. The fact that I struggle to express gratitude in anything like a sincere manner doesn't help.

If scraping up appreciation sufficient to the occasion is a constant trial, then spitting out instructions is my calling. I issue commands with the entitled ease and demanding imperiousness of some sort of deranged medieval monarch. Such callousness isn't meant as casual cruelty. It serves a logical purpose: to give me a modicum of control over my care.

Some—okay, many—people with handicaps find directing others difficult, but not me. No, being demanding falls right in my wheelhouse.

I am, by nature, a contrarian. One of my most uttered phrases is a decisively derisive, "I don't like it!" That phrase is meant in jest . . . mostly. For those who've never been in a position to direct others, you're missing out. It is surprisingly freeing, intoxicatingly empowering, and, above all, addictive.

Let me take a moment to just say that when a guy my size begins throwing his weight around, it's best to get out of the way. More than toes are crushed when my dictatorial momentum builds. It's not uncommon for me to rattle off orders by the dozen, without a pause or a breath, like some sort of over-caffeinated auctioneer. My mouth tends to move at supersonic speed when specifying my all-too-precise preferences, the words emerging in a barely comprehensible blur. Just demand after demand, with nary a "Please" to be heard.

In short, I'm a domineering bastard. Or, as my dad likes to say, "You should have been a boss at CN!"*

My disability might have driven me to become demanding but it was my personality alone that took this trait to such ridiculous extremes. Being a bit OCD didn't help. I need things in my life to be right. That never-defined term is sort of my catch-all. It can be as simple as explaining how I prefer my food prepared or as petty as ensuring my lucky marble elephant always points the proper direction. No one believes quite how demanding I can be, until they experience me. I don't even have to be on worst behaviour. My style is peremptory, domineering, and uniquely annoying. There is never just one demand. No, I utter them in long strings. Many are contingent on the proper completion of some prior step (or steps). And few make the slightest bit of sense to anyone but me.

"More," I usually begin. Adding, "More. More. Moremoremore. Stop!" Then, after a moment's consideration, I say, "No. Too much." Often finishing with, "Start again." Such exactitude and precision have given me a bit of a reputation. My mom has long called me a "Fussy fart" in exasperation. I prefer the term "particular." But whatever words you use to describe me there is no denying that

---

* Canadian National Railroad being his former employer, took to prioritizing profit over people. Management incentivized the white-collar crowd to push, harry, and cajole the blue-collar set relentlessly, earning endless enmity.

my personality leans toward the finicky.

Growing up, I was often given so-called "supervisor" duties on family projects—which was generally code for sit quietly and watch without comment. Somehow, despite my good-natured silence I routinely found myself blamed for "not saying anything sooner" when something invariably went awry.

There's a difference between complaining and criticizing. I *try* not to do much of the former but find the latter helpful . . . if only people would listen to me more often. It's not quite a "Boy Who Cried Wolf" situation. This isn't attention-seeking. None of my criticisms are unmerited. But even legitimate suggestions can grow unwanted when passing my lips. Just as too much of a good thing can overwhelm, so it goes with my well-meaning words.

• • •

Seriousness is not my forte. Especially when it comes to the "Issues." Irreverence, parody, and self-depreciating satire are more my speed. But, having been given this platform—and make no mistake, a professionally published and marketed book like this is a very powerful platform—I feel obliged to use it. For positive purposes, of course. Or, at least, better than my usual smart-mouthed idiocy. This poses me with a significant problem. Balancing humour, especially the juvenile brand at which I excel, with the issues facing the disabled community is a monumental challenge. It doesn't help that I've never really been part of said community.

Living in a remote Northern Ontario town has kept me isolated. I know more about the topics dominating discussion on CNN than I do those plaguing people like me. Ask about international hot-button issues and I can give you a reasoned take but mention some controversy facing the disabled and all I can offer is a blank stare. Living may provide perspective but insight and understanding requires more than I can give. In that, I am not alone. It is estimated that approximately one-in-five humans live with a disability of some sort, well over one billion people. Odds are someone in your family, at your workplace, or among your social circles has a handicap. Many of you might live in ignorance of their struggles—not all disabilities are obvious and not all are crippling. Regardless of the severity, be it debilitating or merely annoying, the chronic conditions still affect our daily lives.

Two minutes of research reveals the plethora of problems facing this often-overlooked community—prevalent among them representation, accessibility, and economic opportunities. Concrete concerns tend to be front of mind for the handicapped. Pocketbook issues dominate among people with disabilities just as it does homes around the world over. It's hard to get too excited about electoral reform when you are worried about where the next meal is coming from or if you can afford next month's rent.

Being born and raised in Canada means the "social safety net" keeps me afloat. Some frugal spending habits and the generous support of family allow me to live a comfortable life. Others aren't nearly as lucky, a fact which remained beyond me for far too long.

Few able-bodied recognize the monumental expense chronic disability brings with it. I should have known better, having seen these bills first-hand. Youth and privilege shielded me from many of the darker aspects facing people of my community—but this is changing. While not actively seeking out examples of hardship, I've come across more and more proof that my charmed existence is the exception not the rule. Which leaves me at a crossroad. I could do the work and use this book to educate readers. Shine a light on the unseen side of disability. Maybe even make the world a slightly better place. Or I can cling to my delusions, write amusing fluff, and hope that I can hide some subtle messages in my entertainingly embarrassing stories.*

They say write what you know, and I'm not one to buck that much ballyhooed advice. I prefer amusement to anger, no matter how righteous. Besides, there are others far better suited to pushing the activist agenda. I'd much rather leave the heavy lifting for people with experience in improving society, sharing lived truths, and recruiting souls sympathetic to the cause.

Millions of people face and overcome hardships daily because of their disability. Many of them still find the time and energy to help others, fight the good fight, and even, yes, change the world. Me? I stick to what I know: telling silly stories and milking my many missteps for cheap laughs. Hopefully I've walked that tightrope—a difficult feat for man who's sense of balance, even back when I could walk, was never all that steady.

Disability may be an undeniable part of me. It is not, however, the defining aspect of my personality. The credit—or blame—for that fact lies with my family and friends.

Finding humour in difficulties is how I cope. Some would argue that there's more to life than amusement and that laughing doesn't actually improve anything. Those people miss the point. Not everyone needs to rage against social injustice. Sometimes sharing a smile is enough.

Smart mouthery and gentle sarcasm make me feel better. So too sharing humiliating anecdotes. And, even though delving through nearly five decades worth of suppressed memories isn't particularly pleasant, it's a sacrifice I am willing to make in order

---

* Ignorance isn't always an impediment. Not knowing the challenges others face has left me free to find my own solutions. Some have proven successful and others less-so, either way these innovations are mine . . . good or ill.

to entertain. To hell with what's left of my dignity! The time to show a stiff upper lip is past. Come look at my scars and laugh at my pain. It's okay, I'm not shy.

If you're reading this, then you know I've chosen to lay myself bare. Better writers than me have been tripped up walking this treacherous path and fallen flat on their faces. I'm certain that won't happen to me. That's not hubris. I fully expect to fail miserably but experience has taught me that, whenever I lose my footing, I will tip over backwards and topple like a chopped tree. So my face, at least, is spared.

Succeed or fail I know my comfort zone and am happy to reside therein. Sure, I'd happily accept a multi-million-dollar winning lottery ticket but, realistically, all of my current needs are well met. What tomorrow might bring, I don't know. In truth, I try not to dwell too much on the future . . . there madness lies.

Or a sequel anyway. And nobody wants that.

Acknowledgements

I owe a great deal of thanks to the Sudbury Writers' Guild. Their enthusiasm and encouragement saw me through this project.

Special mention is owed to my ever-loyal "Brain Trust": Bonnie Ouellet-Mathieu, John Jantunen, Lisa Coleman-Brown, Paul Mandziuk & Vera Constantineau—who provided me moral support, a creative soundboard, and, when needed, brutal honesty. Everyone should have friends like these.

A lot of the credit (or blame) for this book goes to the various editors and publishers who gave my writing regular space: Aonghus Kealy way back at Lambda, Laurentian University's Student newspaper; the late Gary Biesinger, founder and webmaster of www.capreolonline.com; the late David Bateman of The Capreol Press; and Tony Skopyk who ran The Capreol EXPRESS. Then, of course, there's the real power behind this book; Heather Campbell and the team at Latitude 46 Publishing.

Finally, I need to thank the good people of Capreol—the town I'm proud to call home—who have been kind enough to read my stuff for the past twenty years and say mostly nice things.

About the Author

Born with spinal muscular atrophy, Matthew Del Papa has been in a wheelchair since the early 1980s. A graduate of Laurentian University (MA Humanities), past president of the Sudbury Writers' Guild, and currently on the board of directors for Wordstock Sudbury Literary Festival, he has been writing steadily since 2005. An amateur local historian and part-time columnist, his work has been published in newspapers and magazines, as well as anthologies such as *Spooky Sudbury* (Dundurn Press, 2013) and *Nothing Without Us Too* (Renaissance Press, 2022). He lives in Capreol. *Jerry Lewis Told Me I Was Going to Die* is his first collection of humorous essays.